1

The Corporate Transformation
Of Health Care

ISSUES
& DIRECTIONS

J. Warren Salmon, Editor

**POLICY,
POLITICS,
HEALTH AND
MEDICINE**

Series

Vicente Navarro, Series Editor

Baywood Publishing Company, Inc.

Amityville, N.Y. 11701

Copyright © 1990, Baywood Publishing Company, Inc., Amityville, New York. All rights reserved. Printed in the United States of America.

A number of contributions in this book have their roots in articles which originally appeared in the *International Journal of Health Services*. These contributions have been so edited, reworked, rewritten and updated that the most significant resemblance to articles previously published are the titles they bear. Other contributions are original to this volume. Acknowledgement is given to the *American Journal of Public Health* for permission to reprint "Multi-National Operation of U.S. For-Profit Hospital Chains: Trends & Implications."

ISBN: 0-89503-087-x (Paper)
ISBN: 0-89503-088-8 (Cloth)

Library of Congress Cataloging-in-Publication Data

    Main entry under title:

The corporate transformation of health care / edited by J. Warren Salmon.
        p. cm. − (Policy, politics, health, and medicine series)
    Includes bibliographical references.
    Contents: Pt. 1. Issues and directions.
    ISBN 0-89503-088-8. − ISBN 0-89503-087-X (pbk.)
    1. Medical corporations−United States. 2. Medical policy−United
States. I. Salmon, J. Warren (Jack Warren) II. Series.
    [DNLM: 1. Delivery of Health Care−trends. 2. Hospital
Administration. W1 PO211R / W 84.1 C822]
RA410.53.C68   1990
362.1−dc20
DNLM/DLC
for Library of Congress   90-16
                                                                            CIP

Preface

Vicente Navarro

Back during the 1960s and 1970s, the hegemonic interpretation of medicine in the United States was that the evolution of the knowledge, practice, and institutions of medicine was the result of the dominance of the medical profession in the house of medicine. In the pursuit of its interests, the medical profession was shaping medicine in ways that did not always respond to the needs of our populations. This position, much influenced by Professor Freidson, the main voice in the medical sociological circles of the United States, was so dominant that other voices that questioned it were repressed. Those voices—Kelman, Navarro, Salmon, Himmelstein and Woolhandler, McKinlay, and others—kept repeating, however, that medicine could not be explained by just looking at the interplay of visible actors in the house of medicine; nor could medicine be understood by looking only at the professionals' dominance (1-6).

These authors rooted their analysis of medicine in the understanding of the power relations that exist in society and reproduce themselves in the house of medicine as well. They analyzed medicine—the tree—within the context of the forest, class as well as race and gender power relations existent in the United States. They posited that one could not understand medicine without comprehending the society of which medicine is part. And this society is not the outcome of popular wishes, as official rhetoric would like us to believe, but rather the result of heartbreaking struggles in which corporate interests—extremely influential in the political process of the United States—win frequently, and popular wishes are put aside. Medicine reflects this reality.

We have witnessed, for example, how harmful austerity policies in federal health programs have been justified by referring to a non-existent popular mandate. These austerity policies, including cuts in federal health expenditures, have been (and continue to be) carried out not because people wanted them (polls showed that people opposed them), but because corporate America

3

wanted to discipline labor as part of the most aggressive anti-working-class policies this country has witnessed since the early years of this century. This aggression was successful because it was unconstrained by any form of organized resistance due to the absence of a mass labor movement that could reverse those policies.

It is the absence of such a mass movement and of a class instrument of the dominated classes that also explains the invasion of corporate America into all spheres of life, including medicine. Actually, it was the great merit of the before-mentioned authors that they predicted that the next stage in the development of medicine would be its corporatization. The late 1970s and 1980s have proven them correct. It speaks of the potency of the method of analysis those authors used that the evolution of the house of medicine has followed step by step the scenario they predicted. The reality of the corporatization of medicine, recently written about by Relman and Starr, was first discussed and predicted by those authors (7, 8).

The collection of chapters presented here builds upon the tradition initiated by those authors. The *International Journal of Health Services* is pleased to present this collection, specially edited by Professor Salmon. It will no doubt have great influence in the coming debates on the nature and future of medicine in the United States.

Today, we are witnessing major changes in medicine. Never has the gap between what people want and what they receive from their government been wider than it is now. Eighty-two percent of Americans want major changes in the health sector, and 63 percent want a system like Canada's that would nationalize the funding of health care. The United States Congress and the current administration, however, continue policies that take us further away from assuring that access to health care is a human right in the United States, a right denied only to the South African and United States populations among Western industrialized nations. This reality responds to the enormous domi-nance—unparalleled in any other Western democracy—that corporate America has in the political, academic, and media establishments in this country. The chapters in this book provide evidence of that reality. They will contribute to breaking with an ideological monopoly that exists in the interpretation of what is going on in the medical sector of the United States.

REFERENCES

1. Kelman, S. Toward the political economy of medical care. *Inquiry* 8, 1971.
2. Navarro, V. *Medicine Under Capitalism*. Prodist, New York, 1976.
3. Salmon, J. Monopoly capital and the reorganization of the health sector. *Review of Radical Political Economy* 9, 1977.
4. Salmon, J. Corporate attempts to reorganize the American health care system. Doctoral dissertation, Cornell University, 1978.
5. Himmelstein, D. U. and Woolhandler, S. Medicine as industry. *Monthly Review*, April 1984.
6. McKinlay, J. On the medical-industrial complex. *Monthly Review*, October 1978.
7. Relman, A. S. The new medical-industrial complex. *New Engl. J. Med.* 303, 1980.
8. Starr, P. *The Social Transformation of American Medicine*. Basic Books, New York, 1983.

Introduction

J. Warren Salmon

A dramatic alteration in the organization, financing, and delivery of medical care in the United States has been in progress over the past two decades (1). The shift to a corporate mode of production and the dimunition of professional power characterizes the qualitative difference. For this reason, this book describes the change as a *corporate* transformation of health care, rather than merely an unspecified *social* transformation (2).

THE RISE OF THE MEDICAL INDUSTRIAL COMPLEX

In the 19th and early 20th centuries, basic industries, commerce, and finance were brought under corporate auspice with infusions of capital and rapid concentration to a few large firms in most economic sectors. With the flow of funds from Medicare and Medicaid, a concentration and centralization of capital began developing in the health sector, though under much different conditions and in a different pattern. A "medical industrial complex"[1] has now taken grip over most facets of the American health care endeavor, having encroached upon the "not-for-profit" and public providers as well. The roles of the commercial insurance and supply segments of the health care industry have increased in their relative prominence since the turn of the century. Today corporate supply firms wield enormous power as they have chiefly enabled, and benefited from, the technologicalization of medicine and its bureaucratization. A small set of diversified multi-national firms participate in the manufacture and sales of pharmaceuticals, hospital equipment and supplies, computers, and the like. They made available advanced diagnostic and therapeutic regimens, arming

---

[1] With the proper credit given to Robb Burlage, an author in this volume, who actually coined the term back in 1967 for Health PAC.

5

practitioners with a mighty weaponry against disease. Now that the health sector is undergoing a further industrialization, particularly in its organizational and administrative functions, firms providing management information systems, accounting, legal, management consulting and other contractual services are also developing lucrative outlets. With government essentially acting as a guarantor of profit through huge subsidies for patient care, these corporate endeavors have reconfigured the nature of the sector, especially as their share of health care expenditures has ballooned (3). From their vantage in the larger economy come corporate restructurings, leveraged buyouts, hostile takeovers, and consolidations with service providers to mark the new health care marketplace. *Health Week* and *Modern Healthcare* devote substantial space to just tracking such corporate combinations.

ENTRY OF CORPORATE HEALTH PROVIDERS

The large-scale entry of for-profit corporate firms into the *delivery* of services tarried until the late 1960s when social and economic conditions within and without the health sector changed. A cultural climate for explicit profitmaking from services was orchestrated during the Nixon administration in its attempts to induce large corporate enterprises to invest in the operations of health maintenance organizations (4, 5). These attempts were not highly successful, but the lingering traditions of professional altruism and the charitable impulse of religious-sponsored hospitals became undermined. Principally in the hospital arena during the last decade, nationwide proprietary chains staked out less regulated states with growing middle class populations and took advantage of the then favorable reimbursement climates for their phenomenal growth.

Early in the 1980s advocates for "competition" had mobilized media information, developed academic arguments, and followed through with Reagan administration policies to bring the health sector to the marketplace point of view. Their propaganda operated continuously to reverse existing public policy concerns for social equity in health care. What was skillfully orchestrated as "regulation versus competition" never really became a debate; the forces of profit were already established in the medical industrial complex, and the opposing view supporting a stronger government role was easily consigned to a minor position. (Ironically, the most far-reaching regulatory intervention, the Medicare hospital payment under diagnosis-related groups (DRGs), came out of this Reagan supposedly anti-regulation administration).

Most attention has been centered on the "big four" hospital chains: Hospital Corporation of America (HCA) (1988 assets, $5.4 billion with a profit margin of 6.3 percent); Humana ($3.4 billion assets with a profit margin of 6.6 percent); American Medical International ($3.5 billion with a 4.6 percent profit); and National Medical Enterprises ($3.5 billion with 4.6 percent) (6). (These firms restructured in 1988–89 to spin off money-losing hospitals into Employee Stock Option Plans or ESOPs and now focus more on management contracting operations).

These investor-owned firms rose like a phoenix over the 1970s into multi-national enterprises (7). HCA became the second largest health care firm in the world, only surpassed by Johnson and Johnson, Inc. by 1986. Attempts by the largest hospital chains to form integrated health care firms to encompass a fuller range of services were not successful in the mid 1980s due to miscalculation of changing policy conditions, besides managerial difficulties in assembling resources and talents to carry out their strategies. (Likewise, a few nationwide proprietary HMOs faced restricted growth when revenue shortfalls quickly constrained their ambitious expansion plans). Before their declines from the tightening hospital market since 1987, the "big four" chains alone had operated almost 15 percent of all hospital beds in the United States, 70 percent of all proprietary beds, and 2/3 of the foreign hospitals owned by American multi-national companies (7).

Along with about 150 other large national and regional hospital chains, including both investor-owned and the "not-for-profit" ones, the hospital industry giants saw total profits dip 4.8 percent in 1988, a milder decrease from 1987's 47 percent decrease in profits. However, revenues of the hospital systems still grew at an annual rate of 7.5 percent for a total of $56.9 billion (8). The point is that corporate hospital chains are by no means declining as a few policy analysts predicted.

The concentration process within the U.S. health care industry is further shown in dominance by approximately 45 multi-state health maintenance organizations (HMOs), mostly investor-owned, and 74 nursing home chains, almost all operated for-profit. Corporate chains of psychiatric hospitals, ambulatory care facilities, out-patient surgery centers, renal dialysis centers, homecare and durable medical equipment firms, and multi-state preferred provider organizations (PPOs are hybrid HMOs utilizing pre-negotiated fee schedules for selected physicians and hospitals) have also arisen under market competition with profit their supreme purpose. Today there are at least eight health service firms with sales over a billion dollars, far outranking the largest academic medical centers.

LEVELS OF THE TRANSFORMATION

It is important to note the two levels of this corporate transformation. On the one hand, large business purchasers of care, along with the federal government under the Reagan administration, have promulgated cost containment policies that clearly reduce subsidization of care for those unable to pay. In the absence of a federal mandate for universal health insurance, employer-based plans (covering approximately 75 percent of employees' cost for the health insurance) handle the bulk of workers and their dependents, but smaller employers (and a majority within the growing service sector) offer no coverage. Caught in the throws of a changing world economy (and taking advantage of the weakened position of American labor), large corporations over this decade have engaged in "corporate take-backs" to lessen health insurance benefits, forced greater cost-sharing by employees, and reduced health provider payments, which has virtually ended their previous indirect subsidization of hospital care for those unable to pay.

Since the early 1970s large corporations collectively began an unprecedented involvement in health policy and planning on the national and local levels. Numerous initiatives by individual firms—from self-insurance schemes and rearranging employee health benefits within various "managed care" alternatives to workplace medicine and health promotion activities—have been vigorously pursued to stem their rising outlays. With increasing vehemence, purchasers and payors are also challenging providers on cost and appropriateness measures for services to their sponsored patients (9, 10).

Likewise, the federal government as the largest purchaser of medical care services for its Medicare and Medicaid beneficiaries has increasingly restricted payments to providers. There are 32 million aged and disabled persons (including the kidney dialysis patients) on Medicare supported by Social Security taxes on working people. These beneficiaries have been dealt dramatically higher copayments over the Reagan years, most recently with a completely new policy reversal of a direct "tax" on them for catastrophic (sic) care—it doesn't cover long-term care. Medicaid, the federal-state program for the "categorically needy" covers only 21 million of the poor. This program has been slashed at both levels of government, cutting recipients, limiting benefit coverage, and, for many states, not increasing provider payments, which exacerbates patient "dumping" or economic transfers from private hospitals to public hospitals (11, 12). Other federal funding reductions in health programs have removed vital support of local public health care programs. Such cost containment measures must be viewed as part of the ongoing corporate transformation of U.S. health care.

On the other hand, the corporatization of medicine comes from the emergence of large-scale corporate health care enterprise—from the diversifying investor-owned and "not-for-profit" multi-institutional hospital chains, federations, and alliances, as well as the nationwide and regional health maintenance organizations (HMOs) and giant commercial insurance companies which are now actively investing in health care delivery operations. All have been in a mad scramble to integrate and seize larger market shares of the better insured population.

A direct result of this two-fold process is the triaging out of the medically indigent and poor by such bottom-line driven providers at the same time that health care institutions in the inner-city and rural areas, where the bulk of this uninsured and underinsured population resides, are being selectively dismantled (13).

In contrast to this rapid rise of the for-profit sector is the accompanying decline of the public sector's overall delivery of services to the underserved segments of the U.S. population. Public hospitals all across America have been closing since the 1970s, along with hundreds of urban voluntary and small rural hospitals that have tried, or had little option but, to serve surrounding communities of poor, aged, and minority concentrations (14). A comparison between the decline of these provider agencies and the growth of the profit-oriented health care industry represents a condition of underdevelopment amidst development, a reflection of an economic system structured for social inequity in the distribution of services (13).

In essence, this corporatization process entails both the ascendance of profit-oriented health care operations, in addition to the invasion of this host of large corporate parties in the delivery, supply and finance functions. The change is not solely one in ownership, but in the purpose and character of the nation's health care enterprise. Within existing political economic conditions, the social function of the health sector has undergone a reversal in its organizational direction.

RESPONSE AND REACTION

While a wide spectrum of political thought characterizes the critique of this transformation, the major preoccupation of research has focused on the costs, profits, and scale of operations of major "for-profit" health care providers, and mostly hospitals at that (15–18). Yet, the corporatization of medicine has not been confined to just for-profit hospital development. Commentators have recently pointed to lower profit performance and restructuring by certain larger firms to maintain that this overall for-profit direction is on the wane (19); this is a mistaken view. It fails to properly recognize the pervasive organization behavior which became structurally embedded in response to competitive health policy in the 1980s.

Even as the big four national hospital systems prepare for new profit opportunities at home and abroad, the phenomenon of corporatization has revealed itself as a broader social process affecting (and infecting) most health care providers today. Many religious hospitals, visiting nurse associations, and public health departments across the nation today mimic the very same strategies of their for-profit brethren (20). Increasingly, there is a rather blurred distinction between the investor-owned health care firms and the traditional voluntary ones (21). Profit-seeking behavior by the so-called "not-for-profit" hospitals and health maintenance organizations (HMOs) has propelled their consolidation into mostly regional, but some national, systems as well. These traditional providers may still be distinct, but act no differently, from their proprietary counterparts in health care marketplace.

Since the Nixon administration legitimized explicit profit-making, the rate of profit in health care has been significant enough to both reorient traditional providers, as well as attract the cast of outside predators. More recently with the financial contraction, less and less behavioral variance is allowable among hospital, nursing homes, HMOs, and ambulatory care providers of all sorts under different ownership. The same conditions of American capitalism over nearly three decades have reshaped their very existence as institutions for reproduction of a labor force, legitimation, and social control (22, 23).

Critical questions of the for-profit invasion of health care have been raised in many quarters. Of significant concern to many is their very pervasive influence throughout the entire system (24-28). Commentary on the ethical issues stemming from the redirections abound, besides expressions about a perceived insidious loss of passion and compassion among practitioners under the corporatization trend. Clearly the social obligation to care for the poor, sick, and disabled has receded with the rising tide of commercialism and business management. Voices decry the loss of moral responsibility to serve people's needs regardless of ability to pay, let alone rendering services for the objective of a handsome return on provider investment. Such charitable values left over from the religious heritage of health care institutions and the altruism of a professional calling still resonate among many health workers. But more so is the opposite: to accept and capitalize upon the new conditions for profit-making (29).

Physician self-interest has evoked a number of negative reactions to the rise of the "new medical industrial complex" (30-36). From *The New England Journal of Medicine*'s editor to the leadership of the American Medical Association, the defense of quality of care within the constraints of commercialization has become the clarion call of the profession. More at stake, however, is the issue of physician autonomy in a rapidly emerging context of preferred provider and managed care arrangements. Given the abrupt end of government and other third party largess, tighter fiscal scrutiny and a medical management information system capability led to examining what doctors do (10). Physicians fear both managerial dominance over their clinical decision making, as well as a subsequent reduction in their incomes and a gradual depreciation of their status.

THE VOLUME'S CONTRIBUTION

Up until the mid-1970s, the social and institutional changes internal to the health sector were generally observed as having a relative autonomy from the rest of the economy. Today it is common to place health and health care issues within a broader social context based on historical developments that make present happenings appear logical and more explicable in their course. Still, the bulk of observations of the ongoing transformation remain limited by not focusing upstream to the larger process of capital accumulation (37) utilizing a political economic lens to reveal how events in health care today both reflect and extend the fundamental characteristics of capitalist development (38–40).

Because of the social significance of this ongoing transformation of health care, it is timely to investigate differing interpretations of the dynamics before us, as well as to offer fuller descriptions of its processes for theoretical and practical use. The selections in this volume represent a major step toward such an illumination. Many of the chapters appeared previously in the "Special Section on the Corporatization of Medicine" of the *International Journal of Health Services*. These pieces have been edited and updated, while new selections have been added to expand the overall discussion. It is hoped that the chapters in this volume collectively contribute to the needed critique of this corporate redirection and support actions toward a different orientation for health services delivery.

REFERENCES

1. McKinlay, J. B. (ed.). *Issues in the Political Economy of Health Care*, Methuen, New York, 1984.
2. Starr, P. *The Social Transformation of American Medicine*. Basic Books, New York, 1982.
3. McKinlay, J. B. Introduction. In *Issues in the Political Economy of Health Care*, edited by J. B. McKinlay, Methuen, New York, 1984.
4. Relman, A. S. The new-medical industrial complex. *New Engl. J. Med.* 303(17): 963–970, October 23, 1980.
5. Salmon J. W. The health maintenance organization strategy: A corporate takeover of health services delivery. *Int. J. Health Serv.* 5(4): 609–624, 1975.
6. Rayner, G. HMOs in the U.S.A. and Britain: A new prospect for health care? *Soc. Sci. Med.* 27(4): 305–320, 1988.
7. Berliner, H. S. and Regan, C. Multinational operations of US for-profit hospital chains: Trends and implications. *Am. J. Public Health* 77: 1280–1284, 1987.
8. Greene, J. Systems went back to basics in '87, restructuring to stay competitive. *Modern Healthcare* 18(21): 45–117, 1988.
9. White, W. D., Salmon, J. W., and Feinglass, J. Alterations in the agency relationship and implications for the medical profession. *Int. J. Health Serv.* (forthcoming, 1990).
10. Feinglass, J. and Salmon, J. W. Corporatization and the use of medical management information systems: Increasing the clinical productivity of physicians. *Int. J. Health Serv.* (forthcoming, 1990).
11. Schiff, R. L. et al. Transfers to a public hospital: A prospective study of 467 patients. *New Engl. J. Med.* 314(9): 552–559, 1986.
12. Salmon, J. W., Lieber, S., and Ayesse, M. C. Reducing inpatient hospital costs: An attempt at Medicaid reform in Illinois. *J. Health Polit. Policy Law* 13(1): 103–127.
13. Whiteis, D. and Salmon, J. W. The proprietarization of health care and the underdevelopment of the public sector. *Int. J. Health Serv.* 17(1): 47–64, 1987.
14. Sager, A. Why urban voluntary hospitals close. *Health Serv. Res.* 18(3): 450–457, 1983.
15. Ermann, D. and Gabel, J. Multihospital systems: Issues and empirical findings. *Health Aff.* 3(1): 51–64, Spring 1984.
16. Pattison, R. and Katz, H. Investor-owned and not-for-profit hospitals: A comparison based on California data. *New Engl. J. Med.* 309: 347–353, August 11, 1983.

17. Watt, J. M., et al. The comparative economic performance of investor-owned chain and not-for-profit hospitals. *New Engl. J. Med.* 314(2): 89–96, January 9, 1986.
18. Renn, S. C., et al. The effects of ownership and systems affiliation on the economic performance of hospitals. *Inquiry* 22: 219–236, Fall 1985.
19. Ginzberg, E. For-profit medicine: A reassessment. *New Engl. J. Med.* 319(12): 757–761.
20. Salmon, J. W. and Todd, J. W. (eds.). *Proceedings of the Corporatization of Health Care: A Two Day Symposium and Public Hearing.* Springfield, IL: Illinois Public Health Association, 1988.
21. Vladeck, B. C. *In Sickness and in Health: The Mission of Voluntary Health Care Institutions.* New York, McGraw-Hill, 1988.
22. Waitzkin, H. A marxist view of medical care. *Ann. Intern. Med.* 89: 264–278, 1978.
23. Navarro, V. The crisis of the international capitalist order and its implications on the welfare state. In *Issues in the Political Economy of Health Care*, edited by J. McKinlay, New York, Methuen, 1984.
24. Salmon, J. W. The medical profession and the corporatization of the health sector. *Theor. Med.* 8: 19–29, 1987.
25. Schlesinger, M. The rise of proprietary health care. *Business and Health* 2(3): 17–12, January/February 1985.
26. Luft, H. S. For-profit hospitals: A cost problem or solution? *Business and Health* 2(3): 13–16, January/February 1985.
27. Young, Q. D. The danger of making serious problems worse. *Business and Health* 2(3): 32–33, January/February 1985.
28. Young, Q. D. Impact of for-profit enterprise on health care. *J. Public Health Policy* 5(4): 449–452, December 1984.
29. Dreuth, M. R. *The Corporatization of Health Care Delivery: The Hospital-Physician Relationship.* Chicago, American Hospital Publishing, Inc., 1986.
30. Freedman, S. A. Megacorporate health care: Choice for the future. *New Engl. J. Med.* 312(9): 579–582, February 28, 1985.
31. Relman, A. S. Salaried physicians and economic incentives. *New Engl. J. Med.* 319(12): 784, Sept. 22, 1988.
32. Scovern, H. A physician's experiences in a for-profit staff-model HMO. *New Engl. J. Med.* 319(12): 787–790, Sept. 22, 1988.
33. Relman, A. S. Meeting community needs is a major concern raised by for-profit health care. *Business and Health* 2(3): 60, January/February 1985.
34. Wohl, S. *The Medical Industrial Complex.* Harmony Books, New York, 1984.
35. Eisenberg, L. The case against for-profit hospitals. *Hosp. Community Psychiatry* 35(10): 1009–1013, 1984.
36. Moore, F. D. Who should profit from the care of your illness? *Harvard Magazine*: 45–54, November/December 1985.
37. McKinlay, J. B. A case of refocussing upstream—the political economy of illness. *Behavioral Science Research Data Review*, American Heart Association Conference, Seattle, Washington, June 17–19, 1974.
38. Estes, C. L., Gerard, L., Jones, J. S., and Swan, J. H. *Political Economy, Health and Aging,* Little Brown, Boston, 1984.
39. Salmon, J. W. Monopoly capital and the reorganization of health care. *Review of Radical Political Economics* 9(12): 125–133, 1977.
40. Himmelstein, D. U. and Woolhandler, S. Medicine as industry: The health-care sector in the United States. *Monthly Review* 35(11): 13–25, 1984.

TABLE OF CONTENTS

PART 1

Background to the Corporatization of Medicine

The political economic reshaping of the American health care system over the last quarter century has unquestionably been more important and varied than during any former corresponding period in history. The new configuration of the players in health services delivery today is strikingly different than even in the early 1970s.

Since that time U.S. corporations have faced a severe challenge to their dominance in the world economy. No longer is the post-war boom able to sustain rising labor costs, generous health benefits packages, and growing social welfare policies. Decreasing worker productivity with a concomitant rise in health care outlays has added to the general profits squeeze. Amidst the corporate quest for short-run profitability, rampant financial speculation, and a fantastic explosion in private and public debt, declining real wages, reductions in governmental health, welfare and housing programs, and increasing income polarization now characterize the new imposition of austerity.

A wide range of business initiatives makeup a growing wave of corporate involvement in health policy and planning. Economic constraints have forced a re-evaluation of the costs of employees health insurance, absenteeism, disability, workers' compensation, and occupational safety and health. All of these areas have been targeted in attempts to curtail outlays, but also to improve labor productivity. Individual firms are attempting various measures from self-insurance to workplace health promotion activities. Others are setting up computerized surveillance systems to monitor health provider utilization patterns, as well as scrutinize workers' lifestyles. From activities of corporate planning bodies and local business coalitions through reportings in the business press, this collective offensive represents a far-reaching corporate purchaser intrusion into health care (1).

The unending cost increases for employee benefits over the last two decades have propelled these actions. At first, large corporations sought relief in the health cost spiral by rationalizing the system through support for local health planning. Then the Reagan administration's public policy heralded the "market-place" as the solution to rising costs. The *Fortune* 500 firms were swayed by this ideology that "market efficiency" under private control would promote their positioning themselves for greater leverage over providers. Yet the "competitive" policies in health care exacerbated the cost control problematic and sharply divided the corporate class between purchasers whose interests principally lie in cost containment and improved labor productivity on one hand; and the segments of capital, both suppliers and providers, who have cashed in on the continuing bonanza of cost-plus reimbursement on the other hand. These dynamics, of course, led to further constraints through prospective payment by both public and private payers. Needless to say, another unintended consequence of competitive health policies has been the exclusion of those patients from whom providers cannot return a handsome profit—some 56 million uninsured and underinsured Americans (2). The social unrest potential from such neglect and damage looms in the background for the corporate class interest.

Of particular importance more recently are health plan costs for their retirees, which were about $8 billion in 1988, but expected to climb to $22 billion by 2008 (3). The Financial Accounting Standards Board is seeking to require firms to disclose their unfunded health benefits. To do so means that U.S. corporations would have to list liabilities on the order of $1 trillion for funding expected retiree benefits (4). Needless to say, many firms claim they have a right to cut back or terminate health benefits, and they are continually doing so for workers and retirees alike. More of such unpredictable developments may provoke greater pressures to reorganize health care institutions, perhaps returning to utilizing stricter federal regulations, or even getting government to socialize the corporate costs of production for their health care expenses.

To the extent that the ongoing corporatization of medicine emanates from the larger crisis of the international economic order, further restructuring of the welfare state to assure greater accumulation of capital can be foreseen (5). This policy redirection includes withdrawal of the means to pay for services for whom the business press calls the "unproductive." Coincidentally, discussions about rationing care to the (costly) chronically ill and those without adequate insurance coverage have now come to the forefront (6, 7) and the "policy software" is being worked out.

In the first chapter of this section, Tannen outlines a history of planning in the health sector and its functional use for larger economic interests. In the 1970s corporate purchasers of care for their employees sought to reform the system and contain costs through health planning, which was portrayed as an objective and rational mechanism. At a time when the health sector escaped successive control over its growth and development, business groups saw the planning process and health systems agencies (HSAs) as a means to smooth over the implementation of necessary changes. With the demise of federally-mandated health planning and the introduction of market strategies by the Reagan administration, the Washington Business Group on Health, which had supported continuation of the HSA legislation, then stimulated development of local business coalitions, many of which have excluded provider participation.

In "Business and the Pushcart Venders in an Age of Supermarkets," Bergthold presents her research on corporate participation in State policy-making, which clearly links the larger economic crisis to interventions to rationalize the health sector. She explains that the early stage of business coalition activity reinforced the control of health care by the private sector, profoundly limiting policy influence from unorganized consumer constituencies. At their zenith in the early 1980s these local business coalitions numbered over 200 across the nation. Bergthold argues that such business actions serve to continue their class interest over the financing and delivery of health care.

The following selection, "Profit and Health Care: Trends in Corporatization and Proprietarization" by Salmon, explains how profit has always been a motor force for health sector developments, only being unmasked by the investor-owned health care firms dramatic rise since the late 1960s. A historical analysis of these changes provides detail to the growth and influence of the for-profit providers within the more recent ideological and structural conditions in health care. The rapid rise of the corporate hospital chains and other investor-owned operations are examined.

REFERENCES

1. Feinglass, J. and Salmon, J. W. Corporatization and the use of medical management information systems: Increasing the clinical productivity of physicians. *Int. J. Health Serv.* (forthcoming).
2. Salmon, J. W. The uninsured and the underinsured: What can we do? *The Internist: Health Policy in Practice* 29(4): 8–13, 1988.
3. Karr, Albert R. Firms can end retiree health benefits. . . . *Wall Street Journal*, February 7, 1989, p. 1.
4. Weil, R. L. The FASB's healthy proposal. *Wall Street Journal*, March 1, 1989, p. 24.
5. Navarro, V. The welfare state and its distributive effects: Part of the problem or part of the solution? *Int. J. Health Serv.* 17(4): 543–566.
6. Mechanic, D. *Future Issues in Health Care: Social Policy and the Rationing Medical Services*, The Free Press, New York, 1979.
7. Aaron, H. J. and Schwartz, W. B. *The Painful Prescription: Rationing Hospital Care*, Brookings Institution, Washington, D.C., 1984.

CHAPTER 1

Health Planning as a Regulatory Strategy

Louis Tannen

Health planning attained prominence through the National Health Planning and Resource Development Act of 1974 (1). This increased emphasis on planning reflected a widespread demand for health care reform. The burden of rapidly increasing medical costs, coupled with a growing debate over the effectiveness of scientific medicine, made problems especially acute for government, industry, and insurance companies. Although all are hurt by high health care costs, major purchasers are particularly squeezed by soaring medical cost inflation, decreasing industrial productivity, and an increasing prevalence of chronic health problems not alleviated by increased medical expenditures (2).

These major purchasers were the driving force behind the rejuvenated health planning. They have had minimal direct control over the evolution of the health sector which has been dominated by providers and regulated simply by the availability of resources. This pattern of development responded more to the ability of the market to support services (demand) than to the health status of the population (need).

In a medical system where supply generates demand (Roemer's Law (3)), the unplanned expansion of health services has resulted in systematic wasteful duplication, extraneous technology, and insatiable demand. The major purchasers will no longer tolerate such haphazard and limitless expansion and are using their leverage to reform the system and contain costs. Health planning is one of several mechanisms by which health care services are rationalized according to the principles of organizational efficiency found in the business sector.

Planning agencies are a looking glass into the health system, revealing the tensions, stresses, and strategies for change. They are the arena where battles over the reorganization of health services are waged. But not all participants are equal in this arena. Health planning is not a neutral force to meet "true" health

19

needs. Health planning methods are value-laden vehicles through which a particular group or interest can shape the delivery of health services.

While the planning process can be a valuable tool for focusing and mobilizing community interest on specific health problems (e.g., women's health, occupational health and safety) and for getting people to view health as a social phenomenon (more than the interaction between patients and practitioners), it can also be a means of parrying progressive demands. As Piven has observed (4):

> Involving local groups in elaborate procedures is to guide them into a narrowly circumscribed form of political action, and precisely that form for which they are least equipped.

As a mechanism of defusing dissent and deflecting demands, planning loses its visionary thrust and becomes but one more measure of regulation and cost control, serving those who control its use.

Analyses of health planning by Krause (5), Klarman (6), Vladeck (7), and Health/PAC (8) have aided our understanding. They have shown how planning structures and planning ideology can be used to foster the needs of a particular interest group. This paper builds upon these theories by blending the analysis of planning structures with a critique of the uses and effects of planning per se, especially planning driven by the cost containment woes of third-party payors.

HEALTH PLANNING

Classic definitions of planning refer to it as the rational use of knowledge in making decisions concerning future action, directed at some vision of the "good life" (9), or the science of allocating scarce resources for the common good. These definitions describe what is widely referred to as the rational-comprehensive model of planning.[1] Such visions portray planning as an objective science, performed by rational human beings who are not influenced by interest group or ideological biases. The conceptualization separates planning from the reality in which it is done. In a society where "rationality" and "common good" are not the driving force of history, it would indeed be surprising to find these virtues dominating health planning.

Just as hospitals are mirrors of society reflecting the values and priorities of a social order, planning reflects the dynamics at work shaping the future of health services. As an arena where the battles over the reorganization of the health system will be waged, its importance and hence its vulnerability to interest group control is increased. In a society divided by class interests, planning follows suit. As one interest group or class can dominate planning practice, the bias of the

---

[1] See reference (11) for an excellent discussion of these theories.

methodologies and the allocation of its rewards will reflect this influence and control.

Appelbaum (10) describes and critiques the major constructs of the rational-comprehensive model, pointing out its inadequacy in describing the true practice of planning in American society. Summarized, the constructs and their critique are:

> *Theoretical inclusiveness.* Theoretical models do not include all variables which are pertinent. But even if they did, often times the relationships between the variables are not fully known and data for many are not available. Many relevant variables are outside the system over which one has control. Frequently the system being analyzed is evolving and changing so fast that the model simply cannot keep up.
>
> *Predictability of future states.* Many predictions and assumptions about future states assume the continuation of present forms and structures, becoming self-fulfilling prophecies.
>
> *Freedom from constraints on alternatives.* Selection and development of alternatives are often limited by political barriers as to what is acceptable to the group sponsoring the planning (e.g., the city) or by a subjective analysis by the planners of what is feasible.
>
> *Independence of evaluation and analysis.* The delineation of goals and objectives cannot so easily be separated from the evaluation and selection means. One's values grow out of the concrete situations of personal experience. Policy makers choose their objectives and the means of implementing these objectives at the same time.
>
> *Supremacy of technical knowledge.* The assumption that all problems are at their root technical and therefore capable of technical solution is perhaps the most pernicious of all myths shrouding the rational-comprehensive model and will be discussed in more detail later. At this point, suffice to say that "the problems we face are largely political rather than technical; it is not because of inadequate information that we have widespread poverty or insufficient housing or inadequate health care services" (10, p. 20).
>
> *Political pluralism.* In order for planning to serve the "common good," all political and interest groups must have equal access to the political planning process. Such access greatly varies along racial income, class, and sex lines.

If the rational-comprehensive model can be so thoroughly discredited, how is it that all or parts of it continue to dominate planning practice? If "rationality" and "common good" do not explain the nature of health planning efforts, what does? The answer lies in the interrelationship between health planning, the medical care system, and capitalist society.

HEALTH PLANNING, MEDICINE, AND CAPITALISM

Ideology refers to the values and ideas through which people view and interpret the social relations of society. The dominant ideology in a society attempts to legitimize the social structure and authority of the dominant class by justifying the system by which members of that class have acquired their wealth and power (5). To this purpose, the ruling ideology must successfully permeate the social institutions which mold social values (e.g., schools, the family, health care services). Through these institutions, the ideology of the prevailing economic order is transmitted and reinforced throughout the society (11, pp. 119-120).

As a social institution, medicine in the United States embraces an ideology which is compatible with the dominant set of beliefs of capitalism (12). This is evident in the skewed racial and sex composition of the health work force (13); the hierarchical social relations among health workers (14); the substandard care available to "non-productive" groups of population; the focus of medical resources on individual diagnosis, functional ability, and productive capacity (15); and in the medical economy (12, pp. 135-169). Surely medical ideology is shaped and determined by many different forces and is not dictated by any one class, but of the many variations and different organizational forms possible, it is no accident that the prevailing form of medical practice in the United States today is largely compatible with the capitalist mode of production and its social relations. It would be highly unlikely for the medical system to foster ideas relating to the social origins of disease, collective responsibility for health, democratization of medical skills, or community control of medical facilities. These concepts run counter to the prevailing values of the rest of society.

In addition to institutionalizing values compatible with our economic system, medicine can play a more direct role in supporting existing power relations. These functions of medicine include: 1) the reproduction of the labor force and the functional maintenance of workers; 2) social control; 3) legitimation of the society by caring for the mental and physical social pathology caused by capitalism; and 4) the creation of a source of investment, surplus value, and service employment (16). When centered on this basic ideological framework, medicine plays a significant role in the preservation and entrenchment of class relations.

Health planning fits into this scheme of things in two ways. First, planning can ensure that the health system meets these four objectives. If not operating in harmony with these goals, forces outside the health care system will intervene through planning to set it back on track. Planning can be focused on the content of medicine and its effectiveness and the manner in which care is delivered. Specific issues that may be covered include the introduction and effectiveness of new technology (17), new delivery systems such as Health Maintenance Organizations (18, pp. 16-18), productivity of health workers (19), medical care evaluation studies (through Professional Service Review Organizations), and patients' rights.

Secondly, given the health system is adequately performing its roles, the system can be rationalized to perform more efficiently and cost effectively. Planning attempts to manage the problems and internal contradictions caused by the market development of the health sector. These problems include unequal access to, or the uneven distribution of, health services and spiraling costs. To maintain the system's acceptability, rationalization focuses on eliminating the duplication of services and overexpansion, while encouraging the spread of services into underserved areas. At the same time, by limiting expansion, rationalization supports the financial viability of existing institutions.

The view of planning presented above is one not of guiding change to avoid crises but of instituting change to react to crises. Planning has been so intertwined with the regulation of health care that these two processes are now hardly distinguishable (20). By assuming a regulatory posture, agencies are more closely bound to the sources of their regulatory power: generally the major third-party purchasers of services.

As a regulator, one can stop people from doing things but can only indirectly promote activity, if at all. As practiced in the United States, planning is most effective at controlling growth, not at guiding development. Hence, it comes as no surprise that planning has attained perhaps its greatest importance during a severe cost crisis and in the midst of a policy of shrinking the medical care sector.

It is important to reiterate, however, that planning agencies can be used to address a community's real health needs and improve health status. But in assessing the obstacles to their functioning as vehicles for progressive change, the origin of the agencies and the biased structure which has been created for them must be understood.

HISTORY OF HEALTH PLANNING

Rapid, unplanned industrialization and urbanization in mid-to-late 19th century America were accompanied by epidemics of infectious conditions throughout working-class neighborhoods. Workers labored long hours under unsafe conditions. Nutrition was poor and housing overcrowded. The urban infrastructure (sewage systems, waste removal, water supply, etc.) was underdeveloped and overburdened (21).

The response to this problem generally took the form of sanitary reform. Disease was associated with filth, and risk was defined in terms of social, demographic, and economic attributes. Reformers and planners sought to minimize risk and combat disease through sanitary programs, nutrition education, social support, and birth, death, and disease registries. Neighborhoods and people at risk were identified and programs targeted at them.

One reason that social programs were emphasized is that they appeared to be the only workable solution available. Medicine was largely ineffective in dealing with these infectious problems and hospitals had only a marginal therapeutic role. They were therefore largely ignored by the reformers interested in controlling disease. However, this situation was soon to change.

Backed by the American Medical Association, institutionalized by the Flexner report, and advanced by germ-theory-based research, scientific medicine emerged as the dominant medical ideology in the early part of the 20th century (22). This provided impetus for a dynamic new role for hospitals, from the almshouses of the past to the laboratory, workshop, and training center for the expanding medical-care labor force.

As the focus on hospitals increased, so did the number of beds. Between 1909 and 1920, the number of hospital beds increased by 65 percent from 4.7 to 7.7 per 1000 population (23, p. 23). However, coexisting with this huge proliferation of beds was endemic maldistribution. Hospital facilities were not distributed according to need (e.g., morbidity) but on the basis of a real or supposed ability to pay (24). In 1928, of the 3,072 counties in the United States, only 1,765 had general community hospital beds. Concentrations of beds to population varied from one bed for 154 persons in Wisconsin to one bed for 749 persons in South Carolina (24, p. 5).

As hospitals became the center of the health delivery system, hospital construction was fostered through the use of "planning" studies and reports. Efforts directed at guaranteeing health focused on establishing a minimum bed-per-population ratio. Examples of these early studies include: New York Academy of Medicine (1921), Committee on County Hospitals of the American Hospital Association (1927), Duke endowment report (1928), and the Emerson study (1930) (23, pp. 23-30). These fixed ratios, usually of five beds per 1000 population, served two purposes: first, they identified areas which were "underbedded" and "needed" construction; and second, they curtailed overbedding which could bloat the market and threaten the solvency of existing hospitals.

By the late 1920s and early 1930s, hospitals began to suffer the debilitating effects of overexpansion and the Depression. In large numbers, patients unable to afford care in the private voluntary hospitals were forced to use public ones (25, p. 27). The result was badly overcrowded public hospitals and empty voluntary hospitals. Shaped by the more influential hospital administrators who were located in the voluntary sector, planning bodies pressed for the control of bed proliferation, closed proprietary hospitals (23, 26), and organized insurance plans to increase demand by paying patients (the origin of Blue Cross) (27, pp. 6-8).

In 1932, the 26-volume study by the Committee on the Costs of Medical Care was published in response to the excessive financial costs of illness. Some committee members proclaimed the need for increased organizational efficiency along the lines of large-scale industrial production to reduce the unit cost of medical care.

One volume, referred to as the Lee-Jones report (28), carefully tested a technique to estimate resource requirements by examining the health needs of the population. This stands in stark contrast to the mechanical demand-based estimates developed earlier and has been called a "uniquely important landmark in the evolution of planning for health care resources . . ." (23). However, planning for needs was not an idea whose time had come. The occupancy problems in the private sector during the Depression made planning for solvency the top priority. For subsequent decades, planning efforts focused on estimating demand and optimum occupancy rates as the means of projecting the number of beds "needed." The Lee-Jones methodology, which was considered a landmark, "had lain virtually dormant since (1933)" (23).

The crises in the voluntary sector during and following the Depression gave birth to the first voluntary regional planning agencies. As medical technology and the sophistication of hospitals increased, so did the hospitals' need for capital funds. Being largely the product of philanthropy, voluntary hospitals turned to donors for new funds. However, the decreased use of private, nonprofit hospitals raised questions among potential donors about the need for new facilities. As a means of guaranteeing that the requested money would not be wasted on unnecessary construction, regional planning agencies were established in metropolitan areas as a means of setting priorities for the collection and use of capital funds (29).

The model for the formation of the voluntary health planning agencies was based on the councils of social agencies formed in 1920s. These were groups of charity and philanthropic donors who, besieged by many funding requests, came together for the purpose of joint fund raising. Planning was needed to establish fund raising goals, allocate funds, provide insight into community needs, and set priorities. The need for such agencies increased as the major source of funds shifted from individual wealthy families to corporations and foundations (30).

As hospital requests for capital funds increased and swamped these voluntary social planning agencies, separate bodies were created to concentrate on hospital construction. The first such agency, the Hospital Council of Greater New York, was established in 1937. Other agencies were formed in the metropolitan areas of Columbus, Rochester, Detroit, Chicago, Pittsburgh, and others. By 1964 there were 34 hospitals planning agencies (30). As Thompson has observed, "Strong agencies were created where a cohesive group of private donors lived. Hence, the presence of the Mellon interests in Pittsburgh and of Kodak in Rochester made strong central planning agencies possible in these communities" (29, p. 123). Third-party payors were not integrally involved early on because of the limited role they played in health care delivery at that time.

These planning bodies were dominated by corporate executives and wealthy "leading citizens." Thus, "these councils often reflected the economic and social values of the city's wealthier classes" (30). As Gottlieb notes (30, p. 12):

> In their early stages, almost all of these hospital's planning agencies were dominated by representatives of major corporate contributors and their peers who were primarily interested in bricks and mortar developments that were to be financed by contributed capital.

And Klarman observed (25, p. 27):

> The chief executives of these corporations saw hospital planning as a way to rationalize the hospital industry in the manner that one would try to rationalize any large industry.

One of the major effects of corporate domination of planning was the concentration on the hospital bed as the unit of planning. It best reflected the experience of the people on these planning boards, was well defined, and was the area of the greatest interest for the philanthropists (29). Through the review of a hospital's proposal for a capital project, and by helping hospitals create their own planning structure, the planning agencies further reinforced the hospitals' focus on beds at the expense of other types of health services. Generally, little attention was paid to matters other than beds. Nonhospital resource shortages and outpatient care hardly addressed (29, p. 127). Health planning became medical care planning.

The goal of the voluntary planning bodies was to discourage and limit overexpansion. They were largely regulatory bodies controlling the use of donated funds for capital expenditures. Eliminating unnecessary beds was their primary concern. This is not to imply, however, that these agencies were seen as an antagonistic force by the hospitals. Physicians had a high level of involvement on most of the agency boards. Also, many hospitals, severely hurt by overexpansion and falling occupancy rates, sought to limit the self-defeating and wasteful competition among hospitals. The planning agencies were not questioning the need for hospitals and were not a threat to the future of hospital-based medical care. They were quite the opposite. By avoiding overexpansion, they protected the solvency of existing institutions. Stemming from this orientation, planning methodologies developed since the Lee-Jones study in 1933 reflected the growing concern with unnecessary (unused) facilities. However, an unnecessary facility was defined as one that does not have adequate demand to support it; the appropriateness of its utilization or its relationship to health status was only indirectly addressed.

A variety of techniques to more accurately project demand for hospital services emerged to reduce overconstruction and bolster low hospital occupancy rates. These techniques included delineation of hospital service areas, projection of specific types and proportions of services demanded, and determination of the sociodemographic variables which underlie hospital expansion (23, pp. 23–46).

The voluntary health planning agencies became the base upon which later structures were developed. The Hill-Burton Act was passed in 1946 to foster the construction of hospitals in rural areas. Definitely a construction-oriented bill, need was based on a simple arithmetic bed-to-population ration. The act set up, for the first time, publicity created statewide hospital planning bodies. However, in areas where voluntary planning agencies were already in operation (23, pp. 38–44), they played a major role in project review and in advising the state planning agencies established by Hill-Burton. In return, the agencies received financial support (30, p. 125). In 1962 Hill-Burton funds were made available on a 50-50 basis to areas for local planning (25, p. 32) facilitating the formation of additional area-wide health planning bodies.

The Government's first attempt at comprehensive health planning with meaningful enforcement powers came in 1967 with the Comprehensive Health Planning Act (23, pp. 158–161). The establishment of Comprehensive Health Planning Agencies (CHPs) marked a significant change for the voluntary agencies. Some were replaced by the new CHP local agencies; others continued parallel operations until they were absorbed; and still others expanded their boards and were designated CHP local agencies (29, p. 125).

As the hospitals' dependence on contributed dollars for capital projects diminished, so did the usefulness and authority of the voluntary agencies. As the Federal role as a major purchaser of health services increased, publicly created health planning agencies, starting with CHPs, became the dominant force in planning.

But even as planning became a governmentally mandated function, rationalization and cost control remained as goals. The focus of the voluntary agencies on hospital-based medical care, projection of demand, and planned growth continued as the mainstays of planning practice.

HEALTH PLANNING AND THE STATE

Central to understanding the direction of current planning efforts is the role and interests of the State. The primary role of the State in society (31) is that of defending, supporting, and encouraging the health of the economic system, upon which all else is based. In the health sector, the State gives primacy to the impact on the economic system as a whole, rather than on the economic interests of any one interest group in the health system. The preservation of the social order assumes a higher priority than the needs of any single interest group.

The cost crisis in health care and its inflationary impact on the rest of the economy has forced state intervention. This intervention takes three primary forms: cutbacks, rationalization, and planning (31). Planning in regulatory clothing becomes a means of accomplishing the other two political responses. However, the use of planning to resolve the health care crises is somewhat of an enigma. The philanthropic, corporate, and governmental forces which foster and sponsor planning in the health system are the same forces which oppose large-scale planning in other sectors of the economy (25, pp. 28–29).

This apparent contradiction can be explained in three ways. First, planning is one of the more generally acceptable means by which the State and similarly interested groups can exert control over the health care system, a system from which they have been excluded in the past. Although the State is recognized as a legitimate participant in economic and social affairs, medical care was traditionally seen as the province of physicians, scientists, and hospital managers. Because of this, prospects for desired changes originating within the system were slight, so the external imposition of a regulating force was necessary to rationalize the health system. Planning became the most palliative alternative available to the State with which to achieve its goals.

Second, nearly all health planning in the United States has been done on the local level, giving major participants the hope of influencing the planning effort. Growing out of the tradition of the locally originating voluntary planning agencies, there is little central or hierarchical authority. The appearance of local control makes planning more acceptable to local government, corporations, hospital councils, and medical societies.

Third, planning makes the political process of determining the future more predictable. The determination of who is involved, the scope and the power of decisions, and five-year health plans add a measure of predictability to the future structure of the health system (at least through self-fulfilling prophecies). This predictability is an important ingredient to corporate economic planning (18, p. 16).

PLANNING AS STRATEGY FOR REFORM

The value of planning in the reorganization of health services is based on its image as an objective mediator of conflicting interests. Decisions are made under the pretense of a rational, scientific determination and evaluation of alternatives—an image which masks the true ideological orientation of planning decisions.

The legitimacy and impact of planning decisions in many cases depend on this image of objectivity. The "rational evaluation of alternatives" and the "broad sense of participation" support the image. If the ideological and/or interest group control of planning was widely understood, planning agencies would lose their credibility. For example, if a Chamber of Commerce or local hospital council proposed a reorganization of health care services, the bias of the plan would be explicit and resisted by opposing groups. However, when the bias is hidden behind a veil of objectivity or rationalism, the prospects for implementation are increased.

As part of this, planners must have their own body of knowledge, their own jargon, their own methods. Such a mystique sets them apart from the layperson, justifies them as a profession, and legitimates their product. However, since planning as a public pursuit has traditionally not been an accepted concept in the American economy, health planning does not have an historically developed knowledge base of its own (5). It has borrowed techniques from business for forecasting demand and regulating supply. But recently, to both legitimate planners as professionals and to further "objectify" their work, the Federal Government has gone to great lengths to foster the development of the technical aspects of health planning and raise the technical competence of planners. These efforts have concentrated on the development of scientific planning techniques, research methods, needs assessments, and data collection. The growth in scientific planning further separates those without these skills from planning activities.

Adding to the legitimacy of planning is the myth of consumer control. Although the planning act requires that all planning agencies have a majority of consumers on their boards, interpreting this to mean consumer domination is fallacious (32). Consumer members are not a homogeneous group; included in this category are insurance companies, business and labor organizations, public officials, and community leaders. Although "consumers" technically constitute a majority on HSA boards, grassroots community representatives are a minority which moreover lacks the technical experience or financial support that other representatives (consumer or provider) have; they are therefore less powerful. Despite this reality, the image of a regulatory planning agency dominated by consumers—not by people who stand to selfishly profit from planning—adds to the legitimacy of the effort (33, pp. 26–40).

Planning agencies not only mediate conflicts but also serve to bind participants to the decisions of their boards. Federal law mandates the participation of health institutions, insurance companies, direct and indirect providers, labor, major purchasers (business), and "consumers" on planning agency boards and thus ensures that all of the major actors are "involved" in the decision making. Such involvement serves to increase compliance with the final decision of the agency. When a group is formally involved in developing a plan, even though it has bargained or compromised certain things away, it is bound to the plan and less likely to publicly condemn the final product. In accepting the legitimacy of planning and participating in the development of the plan, one accepts the legitimacy of its decisions.

This function is important to policy planners who have an eye to orderly and smooth reform. The functioning of the health care system involves many actors and interests, including providers, consumers, medical supply industries, corporate rationalizers, provider institutions, and health workers (34, 35). The varying interests directly lead to numerous conflicts over priorities. Agreement over organizational forms, financing mechanisms, or public policy is no simple matter.

These debates and conflicts are intensified during times of crisis and organizational stress (36). While government wants all interests involved in planning to ensure they will adhere to the plans developed, the individual groups participate to promote and protect their self-interest. As Krause notes (5, pp. 48–49):

> The Process of planning inevitably and basically a type of power politics involving either the preservation of the *status quo* or change in it. To the

degree that powerful interest groups exist in fields such as health *before* the
introduction of any new attempt at planning, they can be expected to frus-
trate or twist, or coopt the planning process. . . .

As a result of the varying influence of interest groups in different areas,
health planning agencies around the country have different orientations and
goals. Agencies are strongly controlled by either providers, local government,
corporations, or consumers. While differences in control affect the planning
process and its outcome, the variations are still within parameters on agency
activities established by the Federal Government. These limits include the scope
of legislatively mandated duties, the sanctions provided, and nationally established planning priorities. The agencies are evaluated according to federally
determined criteria (e.g., how they have contained health costs in their service
area), not on the basis of how well they have dealt with the local problems of
access, quality, or health status. While there is a local leeway in how the cost-
containment goal is accomplished, i.e., which projects are approved and which
ones are denied, all HSAs must still be guided by cost control. Agencies are
currently given little, if any, sanctions to act in the areas of occupational,
environmental, or public health, and can only peripherally deal with the issue of
quality of care. They are generally limited to tinkering with existing services
rather than given the initiative to foster new and innovative programs.

What is called health planning is really medical care planning. This phenomenon is explained by the recognition that the roots of planning and medicine
are in the social structure in which they are planted. Just as plants absorb
material from the ground into their structures, so does planning absorb from its
social substrate methodologies, priorities, and ideologies. Focusing on health
and why people get sick is an anathema to American medicine because this
would highlight the social origins of disease, origins rooted in the economic and
social relations of our society. Conversely, focusing on an engineering model of
the human body, an individualized germ theory of disease, and the comodifica-
tion of health care has been shown to be compatible with capitalist ideology
and social and economic development.

It has been stated that planning reflects the dynamics and ideology of society
and of the health care system, but that the image of objectivity and rationality
obfuscates the true nature of this ideological orientation. This is accomplished
by the use of planning models which appear to be objective and quantitative, but
in fact embody the bias of ideology of the interests that control planning. A
description of these models follow.

THEORETICAL FRAMEWORK OF PLANNING TECHNIQUES

Planning methodologies may be separated into two major theoretical camps:
resource-based planning, and population-based planning (37). This section will
describe each approach and the health care ideology it embodies. The premise is

that population-based planning permits a social view of health, whereas resource-based planning lends itself to the development of institutionally oriented illness care.

Resource-based Planning

Resource-based planning attempts to match the supply of health resources with the demand for health services (37, 38). The objective of this process is to accommodate demand in the most efficient manner possible, and it relies heavily on service-to-population ratios. This model (shown in Figure 1) dominates planning practice today.

The methodology begins with the selection of the service to be studied (A). This selection is usually generated by problems of under or overutilization of a particular service, or the physical deterioration of a service necessitating its replacement. The current utilization, together with the past utilization trends, is determined (B), so that the potential demand for the service may be forecasted

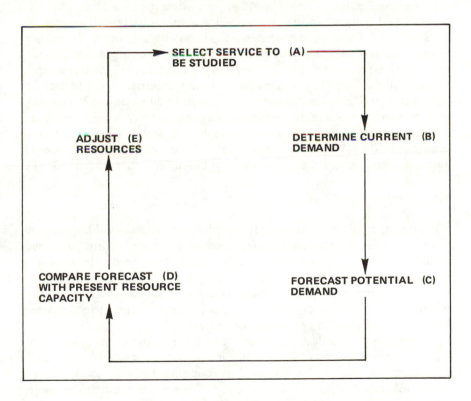

Figure 1. Resource-based planning model.

(C). This potential demand is determined by analyzing who uses the facility and projecting their numerical growth in the future. Also, any expected or desired changes in the hospital's service or market area are included to get the best possible picture of how many people will use the facility in the future.

The projected demand is then compared with the current capacity of the service (D). In determining whether the existing capacity is adequate, any changes in occupancy behavior—such as new standards in minimum allowable occupancy rates (i.e., changing them from 80 to 85 percent) or a lowering of the average length of stay standard—are taken into account. Finally, the expected demand is matched with the expected supply to determine if any resource adjustments (E) are necessary to accommodate the projected utilization.

Two basic problems inherent in the resource-based approach demonstrate the limitations of this methodology. First, resource-based planning embodies the implicit assumption that the purpose of the health system is solely to treat illness. As a result, there is seldom any attempt to link the existence of resources with the actual health status of population they purport to serve.

Second, resource-based planning is inherently linked to a market paradigm and the rationalization or "fine tuning" of the existing resource system. Because resource-based planning focuses on demand and the utilization of services, its implementation is inherently limited to marginal adjustments within the existing delivery system. The system's adequacy is evaluated in terms of how it meets the demand expressed for services. However, demand cannot be equated with the need for health services, as a myriad of factors unrelated to need affect the utilization of the health care system. For example, reimbursement mechanisms shape patterns; inaccessibility, racism, sexism, and inability to pay discourage utilization; and the level of physician supply has been shown to influence demand (e.g., the rate of surgery performed varies directly with the number of practicing surgeons, not necessarily with the "need" for surgery) (39, 40, 41).

Population-based Planning

Population-based planning is a process which determines health needs and establishes resource requirements based upon an assessment of risk levels and health status of a given population. The determination of need is derived solely from attributes of the population, initially ignoring all existing resources.

The first step in the population-based planning model (shown in Figure 2) is the selection of health problems (A). The population is studied to determine the problems which will receive the highest priority. The definition of what constitutes a major health problem and the criteria for ranking them are further examples of the subjective nature of planning.

Following the selection of the problem condition, both the social and the medical risk factors which predispose a population to the condition are ascertained (B). An assessment of the risk levels of the population and its variation

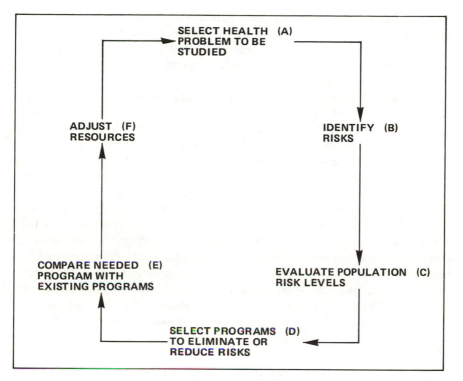

Figure 2. Population-based planning model.

throughout the area is made for each factor (C). The objectives of data collection are to quantify the level of risk in the population, establish the geographic distribution of those at risk, and project their change over time.

At this point, protocols are established to address each risk factor, prescribing programs and standards which will eliminate, reduce, or manage the risks (D). Such programs are not limited to medical services, for the broad definition of risk used in step B requires a correspondingly broad array of social programs to minimize the risks. These programs are matched with the existing programs to determine if changes or additions are necessary in the resources which are provided (E). The resources are adjusted (F) to accommodate the gaps found in step E. The model is circular to emphasize the point that periodic reevaluation is necessary to continually upgrade the system.

By basing its analysis on the subsets of the population and their risk levels rather than on the resource structure, population-based planning facilitates the identification of the social, economic, and environmental problems which predispose a population to high risk of disease. The methodology, therefore, is capable of addressing an array of health problems that extends well beyond the medical care system, and more adequately accommodates the growing aware-ness of the social and environmental determinants of health. It facilitates health maintenance by targeting preventive and health care programs directly at high-risk populations and appears most capable of orienting the health care system toward promotion, prevention, and primary care activities.

There are two major obstacles to implementing population-based-planning. These are the type of data required to carry out the analysis and the method-ology's social orientation. An accurate assessment of health status and risk levels requires data not presently collected in usable form. Data on the dis-tribution of demographic, medical, and environmental risks for geographic areas small enough to be useful for planning do not exist. What is available are data on hospital and clinic utilization, which is compatible with resource-based planning. Hence, a population-based approach is often the unused alternative.

Population-based planning, through its analysis of the underlying risks of disease, identifies the social and environmental causes of ill health, which are not eliminated by medical services. This broadens the scope of health planning into areas such as occupational health, environmental pollution, and social condi-tions. However, the authority of planning to intervene in these areas is not well established. The political implications of encroaching upon the concerns of vested economic interests is perhaps the greatest obstacle to the full implemen-tation of this planning methodology.

As a major vehicle for change in health care delivery, health planning has attracted widespread attention as an arena where the program for health care's future will be developed. However, the emphasis of this program will be cost containment and rationalization, with health status addressed only peripherally. From this orientation, cutbacks, rationing of care, personal responsibility for health problems, and a restructuring of health work will likely become major strategies guiding health planning. Planning agencies and their products are legitimated through images of public participation, scientific evaluation of alter-natives, and consumer control.

Planning is not a neutral force in the reorganization of the health sector. Its methods are value-laden instruments which implement a particular ideology of medical care under a guise of objectivity. Also, by delineating sanctions, per-missible areas of concern, levels of funding, and criteria for evaluation, major third-party payors become the driving force behind the planning effort and control its thrust. Health advocates who work within this structure must constantly struggle against the tide of cost containment priorities to raise pro-gressive concerns of people's health needs.

Yet, when used effectively as a forum for the discussion of health concerns, planning agencies can raise issues and mobilize action to redress problems. Only by understanding and exposing the bias limitation and potential of planning efforts can we effectively use planning agencies for these purposes.

REFERENCES

1. The National Health Planning and Resource Development Act. Act. PL93-641, 1974.
2. Salmon, J. Corporate Attempts to Reorganize the American Health Sector, Ph.D. thesis, Cornell University, 1978.
3. Roemer, M. I. Bed supply and hospital utilization. *Hospitals* 35(21): 36–42, 1961.
4. Piven, F. F. Whom does the advocate planner serve?, In *The Politics of Turmoil*, edited by Piven, F., and Cloward, R., pp. 47–52. Random House, New York, 1975.
5. Krause, E. Health planning as a managerial ideology. *Int. J. Health Serv.* 3(3): 445–463, 1973.
6. Klarman, H. E. Health planning: Progress, prospects, and issues. *Milbank Mem. Fund Q.* 56(1): 78–112, 1978.
7. Vladeck, B. C. Interest-group representation and the HSAs: Health planning and political theory. *Am. J. Public Health* 67(1): 23–29, 1977.
8. Lander, L. HSAs: If at first you don't succeed. . . . *Health/PAC Bulletin* 70: 1–15, 1976.
9. Dror, Y. The planning process: A facet design. In *A Reader in Planning Theory*, edited by Faludi, A., pp. 326–333. Pergamon Press, New York, 1973.
10. Appelbaum, R. P. Planning as technique: Some consequences of the rational-comprehensive model. In *The Structural Crises of the 1970's and Beyond: The Need for a New Planning Theory. Proceedings of the Conference on Planning Theory,* edited by Goldstein, H. and Rosenberg, S. Division of Environmental and Urban Systems, Virginia Polytechnic Institute and State University, Blacksburg, Virginia, 1978.
11. Edwards, R. C., Reich, M., and Weiskopf, T. E. *The Capitalist System: A Radical Analysis of American Society*. Prentice-Hall, Englewood Cliffs, New Jersey, 1972.
12. Navarro, V. *Medicine Under Capitalism*. Prodist, New York, 1976.
13. Kotelchuck, D. (ed.). *Prognosis Negative*, pp. 163–201. Vintage Books, New York, 1976.
14. Ehrenreich, B., and Ehrenreich, J. Hospital workers: Class conflict in the making. *Int. J. Health Serv.* 5(1): 43–51, 1975.
15. Kelman, S. The social nature of the definition problem in health. *Int. J. Health Serv.* 5(4): 625–642, 1975.
16. Rodberg, L., and Stevenson, G. The health care industry in advanced capitalism. *Review of Radical Political Economics* 9(1): 104–115, 1977.
17. Consumer Commission on the Accreditation of Health Services, Inc. Medical technology and the health care consumer. *Consumer Health Perspectives* 5(5,6,8), 1978.
18. National Chamber Foundation. *A National Health Care Strategy. How Business Can Improve Health Planning and Regulation.* Washington, D.C., 1979.
19. Califano announces HEW's new initiative: Productivity standards. *Health Planning and Manpower Report* 7(23): 3–4, 1978.
20. Brown, D. R. Community health planning or who will control the health care system. *Am. J. Public Health* 62(10): 1336–1338, 1972.
21. Rosen, G. *A History of Public Health*. MD Publications, New York, 1958.
22. Berliner, H. A larger perspective on the Flexner Report. *Int. J. Health Serv.* 5(4): 573–592, 1975.
23. Shonick, W. *Elements of Planning for Area-Wide Personal Health Services*. C. V. Mosby Co., St. Louis, 1976.
24. Committee on the Cost of Medical Care. *Medical Care for the American People–The Final Report of the Committee on the Cost of Medical Care*, Volume 29. University of Chicago Press, Chicago, 1932.
25. Klarman, H. E. Planning for facilities. In *Regionalization and Health Policy*, edited by Ginzberg, E. Health Resources Administration, Washington, D.C., 1977.
26. Kotelchuck, R. The depression and AMA. *Health/PAC Bulletin* 69: 13–18, 1976.
27. Law, S. *Blue Cross: What Went Wrong?* Yale University Press, New Haven, 1976.
28. Lee, R. J., and Jones, L. W. The fundamentals of good medical care. *Publications of the Committee on Costs of Medical Care,* No. 22. University of Chicago Press, Chicago, 1933.

29. Thompson, P. Voluntary regional planning. In *Regionalization and Health Policy*, edited by Ginzberg, E. Health Resources Administration, Washington, D.C., 1977.
30. Gottlieb, S. R. A brief history of health planning in the U.S. In *Regulating Health Facilities Construction*, edited by Havighurst, C. American Enterprise Institute for Public Policy Research, Washington, D.C., 1974.
31. Navarro, V. Political power, the state, and their implications in medicine. *Review of Radical Political Economics* 9(1): 61–80, 1977.
32. Marmor, T., and Morone, J. HSAs and the representation of consumer interests: Conceptual issues and litigation problems. *Health Law Project Library Bulletin* 4(4): 117–128, 1979.
33. Bradley, J. A Strategy to Improve the Effectiveness of Consumer Participation in Health Planning: An Educational Approach. Submitted to the Graduate School of Public and International Affairs in partial fulfillment of the requirements for the degree of Masters in Urban and Regional Planning, University of Pittsburgh, 1978.
34. Alford, R. R. *Health Care Politics: Ideological and Interest Group Barriers to Reform*. University of Chicago Press, Chicago, 1975.
35. Salmon, J. Monopoly capital and the reorganization of the health sector. *Review of Radical Political Economics* 9(1): 125–133, 1977.
36. Berliner, H. Emerging ideologies in medicine. *Review of Radical Political Economics* 9(1): 117–124, 1977.
37. Tannen, L., and Lieben, J. Population-based planning as a tool for health plan development. *American Journal of Health Planning* 3(3): 48–55, 1978.
38. Normile, F. R., and Ziel, H. A., Jr. Too many beds. *Hospitals* 44(14): 61–64, 1970.
39. Dowling, W. L. A procedure for rational planning. In *Cost Control in Hospitals*, edited by Griffith, J. R., Hancock, W. M.,and Munson, S. C., pp. 26–38. Health Administration Press, Ann Arbor, 1975.
40. Roemer, M. Hospital utilization and the health care system. *Am. J. Public Health* 66(10): 953–955, 1976.
41. Lewis, C. E. Variance in the incidence of surgery. *N. Engl. J. Med.* 282(3): 135–144, 1970.

CHAPTER 2

Business and the Pushcart Vendors in an Age of Supermarkets

Linda A. Bergthold

BACKGROUND OF BUSINESS PARTICIPATION

In 1973 a representative of big business in the Committee for Economic Development (CED) commented (1):

> Our health care industry is the only major industry that has not had to submit to the discipline of either the marketplace or of public regulation. As a result, the industry has inadequate cost-control mechanisms, and the rate of rise in health-care costs has far outstripped that of any other segment of our economy.

Eleven years later, in testimony before the Joint Economic Committee of Congress in 1984, Joseph Califano, former Secretary of Health and Human Services for President Carter and a current director of Chrysler Corporation, commented (2):

> This month, for the first time in our history, Americans are spending more than $1 billion a day on health care . . . this year Chrysler will have to sell 70,000 vehicles just to pay for its health care bills . . . controlling health care costs has become the Great American Health Care Cost Shell Game. True reductions in costs will come only from fundamental changes in the way we deliver and pay for health care . . . and concerted action by all the players.

Business has been increasingly concerned about the cost of medical care in the United States since the late 1960s, because as costs increase in the medical sector, costs to business increase. The cost to corporations of financing employee health care has increased more dramatically than other indices of growth. Between 1970 and 1982, the nominal growth in the gross national product was 208 percent; U.S. health expenditures increased 332 percent; and business expenditures for employee health insurance increased 700 percent (3). The Bureau of Labor Statistics estimates that fringe benefits have doubled in the past twenty years and private employers were financing nearly one of every five dollars spent on medical care in the United States by 1984 (4,5).

Business concerns about the costs of medical care are not a new phenomenon, however. There have been at least three previous waves of corporate intervention in the medical sector in this century, corresponding roughly to the predepression phases of long-term economic cycles (1888-1893, 1904-1910, and 1925-1933) (6). These periods marked the beginning of a general profit squeeze on business, during which time powerful representatives of big business looked for ways to reduce costs that were affecting their profit margins.

At the end of the 1960s, as Navarro has noted, "the undisputed leadership of U.S. capital began to be threatened" (7). The U.S. economy of the late 1960s was marked by the lowest level of corporate profits in the share of national income since World War II (6). The trade surplus began to decline, turning negative for the first time in the 20th century. What many economists had predicted would be a boom decade in the 1970s started out with a recession in 1969 and 1970, accompanied by increasing inflation rates, shortages of critical raw materials, and a breakdown of the financial markets. In the context of general financial crisis, the generous health benefits plans negotiated by labor throughout the sixties became the target of reform by management. Business leaders began to promote reform of the medical care system as a way of containing rapidly escalating health care costs.

The latest wave of intervention began in the 1970s with the promotion by business of a general rationalization of the medical care system. *Fortune* magazine declared in January 1970 (8, emphasis added):

> The time has come for radical change . . . the management of medical care has become too important to leave to doctors, who are after all, not managers to begin with . . . our present system of medical care is not a system at all. The majority of physicians constitute *an army of pushcart vendors in an age of supermarkets.*

The medical care industry, with its cost-plus structure and resistance to market forces and no claim to the protection of national security like the defense industry, was viewed by business as inherently unstable and out of the control of the state by the mid-1970s. "Basic structural reforms are needed to give the system permanent stability . . . in business, the profit motive spurs efficiency and some believe it could do the same for hospitals," reported one business leader in the same issue of *Fortune* (9).

Business reasoned that if this sector of industry could not be rationalized under public control, then perhaps it could be rationalized under private control. The Committee for Economic Development (CED), an organization of business elites, launched the promotion of privately owned and managed health maintenance organizations (HMOs) as its solution to rationalizing the U.S. medical care industry (1). Although U.S. business was in no way committed to the task of disciplining the medical care sector alone in 1973, a warning note had been sounded to that industry. No sector of industry could continue to grow as fast as medical care if it were to be at the substantial expense of the rest of the industrial community, and no individual entrepreneurs, such as physicians, could continue to control the rate of growth in medical services without accountability to private purchasers. Business underestimated the institutional and legal dominance of the medical profession, however. The pushcart vendors were not about to be brought into the supermarket without a struggle, and business had to become organized politically to wage that battle effectively.

THE ORGANIZATION OF BUSINESS COALITIONS

The policies of the Reagan Administration in the 1980s reflect the expansion and intensification of the efforts of business in the 1970s to restructure the medical care industry. Various organizations representing big business began to become politically organized in the 1970s. As one spokesman for business commented (10):

> The history of American business involvement is that they create "institutional mechanisms" to guide their change after they have identified something as worthy of change . . . the objective is to have big business become a credible participant in national health policy.

The growth of business coalitions formed to deal with health policy issues in the 1980s has historical roots going back to the mid-1960s. In the recent process of organizing themselves politically in the health policy arena, business interests have participated in and in many cases initiated health care "coalitions" around the country. In 1982 there were 25 coalitions in the 50 states; by early 1986 there were almost 200. Almost half of these coalitions had membership that was restricted to employers (purchasers) only. The remainder included labor, government, providers, and insurers in various combinations. In 1982, 80 percent of all coalition members were representatives of business and 50 percent of all coalitions were legally incorporated, many with paid staff and assessed dues. Although the numbers change rapidly, 43 of the 50 states had at least one business/health coalition by the middle of 1984 (11).

All around the country, business representatives were behaving in extraordinary ways. In Boston it was the forceful negotiating style of a Nelson Gifford, the chief executive officer of the Dennison Manufacturing Company, representing the prestigious Massachusetts Business Roundtable, as he placed the President of Blue Cross together with the President of John Hancock in a room and told them to "deal." In Arizona it was the "shoot-em up" confrontation of

Sperry-Rand and other corporations, angry because hospital administrators were flying high in private jets while hospital costs to business soared even higher. In Denver it was a group of expensively suited chief executive officers telling a National Association of Governors' conference, "We employers, whether state, municipal, nonprofit, or private, have a choice of committing suicide or seeing to it that provider behavior is substantially altered" (12). In Iowa it was a small but determined coterie of prominent Iowa businesmen, huddled in the deserted halls of the legislature at midnight, waiting to tackle legislators on their way out of a cost containment hearing. In California it was entrepreneurs in the high-technology industries making deals for cheaper care with unionized physicians. No matter what region of the country or what type of business was involved, activity was visible, measurable, and targeted toward changing provider behavior.

The institutional mechanisms that business created included the coalitions mentioned above and specific national organizations such as the Washington Business Group on Health (WBGH), which is a national policy organization representing large corporations and dealing specifically with business interests in health policy. It was created from the rib of the Business Roundtable, a policy voice of big business in Washington, D.C. to do, as one staff member calls it, "the dirty work of health politics" (13). Although other national business organizations, such as the U.S. Chamber of Commerce and the National Association of Manufacturers are interested in health policy issues and have specific task forces and departments to deal with health, the WBGH is the only national business organization that focuses exclusively on health policy.

Willis Goldbeck, the Executive Director, characterizes the mission of the WBGH in the following way (14; emphasis in original):

> Our biggest job is to change the way business behaves . . . our biggest educational step has not been in dealing with business about government but to *break business away from the providers*. If there was to be a marker of what we have accomplished, it would be that we have broken down the myths that kept business as a passive purchaser and we have made them aggressive buyers. That is a true change and it will not go away.

BUSINESS AND THE POLICY PROCESS

Business interests have helped to change the public policy formation process in health in ways that have been observed in other policy arenas as well: business has participated in *setting the policy agenda* and has encouraged policies consistent with its interests; business has made *strategic alliances with state government* by participating in statewide commissions; business, in some cases, has changed the rules of the public policy process so that they are consistent with *private decision-making* and negotiation modes; and the "public interest" has been made equivalent to "purchaser interests."

Setting the Policy Agenda

"Setting the agenda is the vital first stage of policy formation, which often establishes the parameters for everything that follows," so states the *Harvard Business Review* (15). This and other journals have through the years published articles on ways in which business can have more clout in national policy formation and implementation (16-18). The argument is almost always the same: business does not have enough impact on public policy and needs to become more cohesive, develop better strategy, and intervene earlier and more actively in policy formation. Rarely is there any acknowledgment of the ways in which strategic business elites make informal input into policy all the time and manage to keep certain policy alternatives completely off the table (e.g., socialized medicine), or the ways in which much national policy is often so consistent with business interests that participation is not necessary to ensure dominance (19,20).

As Gabriel Kolko states for the Progressive Era in *The Triumph of Conservatism*, "Business held the reins of the accepted ideology and defined the outer limits of potential reforms" (21). What role did business play in the agenda formation in the early 1980s? The evidence reveals the participation of a few powerful and strategic elites, the work of the Washington Business Group on Health, and to a lesser extent of the U.S. Chamber of Commerce, and the participation of think tanks such as the American Enterprise Institute. The presence and visibility of these elites on key advisory bodies was an indicator of a larger network of business elites aware of the policy agenda being developed.

The policy agenda being developed consisted of two strategies: "the social contract" or corporatist strategy, and the "market strategy" or "capitalism without gloves" (7,22). The choice of strategies depended on the relative strength of labor and the State at the location of policy choices. At the level of the 50 states, and particularly in those states where labor was strong such as Michigan, Ohio, or Illinois, the corporatist strategy was often selected; at the national level, where labor representation was relatively weak, the market strategy of the Reagan administration was dominant. Although not every aspect of Reagan's market ideology benefited every sector of business, and although there are serious strategic conflicts within and between various sectors of business over which policies to support or oppose, the major policy direction in the early 1980s was consistent with large purchaser interests to the extent that these policy changes:

1. preserved the power of the private sector over the financing and delivery of medical care, and thus preserved the basic economic and social relations of capital;
2. increased the purchasing power of the private sector and gave business more control over politics;

3. increased the legitimacy of State power and forced the State to act more as a "prudent buyer" for the poor and elderly;
4. "rationalized" the medical care sector in Kolko's terms; that is, organized the economy so that corporations could function in a more predictable and secure environment (21);
5. encouraged the flow of capital to the Sunbelt and the large for-profit corporations and thus disciplined the individual institutions and entrepreneurs of the medical care industry;
6. stabilized cost increases in the medical care industry;
7. disciplined labor; that is, shifted costs from management to labor wherever possible and developed liaisons between business and the State by means of commissions and other types of planning bodies to buffer corporations from labor reaction and anticipated potential unrest.

At the state level, the relationship between business and policy formation was much more visible that it was at the federal level. In Massachusetts in 1982, although state government initiated private-sector support for its policy changes, business actually defined and controlled the policy formation process as well as its legislative implementation. In California, state government encouraged the participation of business in coalition politics, and while business helped to define the policy alternatives, the state negotiated the policy changes in a more active way, giving itself considerable negotiating power with the private sector through its contracting mechanisms. In Arizona, although state government officials educated the business community in the beginning, business simply stood up and walked away with the process, like "Frankenstein's monster," as one state official commented.

THE ALLIANCE BETWEEN BUSINESS AND THE STATE

The participation of business in public/private sector commissions is not recent nor is it limited to the health policy arena. However, it has been largely a symbolic endeavor in health care politics of past years and business interests have not participated to the degree or intensity which they began to do in early 1980s (23). Between 1982 and 1984, 33 states organized state-level commissions to address issues of health care cost containment. These state-wide cost containment commissions were composed of representatives of government, business, medical care providers, and occasionally labor. They represented to some, a form of "quasi," "middle-level," or "incipient" corporatism. The involvement of "peak associations" of business and government (with a nod to organized labor) in the formation of social policy suggested the corporatist forms of representation in European welfare states (22).

Others viewed any attempts at corporatism in the United States as certain to fail because of the weakness of the State, the lack of consensus about social policy, and the inability of the U.S. labor movement to participate equally with other interests (24–26). Certainly, the latter was true in these cost containment commissions at the state level. At the national level, labor was represented only at the margins of the policy debate. Even though states such as Michigan or New York—with stronger labor movements and a history of tripartite planning arrangements between the state, business, and labor—had some labor partici-pation in their commissions, the result of the corporatist or social contract strategy, even when labor was included as a token member, was to weaken both public and private health benefit packages in the name of "medical care cost containment."

O'Connor and others present a theoretical explanation for the symbiotic relationship between capital and the State (7,27). O'Connor describes three sectors in the U.S. economy: the monopolistic sector (sometimes called "planned"), the competitive (or market) sector, and the state (government) sector. In the monopoly sector, where roughly one-third of the labor force works, production is large-scale, markets are national or international, and the large corporations that comprise this sector favor economic stability and planning. In the competitive sector, where less than one-third of the labor force works, production is small-scale, markets are local or regional, and the small and mid-sized corporations that comprise this sector logically favor competitive policies that allow smaller capital to enter the market. The state sector, which includes a sector that produces goods and services and one that organizes and supervises private industries under contract to the state, employs another third of the labor force and tends to ally itself with the monopolistic sector because of the economic and political power of capital.

O'Connor explains that, contrary to popular ideology that posits a contra-dictory relationship between the two sectors, the State and monopoly capital need each other to grow. Monopoly capital needs the State to provide many costs of social production and other infrastructure costs (medical care, highways, schools), while the State needs capital to foster a healthy accumulation process (27). This mutual need does not deny the contradictions that exist between the State and capital or the publicly adversarial relationships that often emerge in conflict over social policy. In fact, O'Connor explains that the State and capital cannot become aligned too closely, or the myth of pluralist politics may be exposed.

When the State and capital forge close alliances as they did over health policy in the early 1980s, many political observers have wondered if State legitimacy would be threatened by these close links and the identification of overlapping interests. However, there was little or no legitimacy crisis at the level of individual states in the 1980s. Despite the clear dominance of state-level commissions by business, state budget shortfalls, the deterioration of local government funding sources, and the massive cost shifts in health premiums from management to labor, there was little labor unrest or organized opposition of any kind to these public/private commissions or the recommendations they produced.

Was the lack of protest related to the fact that their recommendations were merely symbolic? Friedland and associates have commented on the way in which local government can restructure a potential fiscal crisis into merely a fiscal "strain," by providing symbolic reassurances and solutions, and using policy changes called "reform" to "restructure local government and purge it of obsolete concessions" (28). The use of statewide cost containment commissions was an effective vehicle for turning crisis into strain in the 1980s.

THE PUBLIC PROCESS BECOMES PRIVATIZED

If business has been successful in influencing the parameters of the policy agenda and has developed an alliance with government, what has been the impact of business on the process of policy formation itself? How important is the "public" aspect of the public policy process? The basis of pluralist political analysis is the idea that in a democracy, every organized interest can participate and have an impact and that the state will respond to interest group preferences in an even-handed way. The process of making public policy is portrayed as open and accessible to every citizen, through such democratic mechanisms as voting and public hearings.

There are other viewpoints, however, about how public decisions are actually made. These views describe a decision-making process in which the public aspect is only a small part of the process; in which deals are cut in private, behind the scenes, by a few strategic elites that do not represent all of the affected interests. In California, in Massachusetts, and at the federal level in the early 1980s, hearings and the process of receiving public input to health legislation were bypassed in favor of privately held negotiations. Certain interests were represented (such as drug manufacturers, proprietary providers, and insurance companies) and others were ignored (such as labor, individual physicians, and consumer groups of all types).

Policy alternatives were more often determined by business than by the state. The negotiation process favored the private interests, which could and did shut out the state representatives from their negotiations when private interests diverged from public ones. In Massachusetts, policy was made, as one participant described it, "like a party at your house." Business was the leader in negotiating the policy changes. It was the Massachusetts Business Roundtable that organized and invited the coalition of interests (hospitals, insurers, physicians, state government, and business) to a party that met privately in the offices of the Roundtable itself. At one point, when the public interests were at odds with the private, the coalition simply shut the doors on the state participants and refused to allow them to participate in the discussions.

As one of the participants in the Massachusetts coalition commented (29):

> Public policy development is different from business decision making. The
> Chapter 372 policy changes (the Massachusetts legislation) occurred because
> Gifford (the Roundtable's task force chairman) made it a business decision-
> making process not a public policy process. It was a closed process. Do we
> want business shutting the doors on the state when private interests get
> threatened?

Secrecy, invisibility, extraordinary political maneuvering, and the bypass of
usual legislative procedures, were all indicators of a change by business of the
previous process of health policy formation in Massachusetts. The use of the
ad hoc task force, temporary coalition, or the statewide commission to seal in
the dominant players and seal off "outsiders" was a tool used effectively by
business and by state officials allied with the business point of view.

Another outcome of business control of the public policy process in Massachusetts, in various other states, and at the national level, was the general exclusion of labor from policy discussions. In states where union membership was
relatively high (e.g., Michigan, New York, Ohio), labor was a member of the
various health care coalitions or commissions, but in most states labor was
absent, as a consequence of a weakened organized labor movement in the 1980s.

How is this policymaking process different from previous processes? Although
decisions have usually been made in private and behind the scenes, at least there
were available structures for participation, symbolic or otherwise. Policy alternatives and criteria for negotiation were set, if not completely by the state, at
least with strong state representation, and participation was available to wider
variety of stakeholders in the public process. Although the state representation
of "public" interest is not a perfect one, it may be broader and more closely
identified with the unorganized consumer public than purchaser identification
with public interest. In a few states, such as California, the consumer and
minority interests were represented in the policy process, albeit in a token way.
In the Massachusetts coalition of 1982, however, business as purchaser successfully identified itself as the "honest broker," almost synonymous with consumer
interests. This portrayal was generally repeated and accepted in the press, even
though business was not an equal player but a dominant one, represented
management and not labor, and had conflicts over its own divided interests,
such as its stake in the capital expansion of hospitals and its own role as trustee
of the hospitals with which it was supposed to be negotiating and controlling.

BUSINESS AND THE SUBSTANCE OF HEALTH POLICY CHANGE

What are the policy "solutions" that business has supported and proposed
and that have been hailed as a health care "revolution" in the 1980s? Are there
any patterns of business involvement in the fifty states? Is there any evidence

that business participation has altered provider power? Very few studies have attempted to answer these questions in a systematic way, although the journals and magazines are filled with anecdotal reports about business' role in "radical change in Iowa" or the "road to HMOs" in Richmond, Virginia.

Business supported President Reagan's general "market reform" approach to cost control in the medical care system, which included a major shift from retrospective to prospective payment for Medicare beneficiaries; policies that accelerated the shift to for-profit delivery of medical services; federal waivers that encouraged states to experiment with and restructure Medicaid and hospital payment programs; and a freeze on physician fees. Some segments of business lobbied actively to save the federal health planning and certificate-of-need programs from complete phase-out by the Reagan Administration.

In an effort to make some sense out of this jumble of seemingly contradictory reports, a recent study investigated the associations between the political participation of business and different types of health policy change in the 50 states. Data were analyzed from three 50-state telephone surveys conducted in late 1983 an early 1984 (30–33).

The surveys asked state hospital and business coalition representatives for estimates of the level of business participation in their states. According to the amount of reported business involvement in health care politics, a measure of "business participation" was constructed by combining two qualitative self-reports of business involvement and one quantitative report of actual numbers of business coalitions in each state. Each state was assigned to one of three categories—high, medium or low business participation. Associations were measured between levels of business activity and the kinds of state policy change that had occurred in each state, as reported in these surveys (Table 1).

States in which business participation was characterized as high were more likely to have:

1. financial disclosure legislation challenging the monopoly of providers over information about health care cost and quality;
2. statewide structures in which business could participate, such as state-level cost containment commissions;
3. legislative changes to encourage the growth of alternative delivery systems such as preferred provider organizations (PPOs) or health maintenance organizations (HMOs);
4. legislation to strengthen programs of medical care for the poor and the planning and regulation of health facility expansion.

What do these associations between high amounts of business participation and various state policy changes mean?

Table 1

Combined measure of business participation in the fifty states[a]

Group 1: Low business participation (16 states)

Alaska	Mississippi	New Mexico
Arkansas	Montana	North Dakota
Idaho	Nebraska	Rhode Island
Louisiana	Nevada	South Dakota
Maine	New Hampshire	West Virginia
		Wyoming

Group 2: Medium business participation (16 states)

Alabama	Kentucky	Texas
Colorado	Maryland	Utah Vermont
Delaware	Minnesota	Virginia
Georgia	New Jersey	Washington
Hawaii		Wisconsin

Group 3: High participation (18 states)

Arizona	Iowa	North Carolina
California	Kansas	Ohio
Connecticut	Massachusetts	Oklahoma
Florida	Michigan	Pennsylvania
Illinois	Missouri	South Carolina
Indiana	New York	Tennessee

[a]Sources: U.S. Chamber of Commerce Survey, 1984; InterStudy Survey, 1983; FAH Survey, 1984.

1. States in which business participation was high were more likely to have increased access to information about the medical care system through the passage of financial disclosure laws, either as part of rate-setting programs or as laws that mandated statewide hospital and/or physician reporting of charges and costs. As shown in Table 2, 56 percent of states with high levels of business participation and 44 percent of states with medium participation had some form of mandatory financial disclosure. In contrast, only 13 percent of the low-participation states had financial disclosure legislation. One of the surveys of all 50 states hospital associations asked whether or not business coalitions were involved in the passage of financial disclosure legislation, and the evidence shows direct involvement and pressure from business for disclosure.

As business began to become politically active, its leaders discovered quite early that access to information was key to political power. In states such as Iowa, where it seems unlikely that business would challenge provider power,

Table 2

Existence of financial disclosure laws in 50 states by levels of
business participation, 1984

Financial Disclosure*	High Business	Medium Business	Low Business	Total
None	11%	12%	50%	24%
	(2)	(2)	(8)	(12)
Some	33%	44%	37%	38%
	(6)	(7)	(6)	(19)
Yes	56%	44%	13%	38%
	(10)	(7)	(2)	(19)
Totals	100%	100%	100%	100%
	(18)	(16)	(16)	(50)

*Note: "None" = No financial disclosure laws existed in the state; "Some" = Voluntary disclosure existed or laws were being discussed; "Yes" = Financial disclosure laws existed and were mandatory for all hospitals. Measures of association: Chi square = 11.21; Effect parameter = +21.

Source: Data for Table 2 uses the Combined Measure of Business Participation for the independent variable and data from Cyndee Eyster, "Special Report on Health Issues in Election Year '84: State Roundup," *Review* 17:5 (September/October 1984): 16–35; and Barbara Paul, "State-by-State Hospital Rate Regulation Survey: Movement Toward All-Payers System and the Role of Business in Promoting All-Payers Systems," Memorandum (Excelsior, Minn.: InterStudy, 4 November 1983): 1–26, for the dependent policy variables.

large employers demanded and received state legislation to force the disclosure of medical care cost information on which they could make their purchasing decisions. The financial disclosure issue is one that business, first at the state level and later by introducing legislation at the federal level, has made its major concern. It is also an important indicator of the successful challenge by business of the power of providers.

2. States with high business participation were also more likely to have a partnership between government and business over medical care cost containment through the state-level cost containment commissions discussed above. In 94 percent of the high-business states a cost containment commission had been formed between 1982 and 1984, in contrast to only 50 percent of the medium- and low-business states.

State-level commissions such as the Roberti Health Care Cost Containment Coalition in California, the Joint Legislative-Executive Commission on Hospital Reimbursement in Massachusetts, and commissions in Florida, Michigan, and Iowa, clearly reflected the impact of business interest in health policy change in those states.

3. States with high business participation were also more likely to have more active alternative delivery systems such as health maintenance organizations (HMOs) and preferred provider organizations (PPOs). In 94 percent of the states with high business participation, PPOs were either starting up or highly active, and the pattern was the same for medium-level states. Only 19 percent of the low-participation states had PPO activity by the end of 1984 and 37 percent had no PPOs at all. The fact that many states had laws prohibiting PPO development, and that business lobbied against those laws in many states, is another indicator of business "breaking away from providers."

Other studies have also shown an association between business participation and prepaid health plan development or increased PPO activity (34). Health maintenance organizations (the most popular example of which is Kaiser Health Plan) and preferred provider organizations are both alternatives to the standard fee-for-service type of medical care delivery. In an HMO, the organization assumes a contractual responsibility to an employer to provide a stated range of health services for a fixed monthly fee. The employee cannot use other providers without assuming the extra cost. A PPO is an arrangement whereby a group of providers (sellers) negotiates with a purchaser or buyer to deliver care to a defined set of clients or employees for a discount. If the employee chooses to go to another provider who is not part of the organization, the purchaser will usually require the employee to pay the cost of the care or at least a portion of that cost.

This study supports the assertion that business participation is associated with growth of alternative delivery systems, but raises questions about the association between business participation and various other cost-containment strategies. For example, it has been claimed in states where rate-setting is in effect that fewer alternative systems such as PPOs are developed (34). This study found, however, that Connecticut, Florida, Maryland, New York, Washington, and Wisconsin, all states with rate-setting or review programs, also showed some PPO development, suggesting that rate-setting and PPOs can coexist.

In addition to these strong associations between business participation and information disclosure and development of alternative delivery systems, there were other policy changes that were not as strongly associated with business involvement, but still showed a positive relationship.

4. States with high levels of business participation were somewhat more likely to have strong public health programs, such as state programs addressing the medical needs of the indigent, and increases instead of cuts in Medicaid program budgets. Data showed that 44 percent of the states in which business participation was high had increased their Medicaid budget allocations or made structural changes in their Medicaid programs in 1984, while only 19 percent of the low-business states made such changes. These surveys represent data collected on state policy changes in a single year. More research on Medicaid program changes over a longer period of time would be necessary to clarify the

relationships between business participation and public policy changes, such as Medicaid policy change. Although it appears that states in which business participation was strong also had strong public health programs, the data do not reveal the absolute level of support for these programs or if the state had made drastic cuts and was simply restoring them in 1984 as the economy improved.

5. States with high business participation were also somewhat more likely to be associated with a strengthened state role in health facilities regulation through legislation toughening or strengthening health planning. Thirty-nine percent of the high-business states and 44 percent of the medium-business states made changes in health planning in 1984 that gave the state or local agencies more authority to plan and regulate the expansion of health facilities. Only 25 percent of the low-business states made such changes, and over half actually made changes in health planning laws that weakened or dismantled health planning programs. Although these associations suffer from the same "single year" phenomenon as the associations between business participation and support for public health programs, the fact that the low-business states generally cut back on regulation and the high-business states increased it is consistent with the support of big business for stability, planning, and predictability in the medical care sector.

6. There was no apparent association between the levels of business participation and the existence of regulatory rate-setting programs. An equal number of high- and low-business states had rate-setting programs.

Where the social contract or corporatist strategy is demanded by labor and state government, the purchasers, both public and private, can overwhelm even the substantial power of providers to block this type of regulation and planning. Where the market strategy appears to be more feasible politically, purchasers will select this strategy. Business has not been fooled by the false dichotomies and blurred boundaries in the debate between "competitive" and "regulatory" ideologies of health policy change. As one business advocate commented (14):

> Sure the rhetoric of business supports competition, but the rhetoric means nothing. Business has never been in favor of competition. They want to regulate everything as long as it's not them. This $400 billion issue will not be played out on the basis of rhetoric.

Is business likely to be more active in certain parts of the country, such as the northeast or the west? As Table 1 demonstrates, business participation occurred in all regions of the country, although some areas did have slightly more activity than others. States with high participation cluster in the east north central, mid-Atlantic, and west north central regions. States with medium participation cluster in the south Atlantic and Pacific regions, and states with low business participation cluster in the Mountain, east, and west north central regions.

It has been pointed out by others that geography plays an important role in the implementation of cost-containment strategies (35). New England and mid-Atlantic states have more frequently selected regulatory approaches to cost containment, with HMO and PPO activity more extensive in the mid-west and west. However, this study indicates that it may not be that simple. States as geographically diverse as Maine, Washington, Wisconsin, and New York all have mandatory budget and rate review programs, and Arizona came very close to passing such a program in 1984, yet some of these same states had extensive PPO activity as well.

The associations between business participation and certain health policy changes clearly could have been caused by other factors such as high hospital costs, levels of urbanization or degrees of unionization. However, when these factors were introduced into the equations, they did *not* substantially weaken the original relationship between business and policy changes such as financial disclosure.

This research shows that even where hospital costs are high, state fiscal crisis is severe, and the geography is favorable, regulation of the health care system is unlikely to occur unless there is a "countervailing force" fighting for it (36). The powerful medical and hospital industries prevented regulation throughout the 1970s in a system characterized by "dynamics without change" (23). In the 1980s, U.S. business, in alliance with the state, has provided the countervailing force to break the statement and promote not only regulation but all types of health system change (37).

TO WHAT EXTENT HAS BUSINESS BEEN SUCCESSFUL IN CHANGE?

When the market power of business purchasers is joined with the power of the state in the context of choices defined by the standards of economic theory, the result is a powerful congruence of interests. As Renaud notes in his analysis of health policy changes in Canada, under these conditions the "corporate rationalizers" can make profound changes in the power structure of the medical care system (38). Market relations are extended to the medical care system in a way that relegates providers to a secondary role. Either the state or business tells hospitals how to be organized, who to treat, and how much to charge.

There is evidence in this research that business has become more than the "challenging" structural interest that Robert Alford described in *Health Care Politics* (23). Business, along with other corporate rationalizers, may have become the "dominant" interest in health care politics. Alford defines dominant interests as those that are "served by the structure of social, economic, and political institutions as they exist at any given time" (23).

In a time when the "productivist capitalist logic" has infused the medical care system, the interests of business are well served by existing but changing institutions (38). The previously dominant interests, physician monopolists, no longer control many of the conditions of their work, and their professional autonomy is consistently eroded by trends of corporatization and privatization, trends that business has strongly promoted.

How does business achieve its political dominance? The systemic power of capital allows business organizations and representatives to participate at any level of the State with few constraints and with a powerful impact on policy formation, not just implementation (28). If business has the power to keep issues off the agenda, to determine who will be included and excluded in the policy process, and to ensure that policy outcomes reinforce private power, why participate at all? Is participation to be regarded as a sign of the decreasing power of business?

In one sense, business participation is an indication of the failure of capitalist society to produce policies that favor all segments of capital. The battle over health policy is an example of the emergence of one sector of capital in conflict (and sometimes alliance) with the state and other sectors of capital over the need to rationalize and legitimize efforts to decrease cost inflation in the medical sector. Whether business as purchaser will ultimately challenge and decrease the power of business as provider remains to be demonstrated. What the business participation described in this chapter demonstrates is not an absence of power but just another indicator of the way business communicates and reproduces its power in the political system.

To assert that the power of business alone has changed health policy, however, would be to claim more than the evidence can support. The exercise of business power need not be regarded as causal to be considered important in an analysis of policy change. The most interesting questions that arise from the study of the participation of business cannot yet be answered. What impact will the political and economic power of business have on the fledgling consumer movement in health care, a movement that became considerably stronger with consumer participation in Health Systems Agencies in the 1970s (39)? If corporations and business coalitions become the 1980s' substitute for health planning agencies, as they have become in some areas of the eastern United States, what happens to the unorganized constituencies of minorities, the elderly, and women, who do not have the economic or political resources to promote their interests effectively? What type of policies will be formed and implemented when labor interests are excluded from corporatist arrangements or when management unilaterally makes decisions about health benefits, thus denying labor a strategic and important bargaining tool? What is the impact of corporate power on the professional monopoly of the profession of medicine? What happens when the "boss becomes your doctor" (40)? And finally, what happens to the policy process itself when producers and purchasers ally with the state to monopolize information and the process by which information is collected and disseminated?

REFERENCES

1. Committee for Economic Development. *Building a National Health Care System.* CED, New York, April 1973.
2. Califano, J. Testimony to the Joint Economic Committee of the U.S. Congress, Washington, D.C., April 12, 1984.
3. Shelton, J., Ford Motor Company. Testimony to the Joint Economic Committee of the U.S. Congress, Washington, D.C., April 2, 1984.
4. Fringe benefits grow to 35 percent. *Wall Street Journal,* October 5, 1976.
5. Tell, E., Falik, M., and Fox, P. Private-sector health care initiatives: A comparative perspective in four communities. *Milbank Mem. Fund Q.* 62(3): 357–379, 1984.
6. Salmon, J. Corporate Attempts to Reorganize the American Health Care System. Doctoral dissertation, Cornell University, August 1987 (unpublished).
7. Navarro, V. The political economy of medical care. In *Health and Medical Care in the U.S.: A Critical Analysis,* edited by Navarro, V., Chapter 6. Baywood Publishing Company, Amityville, New York, 1977.
8. It's time to operate. *Fortune* 81(1): 77–80, 1970.
9. Meyers, H. The medical-industrial complex. *Fortune* 81(1): 98–100, 1970.
10. Goldbeck, W. Executive Director of the Washington Business Group on Health. Interview with the author, Washington, D.C., April 1984.
11. Clearinghouse on Business Coalitions for Health Action. Directory of Business Coalitions for Health Action. U.S. Chamber of Commerce, Washington, D.C., March 1984.
12. Loomis, W., Dexter Corporation. Comments at National Governors' Association meeting, Denver, Colorado, January 16–17, 1984.
13. Staff member of the Washington Business Group on Health. Interview with the author, Washington, D.C., June 1984.
14. Goldbeck, W. Interview with the author, Washington, D.C., June 1984.
15. Nolan, J. Political surfing when issues break. *Harvard Business Review,* January/February 1985, pp. 72–82.
16. Banks, L. Taking on the hostile media. *Harvard Business Review,* March/April 1978.
17. Finn, D. Public invisibility of corporate leaders. *Harvard Business Review,* November/December 1980.
18. Fenn, D. Finding where the power lies in government. *Harvard Business Review,* September/October 1979.
19. Domhoff, G. W. *The Powers That Be: Processes of Ruling Class Domination in America.* Random House, New York, 1978.
20. Alford, R. R., and Friedland, R. Political participation in public policy. *Ann. Rev. Sociol.* 1: 429–479, 1975.
21. Kolko, G. *The Triumph of Conservatism: A Reinterpretation of American History, 1900–1916.* Free Press, New York, 1967.
22. Panitch, L. The development of corporatism in liberal democracies. *Comp. Political Studies* 10(1): 61–90, 1977.
23. Alford, R. R. *Health Care Politics: Ideological and Interest Group Barriers to Reform.* University of Chicago Press, Chicago, 1975.
24. Seidelman, R. Pluralist heaven's dissenting angels: Corporatism in the American political economy. In *Political Economy of Public Policy,* p. 59ff. Sage, Beverly Hills, 1982.
25. O'Connor, J. *Accumulation Crisis.* Basil Blackwell Press, Oxford, England, 1984.
26. Estes, C. L., et al. *Political Economy, Health and Aging.* Little, Brown, Boston, 1984.
27. O'Connor, J. *The Fiscal Crisis of the State.* St. Martins Press, New York, 1973.
28. Friedland, R., Piven, F. F., and Alford, R. R. Political conflict, urban structure and the fiscal crisis. *Int. J. Urban Regional Res.* 1(3): 446, 1977.
29. Massachusetts Health Care Coalition participant. Interview with the author, Boston, Mass., June 1984.
30. Bergthold, L. Business and the Politics of Health Policy Change. Doctoral dissertation, University of California, Santa Cruz, June 1985 (unpublished).

31. Directory of Business Coalitions for Health Action. U.S. Chamber of Commerce, Washington, D.C., 1984.
32. State by State Hospital Rate Regulation Survey. InterStudy, Excelsior, Minn., November 4, 1983.
33. A special report on health issues in election year '84: State roundup. *FAH Review* 17(5), 1984.
34. Lewin and Associates. Private sector initiatives—executive summary. As quoted in Hillman, D., and Christianson, J. Health care expenditure containment in the United States: Strategies at the state and local level. *Soc. Sci. Med.* 20(12), 1985.
35. Sloan, F. Rate regulation as a strategy for hospital cost control: Evidence from the last decade. *Milbank Mem. Fund Q.* 61: 195–222, 1983.
36. Starr, P. *The Social Transformation of American Medicine.* Basic Books, New York, 1982.
37. Bergthold, L. Crabs in a bucket: The politics of health care reform in California. *J. Health Polit. Policy Law* 9(2): 203–222, 1984.
38. Renaud, M. Quebec: The adventures of a narcissistic state. In *The End of An Illusion: The Future of Health Policy in Western Industrialized Nations,* edited by de Kervasdoue, J., Kimberly, J. R., and Rodwin, V. G. University of California Press, Berkeley, 1984.
39. Morone, J., and Marmor, T. R. Representing consumer interests: The case of American health planning. In *Political Analysis and American Medical Care,* edited by Marmor, T. R. Cambridge University Press, Cambridge, 1983.
40. Kleinfield, N. R. When the boss becomes your doctor. *New York Times,* January 5, 1986, p. 1.

CHAPTER 3

Profit and Health Care: Trends in Corporatization and Proprietarization

J. Warren Salmon

Throughout this century, profit has been an underlying motor force for health sector developments. However, as the concentration and centralization of health care delivery has proceeded in the United States, the pursuit of profit has become central. No longer camouflaged under an out-moded "not-for-profit" designation, the delivery of health care is now officially to be a "business" run for economic gain.

Nationwide and multinational corporations have become prominent providers of health services to the bulk of the U.S. middle class, with their primary purpose being profit. The rapidity and scope of this trend in the organization of health care is phenomenal in that proprietary corporate forms only began in the United States in the late 1960s. Their extension to other nations further marks their dramatic emergence as a worldwide corporate transformation of health care.

While the American economy is generally characterized by a few concentrated corporations in each sector, the health care system has, until recently, remained based upon thousands of practitioner entrepreneurs and smaller-scale provider organizations. Except for firms in the peripheral supply role (for example, pharmaceuticals, medical equipment and supplies, accounting construction), large capital has not been a major factor in the delivery of services. Urban teaching hospitals, organized "not-for-profit," have dominated here as the largest and most costly institutions. An analysis of the relationships between hospitals and the drug, medical technology, and other supply firms historically reveals lucrative profit streams in this "medical industrial complex," especially since federal subsidization through Medicare and Medicaid. More recently, a vigorous and varied group of investor-owned entities is reshaping the delivery of services for those able to pay and sustain rather their lucrative profit levels.

The editor of the *New England Journal of Medicine* sees this "*new* medical industrial complex" as the "most important recent development in American health care" (1, p. 963). Noting the rapid growth of proprietary providers, he estimated that for 1979 investor-owned hospital and nursing home corporations, diagnostic labs, mental health and home care agencies, hemodialysis centers, free-standing ambulatory and emergency centers, and a variety of other services produced between $35–40 billion, or then 25 percent of personal health care expenses. Another estimate put the gross revenues of for-profit health care providers at $40 billion for 1982 (2). Both figures have climbed greatly in subsequent years under the Reagan administration's policies supporting profit-taking in health care.

For-profit hospital systems own over 19 percent of nongovernment acute general hospital beds in the United States (but more than 50 percent of non-government psychiatric beds). Their growth in number and beds since 1970 contrasts dramatically to the contraction of the "not-for-profit" and government segments of the industry. This figure does not account for the increasing number of "not-for-profit" voluntary hospitals under management contracts with the national and regional for-profit firms. Spurred by rising demands for long-term care, the proprietary hospital systems diversified to compete with or acquire nursing home chains, and began home care programs. They have entered into a wide range of other health-related services.

This proprietary thrust has been mimicked by the "not-for-profit" segment as Reagan policies have removed the historic vista toward a more equitable distribution of care for the American people. In 1983 the 179 centrally-managed hospital chains—whether proprietary, "not-for-profit," or public—expanded their domestic operations 9.5 percent to own or manage 1916 U.S. hospitals (3). As investor-owned health care corporations have become trans-national in scope, foreign markets are rapidly being captured. Moreover, the proprietary and "not-for-profit" hospital integration with finance capital (that is, commercial insurance companies that are quickly diversifying themselves) may predictably lead to a powerful influence over health policy formulation.

Analyzing these trends outside of a clear consideration of capitalist development presents an incomplete, inaccurate, and often apologetic review. Such has been the tendency in interpretative distortions of the history of health care (4). It is necessary to take a perspective of the larger forces impacting on health and health care set in its political economic context (5).

THE MEDICAL INDUSTRIAL COMPLEX

Typological analysis of the array of health care providers and institutions has usually been by ownership: the largest, being the voluntary, private "not-for-profit" segment; the fastest growing, being the proprietary segment; and the severely contracting government segment, including local, state, and federal programs. The private practice of physicians represents the bulk of ambulatory care, right now at least. As with proprietary institutions, profitability governs, though the scope and content of smaller scale physician entrepreneurs differs from the national corporate forms. Before expanding on this point, a brief historical review of the growth of profit extraction from health care is in order.

From the turn of the century onward, dramatic advances in medical technology and key policy developments yielded an elaborate hospital organization central to what became defined as "health care." The American uniqueness to the latter included voluntary health insurance, as well as federal subsidies for hospital construction and hospital-based, post-graduate medical education and allied health professional training. The Great Society programs of the federal government stimulated the expansion of this hospital-centered industry. Medicare and Medicaid were grafted onto the structural arrangement of fee-for-service medicine and cost-reimbursement for hospital care, both of which had been consolidated under retrospective Blue Cross and Blue Shield payment programs (6, 7). Thus, the mode of payment (and its large capital flows to peripheral supply firms) significantly affected the forms of care. Overmedicalization and dependent care-seeking behaviors resulted (8) in disease-focused, technological interventions. Under such a system propelled by profit—not the preservation and maintenance of people's health—the commodification of human needs associated with chronic illness became represented in costly "technological fixes," which by their nature have been generally ineffective.

By the late 1960s the large urban hospitals affiliated with medical schools served as the entry point for a stream of new products and services, from hospital equipment, pharmaceutical, and medical supply firms to construction and computer companies, bankers, lawyers, accountants, and management consultants (9). McClure reports that no change occurred in the market share of medical school and teaching hospitals between 1970 and 1980. Of the total U.S. hospitals, 12 percent account for 50 percent of hospital industry expenditures and 50 percent account for 90 percent of expenditures (10). Labor costs comprise about 60–70 percent of the typical hospital budget, and the bulk of the remaining $179 billion spent on hospital care in 1986 was available to firms from the *old* medical industrial complex. A rapid proliferation of health-related products fashioned around a technological medicine have come from large corporate suppliers.

THE HMO STRATEGY AND CORPORATE INROADS TO DELIVERY OF CARE

Given the promising health care market (growing at approximately 15 percent annually across the 1970s), it was reasonable that corporate capital would eventually extend beyond the supply role. In fact, the Nixon administration attempted to achieve its greater penetration into the delivery of services through the health maintenance organization (HMO) strategy (11). Adding to the involvement of the "private sector" in peripheral supply and insurance companies, the HMO strategy was designed to redirect capital flows within delivery institutions and raise the overall profitability of the industry. Federal contracts to consulting firms were to secure "private sector funding for HMO's," while appropriations for other federal health programs were shuffled into stimulating HMO development across the country. However, the unavailability of substantial federal financing (alongside the Nixon administration's cutbacks and impoundments of health funds) created a situation of almost total reliance on private capital for HMO growth and expansion—investment which was not forthcoming in the face of the economic recession of 1973-75.

Paul Ellwood of Interstudy, a Minneapolis health think-tank, was the chief architect of the Nixon administration's HMO strategy. HMOs were conceived to be the organizational building blocks for a rational, corporate-run delivery system. Being designed for profit-making, the HMO's costs of rendering services contracted in the benefit packages are deducted from prepaid subscriber revenues. Since profitability is key to their survival, Ellwood invited large corporations to lend their "industrial know-how" because "they are experienced in the application of management and have the ability to generate and effectively use capital resources" (12, p. 291). An article by Ellwood and Herbert in the *Harvard Business Review* detailed benefits from corporate-run profit-making HMOs and suggested that industrial medical departments should be converted to HMOs to "realize a substantial saving over present expenditures for employee health care benefits" (13, p. 105). The hope of the HMO strategy was to transform the system to where the "number of health care organizations in the United States would be reduced to as few as 1,000 with each HMO serving from 5,000 to several million persons" (14, p. 363). Local HMOs were expected to "function either as autonomous units or branches of larger national or regional organizations with several subsidiaries" (15, p. 97). Ellwood carried on extensive consultations with large corporations in the development of employee health programs, which led him to express concerns of corporate executives and employee benefit managers (16, p. 13):

> Clearly, fundamental changes are underway in the relationship between medicine and business. Physicians can no longer expect businessmen to accept, without question, the way in which medical care is delivered. . . . But some businessmen are beginning to grumble that medicine imposes a serious threat. In their view, rising employee health costs are no longer a minor concern, for expanded employee health programs, coupled with medical inflation, have become a critical element in a pattern of climbing production costs and rising prices, eroding both corporate profits and the competitive position of U.S. business in the international marketplace.

In addition to opposition by physicians and hospitals, and consumer uninterest and nonparticipation, the HMO program was also hindered by the

Watergate-disrupted federal bureaucracy and the economic recession of 1973–75 and its aftermath. Nevertheless, the HMO strategy helped legitimize profit-making through corporate entities in the delivery of health services. More importantly, it became a means to educate the corporate class to problems of health care and activate them in health policy and planning (17). As purchasers of health services through fringe benefit packages for their workers, business has experienced rampant inflation in health insurance premiums, crimping their profit margins. Moreover, the questioning of the effectiveness of medical care led executives to ponder more closely how the health sector should be restructured and services redesigned to increase labor productivity.

Across the nation, large corporations have greatly expanded their activities in relation to the health care system. Richard Egdahl of the Center for Industry and Health Care at Boston University became one of several chief promoters. Writing in *The New England Journal of Medicine* (18), he detailed three levels for corporate inroads: 1) the in-house programs of medical care, patient education, health protection and promotion; 2) corporate investment in employee health benefits through long-range planning, scrutinizing the cost of benefits administration, monitoring claims, and collecting data; 3) reforming the external health care delivery system. As examples of "industrial sponsored prepaid health plans," he extols the Kaiser-Permanente Health Plan established by Kaiser Industries in the 1930s and the more recent Winston-Salem Health Care Plan, a health maintenance organization opened in 1977 by R. J. Reynolds Company, the tobacco conglomerate. Egdahl consulted with Gillette Company "in the development of a rationalized system of care that permits both greater pluralism than is possible in a closed-panel prepaid group practice, and tighter management controls than most open-panel plans have been able to achieve" (18, p. 1350). This is a "hybrid industry-sponsored health plan" for establishing by either one large firm, or by smaller and more dispersed firms banding together. With the lack of success of the Nixon-Ellwood Health Maintenance Strategy, Egdahl's more practical conceptualization sought to combine occupational and family medicine to serve "as a nidus in which the emergent specialty of primary care in industrial clinics can mature" (18, p. 1352).

A series on *Industry and Health Care* was produced to inform corporate leaders on how to affect major change in the delivery system (19). Resulting from several conferences and collaboration among these corporate medical representatives, these books were developed in close association with the Washington Business Group on Health (WBGH) which was created by the Business Roundtable, a major planning organization comprised of chief executives of the top 200 U.S. corporations. The WBGH's identification of its class interests, and its strident attempts to pressure government and provider officials, coincides with efforts of other corporate planning bodies, such as the U.S. Chamber of Commerce, the American Enterprise Institute, and the Conference Board. These groups have carried out extensive investigations of health care over the past decade, while the business press has publicized activities of various firms in addressing health care issues for their workers (20).

Extending beyond the powerful influencing of national policy are more practical interventions on the part of the corporate class. In numerous locales, provider organizations have been bracing for a fight with "employers (who) are banding together, hoping to meld their market power as large-scale purchasers of health care services in order to keep costs down" (21, p. 55). Just as the Reagan administration was emasculating the nationwide network of health systems agencies, 123 business coalitions on health care have been started to watch over their $77 billion health outlay in 1983 (22). Twenty-five percent of these business coalitions, particularly those sparked by the WBGH, excluded doctors and hospital representatives.

Since a general corporate inability to control professional and institutional behavior has existed over time, the implementation of "managerial solutions" utilizing "marketplace economics" masks the outright effort to wrest control over the delivery system. Substantially reducing the federal health role, setting financial limitations on care, and creating profit "incentives" are now strategic, all the meanwhile the public is alarmingly told of skyrocketing costs, wasteage and inefficiency, wide variations in medical and surgical practice rates, etc. "Not-for-profit" rationalization, substantial dissolution of the public hospital system, continual federal cutbacks, stiffer consumer copayments, and multi-hospital systems growth and amalgamation are all being orchestrated through federal policies in a rather haphazardous manner.

Business spokespeople argue their interest lies in curtailing corporate outlays for employee health, to reduce absenteeism and to improve worker productivity: all directly affecting the level of corporate profits. Moreover, the segments of people whom the business press calls the "unproductive" have increasingly suffered from inadequate services in this reallocation of health resources under the "Reagan revolution." Whereas health needs among the underserved were previously given at least lip service in policy circles, the "health cost crisis" now overshadows issues of access, quality, and equity in a health system geared for profit maximization.

The corporate class may come to further realize a strategic necessity to integrate health services for valued employees under tighter control. There are surely different dimensions of corporate involvement in health care, with diverse capital groups often taking conflicting positions to the larger class interest. The corporate class as a whole is concerned with rationalization of the delivery system and reallocation issues, while segments of capital, who divide the billions of health care spoils, oppose this overall interest, or work their best within the constraints set. Most specifically, "purchasers" versus "providers" clash over cost containment policies, and "suppliers" and "insurers" often resist overall class policies also. As with all aspects of capitalist development, the entire process over time yields many short-term contradictions to the larger corporate class interest.

Navarro analyzes (23, p. 172):

> What we are witnessing is not so much a dismantling but a restructuring of the welfare state, with the intention of reducing the level of collective consumption actively intervening in the restructuring of capital to enable it to better respond to the international capitalist crisis. This restructuring the welfare state takes place by: (a) large transfers of funds within the public sector and also from the public sector to the private sector; (b) changes in the management and control of certain state apparatuses; and (c) changes in the criteria by which decisions are made and funds are allocated.

COST CONTAINMENT EFFECTS ON HEALTH PROVIDERS

The Reagan administration ushered in a dramatic alteration in American domestic as well as foreign policy. Promises of a reduction in government role, regulatory reform, and private sector involvement have been fulfilled. Massive cutbacks in nearly every public health program and the phasing out of the two regulatory programs (the Professional Standards Review Organizations and the Health Systems Agencies) have been achieved to create a "free market." Funding for Medicare and Medicaid has been continually slashed, with higher co-payments and stricter eligibility requirements being instituted. Medicare reimbursement rates to hospitals have been reduced through prospective payment according to diagnosis-related groups (DRGs). Health provider reductions and higher consumer out-of-pocket payments as a means to contain costs have been instituted (24). Through these actions to shrink the growth of health care expenditures, large-scale entities, have staked out opportunities for profit. The president of the Federation of American Hospitals, the lobbying arm for the proprietary hospital chains, explained that for the first time there is (25, p. 2):

> . . . an administration opposed to government regulations of our industry, opposed to comprehensive national health insurance, opposed to cost controls, opposed to planning, and receptive to new ideas. . . . We have never been in a better position in our history.

Even before the enactment of Republican policies, federal and corporate constraints on health expenditures had brought upheaval to the hospital industry. In the face of deterioration of the public hospital system and financially-distressed urban voluntaries, "not-for-profit" hospitals have sought survival strategies through the financial crunch by mimicking their proprietary counterparts.

Between 1974–77, eighty-five public hospitals closed. Twenty-one county hospitals in California were closed or sold during the last six years of the past decade. In New York City alone, twenty-nine hospitals were closed between 1976 and 1980, and seventeen were considered "financially distressed" in 1982 along with a total of 160 hospitals nationwide according to the U.S. Department of Health and Human Services. Over the six years up to 1980, the American

Hospital Association (AHA) showed a net loss of 186 hospitals (26), and this was before the Reagan administration health budget cutbacks. The AHA reported a continuing decline in the total number of hospitals in 1981 to 6,933 and approximately 1,360,000 beds—a decline of thirty-three hospitals and more than 3,000 beds less than 1980 (27). Much of this decline represents an adjustment to the widespread over-bedding up through the 1960s; however, Sager has found that the increased rate of urban hospital closings is primarily confined to smaller institutions located in substantially minority neighborhoods (28, 29).

Can it be readily assumed that hospital closings mean reduced aggregate cost? More sophisticated, higher level institutions that remain open find their caseload heavier, and with more patients who have little means for paying. While teaching and public hospitals have historically been the "providers of last resort" to the disadvantaged, many voluntaries no longer accept, or limit, the uninsured indigent (including many employed), or the Medicaid population whose reimbursement is much lower than private health insurance. Indirectly complicating fiscal dilemmas of teaching institutions, numerous community general hospitals are reducing their mix of services to cut losses and maximize reimbursement. Many voluntary hospitals, particularly those serving minorities and low-income populations, hold options of either bankruptcy, relocation, or conversion of facilities.

"Not-for-profit" voluntaries have become more obviously profit-seeking. Their true organization behavior is now unveiled, reflecting a convergence to that of the proprietary competition. Etzioni and Doty (30) previously found that budget surpluses of voluntaries went mostly into exotic technology and duplication of facilities in their communities, which was partly to blame for cost inflation. More specifically, the generation of surplus by a voluntary hospital is realized by its medical staff (mostly indirectly), administrative personnel (in high salaries and expense accounts), trustees (and their business associates who furnish services or products to hospital operations), and, as mentioned previously, an array of medical industrial complex suppliers (31). Past behavior of voluntaries has significantly resulted from the conditions for their development, including the advent of Medicare and Medicaid, physician and administrator desire for increased technology and growth in size, changes in their labor force, government regulation, and even community and consumer influences. With philanthropic funds now inconsequential, the problematic ethical issues surrounding the profit motive apply only to governmentally provided services. *Medical World News* has reported (21, p. 58):

> The corporate chains' success has elicited a compliment from the nonprofit sector: imitation. Non-profit hospitals are also forming multi-hospital systems, and there are now 225 non-profit systems that manage 1,131 hospitals. "The same ingredients that propel such companies as Sears, McDonald's and Exxon are also applicable to the institutional health care sector," [comments an officer of Hospital Corporation of America].

Over the past several years, the hospital industry's trade magazines have extolled the necessity of changing their historical role through diversification into new "markets." Forward-looking hospital executives are urged to partake in long-range strategic planning, set up "profit centers," and seek out "captive distribution systems" to guarantee patient flow. Nonprofitable patients are not to be "targeted" in marketing new services.

In order to cope with lagging revenues from unfilled beds, voluntaries have engaged in acquisitions, mergers, and a variety of diversification schemes. Several across the nation have offered stock in these new services. Corporate restructuring is common, to set up a holding company or parent corporation and to spin off "new lines of business" in, for example, hospice care for the terminally ill, occupational medicine programs, sports medicine clinics, biomedical engineering businesses, mobile diagnostic units, alcoholic recovery centers, clinical labs, surgicenters, nursing homes, home health care, housing for the elderly, restaurants, parking lots, health spas, flower shops, shopping centers, and more. Some diversification is only remotely related to the original mission of health care, contributing to the blurred distinction between "not-for-profit" and proprietary segments.

Writing in the *Harvard Business Review*, Goldsmith urged hospitals to analyze and adapt to the "new health care market" or face severe difficulties and be absorbed (32). For a more "cost-effective, business-like basis" to voluntary hospital operations, multi-institutional arrangements have become prevalent in medical facilities and care; staffing resources; administrative and other services; continuing education and inservice training. Over the last two decades, there has been a trend toward combining various clinical services (for instance, blood-banking), as well as a range of administrative services, just as proprietaries have done to achieve "economies of scale" (for example, group purchasing, management information systems, personnel, laundry and linen).

David Stockman, Office of Management and Budget Director under Reagan, predicted that the "health care market," once put back on competitive terms to "normally" handle "supply and demand," will force voluntary hospitals to become part of larger for-profit marketing operations; if they fail to make good investment decisions in beds or equipment, they can go bankrupt, or be taken over by more efficient concerns (33). Huff and Sharrer (34) maintain that the Economic Recovery Tax Act of 1981 and reimbursement policies for Medicare and Medicaid have created a competitive imbalance for the "not-for-profits." Since "government resources are increasingly being channeled into the for-profit health sector . . . and voluntary hospitals' ability to survive is jeopardized," these authors urge conversion to for-profit status by voluntaries.

THE GROWTH OF MULTI-HOSPITAL SYSTEMS

Only four of the thirty-nine proprietary hospitals listed in the first U.S. Hospital Census in 1873 survived into the twentieth century. By 1928, 2,435 were in operation, constituting about 36 percent of hospitals of all types in the country (1). Many were extensions of group practices of physicians and surgeons, serving either small towns or catering to well-to-do patients who wish not to be admitted to large urban centers.

Last decade, a university hospital representative expressed concerns that were echoed throughout the health care system (35, p. 65):

> There is considerable evidence to indicate that many of the institutions owned by such corporations seek to gain their profit margin through the exclusion, by one technique or another, of patients who cannot pay the full cost of their hospital care; by using methods of patient selectivity to ensure that the institution does not care for the more complex type of medical and surgical conditions; through the exclusion of such services which have traditionally been money-losers for hospitals; or through a combination of all the above factors. This obviously brings the profit motive of the proprietary hospital directly into conflict with the total community medical needs in a particular locality.

In a 1973 policy report on proprietaries, Blue Cross summed up (36, p. 5):

> The provision of health care has traditionally been considered a social undertaking. . . . In recent years, lack of confidence in the ability of profitable enterprises to maintain quality in health care has helped maintain dominance by nonprofit hospitals.

Today, arguments questioning the proprietaries' quality of care, "cream-skimming" practices, and whether they achieve their purported efficiency have, for the most part, subsided with the acceptance of "competition" conditions. The convergence of hospital behavior in both segments of the industry has led the proprietaries to criticize the tax-exempt status of their counterparts. Representatives of the corporate chains claim that their hospitals are more efficient and cost effective (37) but evidence suggests that they have slightly higher costs and charges. Lewin, Derzon, and Marguiles (38) found that proprietaries have a higher income per day and higher total operating cost per case; their Medicare and Medicaid reimbursements also tends to be a little higher per day. (Medicare pays an additional return on equity to for-profit firms.) Pattison and Katz found California proprietaries having higher total operating expenses, but only slightly higher per patient stay costs (39). Both studies showed not only higher costs and charges in the investor-owned hospitals, but also higher profit levels. Multi-hospital systems, particularly the for-profits, tend to increase the costs of care especially during the years following a merger (40). It should be noted that such studies are becoming immaterial under the present political economy.

Medical education and postgraduate training are absent in proprietaries, though just recently the largest hospital management corporations have ventured into selected teaching institutions for management contracts. For-profit hospitals generally avoid the most sophisticated and costly technological care, emphasizing profit-laden services to usually more affluent, growing communities in states with fewer regulatory constraints. An exception to this has been the Humana Heart Institute's artificial heart transplant activities, though this "loss leader" reaped a worldwide public relations benefit. Due to all of these, teaching institutions have argued they have an almost exclusive burden for training future professionals and for caring for the most severely ill and inadequately insured.

The investor-owned hospital chains have clearly become the phenomenon of the 1970s and 1980s. From 1968 to 1975 the number of proprietaries in corporate chains increased from fifteen to 300. By 1978, there were 399 hospitals with 84,000 beds owned by thirty-one major entities. While the hospital industry recently as a whole is shrinking, proprietaries keep expanding rapidly. From 1977–82, the total number of owned and managed hospitals by the for-profits in the U.S. and abroad increased by 42 percent, with beds jumping 62 percent (27, p. 6). In 1981 alone, the ten largest proprietary hospital corporations expanded by an average of 42.5 percent (41). In 1982, a total of 120,848 beds in 1,045 hospitals were held by investor-owned firms (27). Nineteen investor-owned systems increased their revenues over the year in 1982, by 34.2 percent and their profits by 51.7 percent (42). The largest, Hospital Corporation of America (HCA) based in Nashville, Tennessee, was a $4.2 billion concern (1984), owning over 355 hospitals in the United States, United Kingdom, and several other countries. (This transnational health provider managed another 35,303 beds in 294 hospitals under contract in 1983, an increase of 11.4 percent over 1981.) With the Reagan administration's change to prospective payment under Medicare, HCA saw an increased demand for its contract management services— about $8 million profit on $27 million in 1982 revenues (42). In fact, that year it did expand its contract business 20.3 percent from 1982 (3).

The growth strategies of the proprietary chains have been altered with great flexibility. In the late 1960s, they raised equity capital in the stock market for the construction of new facilities. Later, contract management became predominant with higher interest rates, capital shortages, and escalating construction costs. Voluntaries and public hospitals with financial problems were then targeted for acquisition. Hull reports that twenty-three public hospitals have been absorbed from 1979 to 1982 (43). Punch states: "Catholic hospitals are prime acquisition targets" as religious orders rethink their mission when confronted with financing difficulties (44). HCA, the leader in the "public-to-private" conversion, brought sixteen city or country hospitals between 1975–80 (45). American Medical International (AMI) (1983 sales of $1.57 billion and $130 million profit) owns over ten former public hospitals; it acquired Hyatt Medical Management Services, which had managed Cook County Hospital in Chicago until they were dismissed. The proprietaries have been particularly aggressive in obtaining psychiatric hospitals: HCA has twenty-five and National Medical Enterprises (NME) has twenty-two. Of non-government psychiatric beds in the U.S., 50 percent are owned by proprietaries.

Concentration and centralization characterize the investor-owned hospital chains. Within the past few years, a wave of mergers has reduced the number and dramatically increased the size of the top firms. HCA brought Hospital Affiliates International; Humana merged with American Medicorp to become the $1.9 billion second largest; and NME ($1.765 billion in 1983 sales) acquired National Health Enterprises and Hill-Haven Corporation of Tacoma, Washington, two nursing home chains. The Forum Group, Inc. of Lexington, Kentucky, now controls American Medical Centers, Somerset Corp., Medical Corporation of America, National Psychiatric Institute, Exception, Inc. (home for the retarded), and Retirement Living of Wilmington, Delaware. American Medical International and Lifemark merged in 1984, yielding a combined 12,000 beds for hospital care, besides alcoholism treatment and ambulatory care facilities. AMI also bought PSL Healthcare in 1985; PSL was a "not-for-profit" holding company in Denver— another example of the proprietary takeover. The top ten chains now operate over 70 percent of all proprietary hospitals, with each diversifying into other areas, mostly nursing homes, free-standing ambulatory care centers, health maintenance organizations, and preferred provider organizations. This concentration trend follows a series of financial advantages that accounted for their rapid growth.

During the inflationary 1970s investor-owned firms were able to service their long-term debt in cheaper money. The use of tax-exempt industrial revenue bonds greatly aided construction projects, which have lessened with the subsequent rise in contract management and "not-for-profit" acquisitions. Wall Street found their stocks glamorous back then (46). Even under Medicare prospective payment and declining hospital admissions in the first half of 1985, their stocks stayed high because analysts reported their earnings gain of 15 to 20 percent and their increased profit margins "prove the industry isn't only surviving cost cutting but thriving. They note that after a year of consolidation these companies are finally moving to expand and recapture their patient base" (47, p. 52). (After 1986 they were no longer "darlings" of Wall Street with their subsequent crash). Other prior financial expansion through debt instruments included bank and insurance company loans, commercial paper, subordinated debentures, and Eurodollar financing. These firms became one of the most highly leveraged industries in the U.S. (48). Compared to the stock market as a whole, the stock of hospital chains prior to 1986 sold at higher price earnings multiples, which aided equity building across the 1970s. Given these favorable conditions, they were positioned to move much more quickly than voluntaries whose outlook for funding expansion remained bleak.

The proprietary chains searched out viable markets in the southwest, midwest, California, and Florida. By positioning themselves in these regions, they not only found greater acceptance of for-profit systems, but also avoided hospital unions and stiffer state regulations. It must be remembered that the expansion by proprietaries was supported by public funds in previous cost-plus reimbursement with an added amount for building equity.

The proprietary systems have found more lucrative profit opportunities in managing voluntaries and public hospital without tying up much capital. In the last decade, the latter hospitals needed numerous improvements in financial management, management information systems, credit and collection, industrial engineering, and materials management. Investor-owned firms provided management consulting in these areas for individual hospitals, which often led to management contracts replacing the hospital administration. By 1981, investor-owned firms managed 278 hospitals, an increase of 40 percent over the previous year (41). Between 3-9 percent of gross hospital revenues is usually charged for the chain to institute revenue-enhancing and cost-cutting measures. What this means is that the hospital is brought into the chain's purchases of drugs, supplies, and insurance, and higher reimbursement from third parties and increased collections from self-pay bills are sought. *Business Week* reported that savings to the managed hospital can be three to five times the contract cost (49); however, critics maintain the real savings comes from lowering staff/patient ratios and eliminating some services (50).

The proprietary hospitals have undertaken foreign expansion for similar reasons to other multinational corporations: profit margins usually exceed those in the United States, besides tax advantages and less regulation. Nine chains operate hospitals overseas in seventeen different countries, with the most rapid investment being in the last few years. Even with its National Health Service, Great Britain is not exempt from this proprietary penetration. In anticipation of a growing "market," American multi-national hospital management companies have staked out Great Britain for their greatest foreign investment. The Federation of American Hospitals claims (27, pp. 24-25):

> Selection of a country for hospital development and ownership is a careful, painstaking and often lengthy process for the companies. In addition to the customary feasibility and economic studies, they usually do a political and cultural assessment and other exploratory research that would provide a good feel for the stability and future direction of the country in question. These steps are regarded as an integral part of the decision-making process.
>
> Companies that are mainly interested in equity investment and long-term development concentrate on countries where there is impetus in the private sector. For example, opportunities are especially bright in countries with ailing national health programs, such as England. Government support for private sector hospital build-up has been especially encouraging for the American companies operating there.

Six U.S. hospital corporations own and operate fourteen hospitals (1132 beds), with seven under construction; one other hospital is under a management contract. AMI owns and manages nine.

HCA has six British hospitals with several other countries being studied as potential targets for development. Whitaker Corporation gained 50 percent of the top rating profit from foreign work, including Saudi Arabia (51). Mannisto reports that (52, p. 52):

> American health care expertise not only upgrades the quality of health care in the countries that these corporations serve, but foreign operations also provide the opportunity for U.S. companies to become familiar with different medical philosophies and techniques that can be applied to their domestic operations.

The proprietary systems are still dwarfed by the total "not-for-profit" segment, which has itself concentrated into multi-institutional provider systems. The formation of hospital coalitions and alliances by voluntaries, as well as by local governments, parallel the nationwide proprietary chains (well over 30 percent of "not-for-profits" are owned or leased by multi-institutional providers).

The Modern Health Care survey (3, 41, 42) reported a 10.3 percent, 11.5 percent, and 6 percent respective growth in the number of beds owned, leased, or managed by the "secular non-profit chains" in 1981 (66,476 beds), 1982 (80,159), and 1983 (86,266). While not growing substantially in 1981, Catholic chains controlled 80,737 beds, and other religious chains grew 7.2 percent to a total of 23,658 beds. This growth, besides the phenomenal larger increases by the investor-owned systems, contrasts to the declines in the public hospital systems reported in the annual survey. The Seventh Day Adventist Health System, with three regional networks, ranked second to the Kaiser Foundation, the $2.9 billion HMO as the largest "not-for-profit" system. The Sisters of Mercy Health Corporation in Farmington Hills, Missouri, is the largest Catholic system, with 5,869 beds in 1983. Several other religious systems have combined under Catholic orders and Protestant sects. An example of a hospital coalition is the Voluntary Hospitals of America, Inc., based in Dallas, Texas. It is owned by over thirty large tax-exempt hospitals and expects to be a $8 billion holding company of 100 shareholders by 1985. In the public sector, the New York City Health and Hospital Corporation held 7,778 beds in 1983, and the County of Los Angeles Hospital had 4,506 beds, though both are continuing to close hospital units due to severe fiscal problems. Johnson reports that in 1983 the top ten systems had 40 percent of the hospitals affiliated in the 179 centrally managed multihospital systems (3). So it can be seen that concentration is significantly developing.

Substantial growth awaited these inter-organizational arrangements among the for-profits and voluntaries up until the Reagan administration and corporate purchaser squeeze on hospitals, which hit a continually contracting public hospital sector. Johnson maintains: "The standard forecast is that more than 50 percent of the nation's hospitals will be part of systems in five years" (42, p. 93). Reasons given for this tendency toward multi-institutional providers are the supposed economies of scale and greater availability of clinical and managerial expertise for participating units, though these have been empirically questioned (40). Larger operating and monetary base does however strengthen their political power and increases access to private capital markets. Moreover, prospective reimbursement payments are forcing independents into this pattern of consolidation, or they may face closure.

CONCENTRATION DISGUISED AS COMPETITION

The Reagan administration has taken steps to severely tighten hospital care financing, besides efforts by corporate purchasers and insurance companies, to intensify "competition." According to Wennberg, local hospital areas have varied extensively in reimbursement rates by Medicare and Blue Cross, in per capita expenditures for hospital care (53). Part of these variations are due to fixed costs from past expansions and differing intensities of service to more ill-patient populations; however, corporate class representatives among other sources today are seeking a modification of physician behavior as a principal means to curbing climbing costs in hospitals (54).

Toward this end, prospective payment under the diagnosis-related groups (DRGs) has reallocated internal hospital expenditures and forced administrators to police their medical staff. DRGs promote incentives for profit when patients are promptly discharged and ancillary services utilization is reduced. In effect, the DRG system, like "vouchers" to allow Medicare patients to join prepaid arrangements like HMOs, promotes consolidations since greater profits go to providers most able to control their marginal costs (that is, large-scale multi-institutional systems). Of note, the Federation of American Hospitals, which had opposed the Carter administration's proposal for a "cost-cap" over hospital expenditures, was the only staunch backer of the DRG legislation.

By making profit incentives central to promoting provider efficiency, Reagan's health policy has favored concentration, not withstanding the rhetoric of "competition." As a result of the combined actions by purchasers and providers, the multi-institutional provider systems have emerged as the foremost contender for arranging for a fuller range of personal health services; their domination of the delivery system is virtually assured, despite the adverse effects on the total population's health from the unplanned character to these developments.

Besides this upheaval in hospital care, dramatic changes in ambulatory care led for-profit health firms to seek "unification." Steps were taken to coordinate primary care clinics, urgent care centers, hospitals and nursing homes, home care and hospice services. The greater number of medical graduates each year presents an employee pool to systems who vertically integrated to set up free-standing clinic operations (55). Humana operated 80 MedFirst centers by 1983, to be the foundation of Humana Care Plus, an insurance company to offer an integrated benefit package across the country to large corporate purchasers (56). National Medical Enterprises and American Medical International sought similar insurance ventures. HCA associated with PruCare, the health maintenance organization owned by Prudential Insurance Company. HCA has also operated an HMO in Brazil serving over 650,000 people.

Several multi-state HMOs also expanded rapidly (57). Regional and national networks include the Kaiser Foundation Health Plan, CIGNA Health Plan (the largest investor-owned HMO), MaxiCare Health Plans, US Health Care in Pennsylvania, Health-Plans of Nashville, Tennessee, John Hancock, and PruCare. The *Modern Health Care* survey listed eight investor-owned firms and four secular "not-for-profit" HMOs in 1982 (58). As with hospitals, there have been significant mergers and acquisitions, and the largest "not-for-profit" HMOs (Group Health Plan, Minneapolis; Harvard Community Health Plan, Boston; Group Health Cooperative of Puget Sound, Seattle; and Health Insurance Plan of Greater New York) affiliated and set up a profit corporation to market to large corporate purchasers and develop HMOs in other cities. Blue Cross–Blue Shield Plans likewise sought nationwide marketing.

For the explicitly for-profit HMOs, little upfront capital is actually required if these corporations take over HMOs that were originally set up as nonprofit entities (e.g., Philadelphia Health Plan by John Hancock; Health Service Plan of Pennsylvania by Health-Plans; North-Care in Evanston, Illinois, by Prudential, among numerous others). This follows the same pattern as in the takeover of public and "not-for-profit" hospitals. These existing health care organizations have been highly subsidized out of the public purse, but are now being virtually given to the for-profit sector. Many commercial insurance companies began PPOs as a means to capture new "patient markets." In a PPO, the consumer is allowed to choose his or her own primary care physician, but must use prescribed hospitals and their specialists for referral care. California saw many PPO beginnings with other state governments quickly following suit with enabling legislation (41).

IMPLICATIONS FROM COMPETITION

By looking at other U.S. industries that have become concentrated, it can be seen that larger firms have distinct market advantages over others. They possess ready organizational and financial resources to systematically searchout possible modifications in their activities to reap big cost savings. By virtue of their domination of the market, these larger corporate entities can also risk the installation of more efficient, but expensive new systems and technology because of their ability to sell their product lines. The larger and more dominant the firm, the greater its marketing strength and the greater its manipulation of the market to its terms. Needless to say, their political power outweighs the smaller firms.

Of course, corporations in concentrated industries, particularly in times of economic downturn, have little incentive to pass their cost savings on to consumers. Rather, innovations in production, and reductions in labor costs, will just increase profits. In health care, concentration over time may tend to work *against* organizational innovations and advances in science that are not profitable, but are in the interests of improved health.

In 1980 *The New England Journal of Medicine* editor, A. Relman, had urged the American Medical Association to "act defensively in separating physicians from the commercial exploitation of health care," though he does not see similar issues in the private practice of medicine, nor in the pharmaceutical, hospital equipment, and supply industries: "no one has seriously challenged their social usefulness" (1, p. 963). As in the response in the 1930s by the medical profession to the "corporate practice of medicine" under the prepaid group practice form, Relman's principal concern appears confined to the increasing control over physician behavior by large organizational structures managed by non-physicians. Expressing his academic medical perspective, Relman questions "whether competition from profit-making providers is really threatening the survival of our teaching centers and major urban hospitals" (1, p. 963). However, by pitting for-profit against "not-for-profit," he fails to note similarities in their respective organization behaviors, most notably that under present conditions both segments are interested in "increasing its total sales," and both are now "cream-skimming," and overemphasizing procedures and technology, with "excessive fragmenting of services."

Recent encroachments into academic medicine have come from proprietary hospital systems. Humana signed a management contract for the University of Louisville Medical Center in 1983, and American Medical International purchased the teaching affiliate of Creighton University in Omaha, Nebraska. Harvard Medical School's Massachusetts General Hospital considered selling the prestigious McLean Psychiatric Hospital to HCA. More universities are thinking about dumping their costly teaching hospitals, either by outside contract or direct sale (59). Humana has contracted to build and operate Chicago Medical School's teaching hospital.

Through the twentieth century, physicians as a profession have postponed or minimized their "proletarianization," a process inherent in modern corporate society—one that has quickly and more easily engulfed most other workers (60). This current transformation of the health sector, coupled with an "over-supply" of physicians by the year 2000, appears to be leading a reduction of the physician to a proletarian function within large bureaucratic organizations. Given the continuing industrialization of health services, small-scale medical practice has become untenable and professional perogatives are quickly eroding in these management-controlled structures. Fuchs' notion of physician as the "captain of the team" seems absurd under the impending changes (61), as medical activity moves closer and closer to the service capital accumulation by large-scale multinational capital. Unfortunately, given the apparent acceptance, or in some instances an outright embrace, of a profit-centered health care system by professionals, Americans may come to have little alternative.

Production for profit in medical care means much less emphasis on equity in the distribution of services and less concern for the individual regardless of class, sex, race, age, culture and language. Patient-practitioner interactions can be expected to be redesigned. It remains to be seen how mutual trust and respect, which are integral to healing, will be supported under altered economic relationships between patients and their providers of care. Profit maximization tendencies are likely to influence how numerous bioethical issues are viewed and resolved. Future medical research priorities, and ideological orientations in health services research, will likewise be shaped by profit maximization. Moreover, the next decade's "information systems revolution" will enable a concentrated health care industry not only to modify the content of medical practice, but to possess a pervasive power to define the parameters of "proper health." This prospect is made more ominous given the political nature of the inexorable expansion of socially and environmentally generated health problems (62, 63). It is also doubtful that managerial talent will yield benignly beneficial results in lessening demonstrated ineffective procedures, wasteful use of biotechnology, unnecessary ancillary testing, ritualistic surgery, and the like (64). Profit has accounted for their embedding into the delivery system; they may be predictably prolonged to recover costs, even while corporate purchasers of care for employees demand efficiency and cost effectiveness. Moreover, new profit opportunities are continually generated as the world now knows from the artificial heart hoopla among medical suppliers and Humana (65).

SUMMARY AND CONCLUSIONS

The process of capital accumulation has always been central to health sector developments, only now have a wider range of observers and the public come to see this—the problem lies in the lens used to interpret it.

Most importantly, the context of the continuing economic crisis of western capitalism portends significant readjustments to the cumulative nature and structural fit of medical care in all advanced nations. The weakness of capital in the United States is reflected in the retarded growth of investment and significantly lower rates of return than in previous decades. International monetary instability, political realignments among nations, continued economic challenges from other advanced countries, and military adventurism will influence domestic policies.

The Reagan administration has eroded previous full employment goals and income redistribution attempts in order to strengthen the material base of corporations. The renegotiation of the social contract between labor and capital is signified by governmental reductions of social welfare spending and unilateral revocation of health benefits for certain workers. This erosion of the social wage, and decline in the standards of living of the American people, are not short-term aberrations soon to be corrected. To the extent that health emanates from social structural and ecological conditions arising from the overall process of capital accumulation, the divergence between the social production of disease and for-profit medical care will increasingly indicate limitations in medical interventions (66).

On the one hand, the proprietary thrust in medical care has been gaining legitimacy by appeal to the corporate class and federal government with promises of efficiency, cost-controls, and economic returns. These parties may recognize their apparent inability to overcome the disease-producing aspects inherent under capitalist development other than through market creation. On the other hand, there have been deep economic affinities between institutionalized services under the existing "medical model" and other ideological characteristics of corporate expansion into the service sectors. The larger corporate entry into medical care has escalated with the rising imbalances between a "socially inefficient" health system and the overall corporate profit squeeze over the last decade.

The probable convergence between the corporate class interest for cost containment and for-profit reorganization lies in the legitimation of a chaotic system of health care consistent with dominant principles of economic production; yet antagonisms will inevitably persist. What may come to pass with this entry are new forms of class control, whereby a reorganization strategy will gradually reshape the ideology of medicine and the specific content of health services over the next few decades. The loss of relative autonomy by health sector parties in the economy threatens the medical profession, which is the point that concerns the editor of *The New England Journal of Medicine* (1). The growing influence of corporate planning bodies in health policy formulation and numerous local business coalitions signifies a new context for future health sector developments.

Earlier last decade O'Connor maintained that a "social industrial complex" may eventually emerge to organize more "rationally" health, education, and social welfare services, and even other aspects of family and social life (67). All necessary for the reproduction of labor power under a capitalist economic system, he analyzed it would make sense for class-conscious corporate policy to redesign them to lessen their absorption of the social surplus. Marginally productive and disenfranchised populations serve little purpose in the generation of profit from these services, or in the allocation of societal resources in the first place. Thus, discussions of rationing medical care resources assume a logic beyond the individual clinical level. What may have seemed reprehensible a mere decade or so ago, this topic has come into vogue in both the United States and the United Kingdom (68, 69).

The imposition of such a framework for the health and health care for our nation is being resisted. A changing public consciousness indicates that many people will not be satisfied with their own health levels resulting from an economic transaction dependent on the value of their labor. Navarro has presented evidence that no popular mandate exists in the United States for the withdrawal of services for the aged and unfortunate, nor for the weakening of government protection for the worker, consumer, and our ecology (70).

As greater numbers of people more broadly define their health, demands for more meaningful and sensitive encounters with health practitioners will surely escalate. Ideologically, the medicalization of a whole array of political, cultural, and personal conditions leading to chronic degenerative illnesses are presently being manipulated to obscure the social and ecological origins of disease. While not always countering this, commentaries from the aged and women's health, self-care, and holistic health movements, and from ecological, spiritual and "New Age" circles, are articulating the political and social issues. From these quarters have come attacks on the "medical model," which has been most amenable to commodified services for repair of acute illnesses (71, 72).

If a large enough segment of our population seeks an altogether different orientation in the purpose and meaning of health care; if health becomes more viewed in its proper social and ecological framework; if people demand decentralized health services organized under the democratic control of their community; if communities attempt to relate health services with other aspects of community and social life, then profit-making opportunities will be undermined and progress toward our collective health may be achieved.

REFERENCES

1. Relman, A. S. The new medical industrial complex. *New Engl. J. Med.* 303: 963–970, 1980.
2. Gray, B. H. *The New Health Care for Profit: Doctors and Hospitals in a Competitive Environment.* National Academy Press, Washington, D.C., 1983.
3. Johnson, D. E. L. Multi-unit providers: Survey plots 475 chains' growth. *Modern Healthcare* 14(5): 65–110, 1984.
4. Starr, P. *The Transformation of American Medicine.* Basic Books, New York, 1982.
5. Navarro, V. Medical history as justification rather than explanation: A critique of Starr's "The Social Transformation of American Medicine." *Int. J. Health Serv.* 14(4): 511–528, 1984.
6. Kelman, S. Review of "The Rising Cost of Hospital Care" by M. S. Feldstein. *Int. J. Health Serv.* 3(2): 311–314, 1973.
7. Brown, E. R. Medicare and Medicaid: The process, value, and limits of health care reforms. *J. Pub. Health Policy* 4(3): 335–366, 1983.
8. Renaud, M. On the structural constraints of state intervention in health. *Int. J. Health Serv.* 5(4): 559–571, 1975.
9. Ehrenreich, J. and Ehrenreich, B. *The American Health Empire: Power, Profits and Politics.* Random House, New York, 1970.
10. McClure, M. Hospital management companies expand foreign operations. *J. Am. Hosp. Assoc.* 55(3): 52–55, 1981.
11. Salmon, J. W. The health maintenance organization strategy: A corporate takeover of health services delivery. *Int. J. Health Serv.* 5: 609–669, 1975.
12. Ellwood, P. M. Health maintenance strategy. *Medical Care* 9(May/June): 291–298, 1971.
13. Ellwood, P. M. and Herbert, M. E. Health care: Should industry buy it or sell it? *Harvard Business Review* 51(July/August): 99–107, 1973.

14. Ellwood, P. M. Testimony before the Senate Subcommittee on Public Health and Environment. Series no. 97-90, part II. Washington, D.C., U.S. Government Printing Office, 1972.
15. Ellwood, P. M. Models for organizing health services and implications of legislation proposals. *Milbank Mem. Fund Q.* 50(October): 73–101, 1972.
16. Ellwood, P. M. Big business blows the whistle on medical costs. *Prism* December: 12–15, 1974.
17. Salmon, J. W. Monopoly capital and the reorganization of health care. *Rev. Rad. Polit. Econ.* 9(12): 125–133, 1977.
18. Egdahl, R. H. and Walsh, D. C. Industry-sponsored health programs: Basis for a new hybrid prepaid plan. *New Engl. J. Med.* 296(22): 1350–1353, 1977.
19. *Springer Series on Industry and Health Care* (5 vols.), edited by R. Egdahl. Springer-Verlag, New York, 1977.
20. Salmon, J. W. *Corporate Attempts to Reorganize the American Health Care System.* Unpublished doctoral dissertation, Cornell University, 1978.
21. Rhein, R. W. The new cost-control 'coalition': Will big business run the show? *Medical World News* 23(3): 54–64, 1982.
22. Meyerhoff, A. S. and Crozier, D. Health care coalitions: The evaluation of a movement. *Datawatch* 3(1): 120–127, 1984.
23. Navarro, V. The crisis of the international capitalist order and its implications for the welfare state. *Int. J. Health Serv.* 12(2): 172, 1982.
24. Salmon, J. W. The competitive health strategy: Fighting for your health. *Health and Medicine* 1(2): 21–30, 1982.
25. Federation of American Hospitals. *Federation of American Hospitals 1981 in Review: Annual Report.* Federation of American Hospitals, Little Rock, Arkansas, 2, 1981.
26. Rhein, R. W. Hospitals in trouble: Crisis for doctors. *Medical World News* 21(24): 58–68, 1980.
27. *The 1983 Directory: Investor-owned Hospitals and Hospital Management Companies.* Federation of American Hospitals, Little Rock, Arkansas, 1982.
28. Sager, A. Why urban voluntary hospitals close. *Health Serv. Res.* 18(3): 451–481, 1983.
29. Sager, A. The reconfiguration of urban hospital care: 1937–1980. In *Cities and Sickness: Health Care in Urban America* (Urban Affairs Annual Review, vol. 25), edited by A. L. Greer and S. Greer. Sage Publications, Beverly Hills, 1983.
30. Etzioni, A. and Doty, P. Profit in not-for-profit corporations: The example of health care. *Polit. Sci. Q.* (Fall): 433–453, 1976.
31. Health Policy Advisory Center. *The Profits in Non-Profit Hospitals.* Health Advisory Center West, San Francisco, 1979.
32. Goldsmith, J. C. The health care market: Can hospitals survive? *Harvard Business Review* (September/October): 100–111, 1980.
33. Inglehart, J. K. Report on the Duke University Medical Center private sector conference. *New Engl. J. Med.* 307(1): 68–71, 1982.
34. Huff, J. S. and Sharrer, K. I. Government policies force non-profits to go profit. *Modern Healthcare* 12(6): 81–83, 1982.
35. Cannedy, L. L. An historical analysis of the viability of for-profit hospitals. *Hospital Progress* 51(November): 64–71, 1970.
36. Stewart, D. A. *The History and Status of Proprietary Hospitals* (Research Series No. 9). Blue Cross Association, Chicago, 1973.
37. Eamer, R. K. Why proprietary hospitals are more efficient and cost effective. *Modern Hospital Care* 8(4): 60–63, 1978.
38. Lewin, L. S., Derzon, R. A., and Marguiles, R. Investor-owned and nonprofits differ in economic performance. *Hospitals* 54(1 July): 52–58, 1981.
39. Pattison, R. and Katz, H. Investor-owned and not-for-profit hospitals: A comparison based on California data. *New Engl. J. Med.* 309(6): 346–353, 1983.
40. Ermann, D. and Gabel, J. Multi-hospital systems: Issues and empirical findings. *Health Aff.* 3(1), 1984.

41. Johnson, D. L. and Punch, L. Multi-hospital systems survey. *Modern Healthcare* 12(5): 74–122, 1982.
42. Johnson, D. E. L. Multi-units are ready to boost their market share. *Modern Healthcare* 13(5): 89–122, 1983.
43. Hull, J. B. How ailing hospital in south was rescued by a for-profit chain. *The Wall Street Journal*, January 28, 1983, p. 1.
44. Punch, L. For-profit nursing homes systems consolidate: Beds grow by 18 percent. *Modern Healthcare* 12(6): 74, 1982.
45. Lancaster, H. More public hospitals are sold to firms despite objections from poor and aged. *The Wall Street Journal*, November 11, 1980, p. 48.
46. Loeb, M. Hospital corp., similar stocks remains favored by analysts despite Medicare cuts, trust suits. *The Wall Street Journal*, August 30, 1982, p. 31.
47. Hull, J. B. Hospital-management stock prices expected to rise despite pressures of Medicare, insurers. *The Wall Street Journal*, January 30, 1985, p. 52.
48. Siegrist, R. Wall Street and the for-profit hospital management companies. In *The New Health Care For Profit*, edited by Gray, B. National Academy Press, Washington, D.C., 1983.
49. *Business Week.* How outsiders manage hospitals for profit. November 24, 1975, pp. 50, 55–56.
50. Dallek, G. The private (mis)management of public hospitals: Feeding at the public trough. *Health Law Proj. Library Bull.* 6: 62–76, 1981.
51. Hull, J. B. Hospital firms are expanding foreign work. *The Wall Street Journal*, July 9, 1982, pp. 19, 33.
52. Mannisto, M. Hospital management companies expand foreign operations. *J. Am. Hosp. Assoc.* 55(3): 542, 1981.
53. Wennberg, J. E. Should the cost of insurance reflect the cost of use in local hospital markets? *New Engl. J. Med.* 307(22): 1374–1381, 1982.
54. Doctors and the state. *The Wall Street Journal,* January 16, 1976, p. 23.
55. Weiss, K. Corporate medicine: What's the bottom line for physicians and patients? *The New Physician* 9: 19–25, 1982.
56. Punch, L. M.D.s, hospitals beat out systems in the alternative service market. *Modern Healthcare* 13(5): 126–128, 1983.
57. Inglehart, J. K. HMOs (for-profit) on the move. *New Engl. J. Med.* 310(18): 1203–1208, 1984.
58. Kuntz, E. F. Systems scoop up nursing homes. *Modern Healthcare* 12(5): 102–103, 1982.
59. Evangelauf, J. Many universities are weighing sale of their hospitals. *Chron. Higher Educ.* 29(21): 1, 20, 1985.
60. McKinlay, J. B., and Arches, J. Toward the proletarianization of physicians. *Int. J. Health Serv.* 15(1): 161–195, 1985.
61. Fuchs, V. R. *Who Shall Live?* Basic Books, New York, 1975.
62. Eyer, J. and Sterling, P. Stress-related mortality and social organization. *Rev. Rad. Polit. Econ.* 9: 1–44, 1977.
63. Eyer, J. Capitalism, health, and illness. In *Issues in the Political Economy of Health*, edited by McKinlay, J. B. Tavistock, New York, 1984.
64. McKinlay, J. B. From 'promising report' to 'standard procedure': Seven stages in the career of medical innovation. *Milbank Mem. Fund Q./Health and Soc.* 59(3): 374–411, 1981.
65. Richards, B. and Mills, D. Humana's inplant of artificial heart brings capital and competition to growing industry. *The Wall Street Journal*, February 7, 1985, p. 4.
66. McKinlay, S. and McKinlay, J. B. Examining trends in the nation's health. Paper presented at the American Public Health Association Annual Meeting, New York, November, 1979.
67. O'Connor, J. *The Fiscal Crisis of the State.* St. Martin's Press, New York, 1973.
68. Evans, R. W. Health care technology and the inevitability of resource allocation and rationing decisions. *JAMA* (Part 1) 249(15): 2047–2053; (Part III) 248(6): 2208–2222, 1983.

69. Aaron, H. J. and Schwartz, W. B. *The Painful Prescription: Rationing Hospital Care*. Brookings Institution, Washington, D.C., 1984.
70. Navarro, V. Where is the popular mandate? *New Engl. J. Med.* 307(24): 1516–1517, 1982.
71. Berliner, H. and Salmon, J. W. The holistic alternative to scientific medicine: History and analysis. *Int. J. Health Serv.* 10: 133–147, 1980.
72. Salmon, J. W. (ed.). *Alternative Medicines: Popular and Policy Perspectives.* New York, Tavistock, 1984.

PART 2

Impacts on Health Care Institutions

The increasing bottom-line orientation to overall health care provider operations arose quickly and unashamedly under the competitive health strategy during the Reagan administration. The ideological supposition of the market advocates was that benefits of improved management, economies of scale, inter-organizational linkages, and infusion of private capital would address the inflationary costs of care problem. Profit would be the determiner of success as the market would reward the efficient.

Yet too much greed and grasping for market share kept costs climbing, all the meanwhile unleashing a whirlwind spurt in administrative overhead (1). Traditional "not-for-profit" providers, as well as the explicitly for-profit hospital chains, nursing homes and health maintenance organizations, joined in a bitter fight for middle class markets of paying "customers" while limiting or eliminating any underfunded patients. Acquisitions, mergers, and takeovers consolidated institutions into nationwide and regional systems. Most providers sought diversification in their "product lines" while the investor-owned firms got caught up in leveraged buyouts, stockholder suits, and later divestitures. In short, with injection of competition, capitalism had spread heartily throughout health care.

Predominant liberal analyses have held, given recent declines by the "big four" corporate hospital chains, that the for-profit medicine phenomenon has ebbed and may have run its course. These kinds of analyses fail to recognize the presence and growth of the smaller regional hospital systems, both proprietary and "not-for-profit," many of which are still doing financially quite well. While overall profits continued to decline in 1987 for the 155 multi-hospital systems in the *Modern Healthcare* survey (though marginally so compared to 1986), revenues were up to $56.9 billion, particularly rising for the secular "not-for-profit" chains (2). But for the fifteen investor-owned companies, profits were up 44.8 percent over 1986. And while Hospital Corporation of America (HCA), Humana, American Medical International, and National Medical Enterprises divested a total of 127 acute-care hospitals in the United States, almost all were sold to other for-profit organizations, including leveraging their own employees' retirement funds by selling off their unprofitable and marginally profitable institutions to their Employee Stock Option Programs. Management-buyouts have been also orchestrated by HCA, Charter Medical Corp., and Republic Health Corp. Thus, the for-profit health care firms through restructuring have adjusted to the tightening financial constraints on the health sector and are ready for continued profit-taking less concentrated in hospital ownership.

Such analyses of the proprietary development also downplay the continuing significance of the broader corporatization trend when focused mainly on the hospital sector. Such perspectives neglect many of the larger impacts throughout the entire health care system. For example, to remain price competitive with Preferred Provider Organizations and other managed care alternatives, about 50 percent of HMOs across the nation lost money over the past few years. Facing these harder times, many HMOs are cutting corners in care provision, given incentives for an under-provision of services. Similar bottom-line obsessions have spread outward through a wide range of public and voluntary health providers too.

This section offers five chapters that begin to detail how the ongoing corporate transformation has affected health care institutions. In the first selection on "The Health Maintenance Organization Strategy," Salmon examines the policy context for profit-making in health care set in place during the Nixon administration. Detail is provided on the origins of legitimating this direction in a traditionally non-profit delivery mode (excepting physicians) and how the federal government educated, and initially led, the corporate sector to become more involved in health care activities and health policymaking.

Berliner and Burlage in "Proprietary Hospital Chains and Academic Medical Centers" examine the interpenetration of the four largest proprietary hospital chains and academic medical centers for the legitimation, as well as a vertical integration, of these firms' former strategies. Prior to 1987 these companies had begun to buy, manage, or build a few teaching hospitals. The authors here lay out potential consequences of such linkages for academic medical centers in terms of the continued educational mission, amounts of indigent care to their surrounding communities, and research programs. They also explore larger social implications, which are still relevant today despite the relative insignificance of these arrangements today.

With the issue of uncompensated care plaguing hospitals and the plight of the poor and medically indigent at a critical stage, the condition of the public sector and its responsibility for care to the underserved is evermore vitally important. In "The Proprietarization of Health Care and the Underdevelopment of the Public Sector," Whiteis and Salmon define the social relationship between the rapid growth of the for-profit providers and the dismantling of the health care institutional structure left chiefly to serve the urban poor minorities, chronically ill, and aged with little means to pay for services they need. A record number of 81 hospitals closed in 1988 eclipsing the previous record of 79 the year before. Since 1980, 445 hospitals have closed their doors, with many in communities where services are still needed (3). Whiteis and Salmon make a case that reveals the underdevelopment of public hospitals, certain inner-city voluntaries, and community-based clinics, in the face of rampant success by proprietary providers catering to middle class clienteles requiring less intensity of services.

These developments in the health sector have dramatically transformed the medical workplace and profoundly altered the everday work of the doctor. In the next chapter, "Corporatization and the Social Transformation of Doctoring," McKinlay and Stoeckle discuss the impact of recent changes and critique prevailing views of professionalism. They see a movement toward proletarianization of physicians as the profession loses control over certain perogatives, thereby subordinating it to the broader requirements of production under advanced capitalism. Organizational changes in delivery institutions are producing a myriad of consequences for patients, and the authors here address how doctors may respond over time.

REFERENCES

1. Himmelstein, D. U. and Woolhandler, S. Cost without benefit: Administrative waste in U.S. medicine. *New Engl. J. Med.* 314: 441–445, 1986.
2. Greene, J. Systems went back to basics in '87, restructuring to stay competitive. *Modern Healthcare* May 27, 1988, pp. 45–117.
3. Burda, D. Record 81 hospitals close. *Modern Healthcare* January 20, 1989, p. 2.

CHAPTER 4

The Health Maintenance Organization Strategy

J. Warren Salmon

Significant structural reorganization of health services delivery in the United States has been taking place, providing for a totally new configuration for the entire health services industry. Yet most health policy analysis provides little understanding of the true nature of this development, simply because it ignores the macroanalytic dynamics of the overall society.

This paper suggests that a new structure for health services delivery is emerging, a major component of which is the health maintenance organization (HMO). The extent of possibilities for and the implications of a major corporate takeover of the health care delivery institutions are examined.

CONTEXT FOR HEALTH SERVICES DEVELOPMENT

Political economic analysis begins with the premise that the economic structure of the society serves as the underlying context for the functions and organizational development of its various support sectors (e.g., social welfare, education, military, civilian police). Given the primacy of the accumulation of capital and general economic expansion (1, 2), capitalist societies periodically experience severe crises of various kinds. In the 1970s the United States was faced with a number of crises which grew out of the structural contradictions of its social organization. In international terms the American economy has been in its most precarious situation since before World War II (3). This in turn places constraints on the domestic economy, and, conversely, the acute domestic economic stagnation exacerbates the international situation (4). World economic policies must be coordinated to assure stability and continued U.S. dominance, and at the same time critical domestic social needs must be addressed while an attempt is made to stimulate economic recovery within the constraints of the new international economic order.

Such tendencies generally necessitate the active intervention of the state (5). In earlier attempts to ameliorate various of the difficulties on a piecemeal basis, the state engaged in a variety of forms of financial subsidization. The accumulated experience of this approach, however, has contributed to the fiscal crisis of the state: the tendency for government expenditures to outrace revenues (6, 7). Consequently, since 1968, with the advent of the first Nixon Administration, a more sophisticated approach to the resolution of American economic difficulties emerged, with implications for the future of health care.

RESTRUCTURING HEALTH SERVICES FOR SOCIAL EFFICIENCY

International conditions and acute domestic stagnation produced an immediate concern for the efficient functioning of American capitalism. Efforts to expand productive capacity and increase the productivity of labor are becoming paramount. Social investment decisions for the economy take on greater importance. Further, higher levels in the productivity of labor can be promoted by reorganizing the social welfare sector and consolidating institutions which provide for the reproduction of the labor force. Accordingly, the state adjusts budgetary priorities to favor corporate expansion and implements new state programs.

O'Connor (7, p. 54) maintains that these conditions and subsequent action "may lead to the development of a full-scale 'social-industrial complex' under the auspices of state and monopoly industries." The emergence of the "medical-industrial complex" (8, 9) may be viewed as a part of this larger shaping of the social welfare sector. State subsidization of the present health care providers is promoting greater inroads by large corporations to participate in the industrialization of health services. The rising percentage of the gross national product spent on health care has been considered excessive by policy makers given the present economy, and the state's financing burden exacerbates its fiscal crisis. The rising cost of medical care has been clearly related to the present structural elements of fee-for-service medical practice and cost-reimbursed hospital care. Therefore, state policies are now attempting to reorganize health care delivery for greater social efficiency and at the same time allow for the infusion of monopoly capital to redirect capital flows within the health services industry. Given the magnitude of the social crises facing America today, health policy additionally serves to legitimate the present social order.

One immediate outcome of the Medicare and Medicaid financing was the market expansion for the peripheral supply firms (e.g., construction, drugs, hospital equipment and supplies, systems and communications) and the financial intermediaries (Blue Cross, Blue Shield, and the commercial insurance companies). In commenting on investment possibilities in medical care, *Forbes* magazine (10) proclaimed in 1968 that "big business is looking for ways to get in." Large corporations who will not be limited to financing and peripheral supply roles are entering health services delivery also.

CORPORATE INTERVENTIONS IN HEALTH SERVICES
DELIVERY

It is important to distinguish between the two levels upon which the restructuring of health services delivery is occurring. As described, adjustment within capitalism represents the long term macrosociological process. This level provides the institutional context within which individuals and organizational entities in the health care sector will tend to be generally consistent, although not always directed and deliberate, with the resolution of present contradictions.

It has been stated that international and domestic economic conditions have given rise to a pressing concern for greater social efficiency in the social welfare sector. As this relates to the health services industry, state subsidization facilitated the beginning industrialization of the delivery system and coincidentally encouraged greater corporate involvement. These dynamics yield more meaning when some particulars in their historical perspective are traced.

Capitalist intervention in health services manifested itself in a number of ways, both obvious and subtle, since the Carnegie Foundation sponsorship of the Flexner Report in 1910 and the follow-through of grants from the Rockefeller Foundation to reorganize medical education. Most direct involvement by corporate capital has evolved over the past few decades in the financing role by commercial insurance firms and in the peripheral supply role. Various foundations have redesigned many facets of the organization of medical care, today significantly influencing delivery forms (11, 12). Industrial and financial interests were presented in the Committee on the Cost of Medical Care, which in 1933 proposed a precursor form to the health maintenance organization (13). Nearly all subsequent voluntary and governmental commissions on medical care include executives from large corporations in leadership roles. Hospital and medical school boards of trustees have always been vehicles for corporate interest to provide a rather substantial influence on the local health services delivery (14). Needless to say, corporate interests have been shown clearly in both the formation of Blue Cross plans and their continued regional operations throughout the country.

The emergence of a "class-conscious corporate directorate" (10, p. 111) which has devoted major attention to health policy matters arose with the waning influence of the American Medical Association, the American Hospital Association, the American Public Health Association, the Association of American Medical Colleges, and other traditional health interest groups. Discussions within the corridors of corporate power have been considering new structural elements to address monopoly capital's needs in the 1970s and after. The Committee for Economic Development published a major report in April 1974 entitled *Building a National Health Care System* (15). The American Enterprise Institute, the United States Chamber of Commerce, the Washington Business Group on Health, the National Association of Manufacturers, the

Conference Board, and other policy groups known to exert great influence in state matters were active in discussing the restructuring of the health services industry (16-19). *Fortune, Business Week, Forbes,* and *Wall Street Journal,* in contrast to earlier times, now devote great amounts of news and editorial space to problems in health care, and all strongly endorse the health maintenance organization strategy (20-27).

Since the 1960s a new development in health services delivery is represented in the investor-owned hospital and nursing home corporate chains, e.g., American Medicorp, Hospital Corporation of America, AID (a subsidiary of the Insurance Company of North America), Extendicare, American Medical International (28). This proprietary development must be viewed in terms of its significance to the breakdown of the "not-for-profit" orientation and the rise of large-scale administrative efficiency.

THE HMO STRATEGY

The HMO strategy of the Nixon Administration demonstrates the state's role in bringing about a new organization form for health services delivery. Dr. Paul M. Ellwood Jr., the chief architect of the HMO concept, participated in the early discussions convened by the Department of Health, Education, and Welfare in January 1970 (29). Ellwood has served the function of an ideological entrepreneur through his writing and consultation to large corporations and the technical research and development of his organization, Interstudy. No news article on HMOs fails to mention his extensive activity. The Center for Political Research, a Washington-based research group for business, reported that "key factors in this effort [to sell the idea of for-profit HMOs] have been, and will continue to be, the activities and ideas of Dr. Paul Ellwood . . ." (30).

In his 1971 State of the Union message and subsequent health message to Congress on February 18, 1971, Richard Nixon declared the HMO strategy to be the cornerstone for restructuring the health care system. Briefly defined, the health maintenance organization is to bring together a comprehensive range of medical services in a single organization and provide the services purchased in a benefit package for a fixed contract fee which is paid in advance. Through changing the financing mechanism from the sickness-oriented, piece-work basis of the present delivery system, the HMO structures an economic incentive "to concentrate on keeping people healthy" and provide "greater efficiency" (31). According to Ellwood, the HMO strategy will strengthen the role of "competition" by introducing "economic incentives" and minimize the need for "regulation" by relying upon "market mechanisms" (32-34). The promise of a rational, well-organized delivery system of HMOs sounds convincing to cost-conscious employers who purchase the bulk of health insurance for their employees (35) and to individual consumers who face problems of cost, quality, accessibility, and availability of services. As Alford (36) points out, those proposing "solutions" of corporate rationalization gain support from consumers who are hard-pressed for improved health care services.

The HMO concept as described by HEW and Ellwood should not be taken literally. Sifting through the rhetoric and associated debatable "issues" concerning HMOs, it becomes clear that the HMO embodies a certain organization form that is ideologically and organizationally consistent with the dominant production institutions in the society. It encompasses the increased technological and scientific advancement in medicine, the extensive specialization and division of labor within large scale, complex organization, and the control by administrative and financial management. Its very structure is designed for profit making: the costs of providing the services under contract in the benefit packages are deducted from the prepaid revenues, yielding the profit.

Since profitability is the key to survival, Ellwood invited private corporations to lend their "industrial know-how" because "they are experienced in the application of management and have the ability to generate and effectively use capital resources . . ." (32). Writing in the *Harvard Business Review*, he detailed the strategy for corporate involvement in profit-making HMOs and suggested that industrial medical departments are easily convertible to an HMO to "realize a substantial savings over present expenditures for employee health care benefits . . ." (37, p. 106). What Ellwood imagines is an eventual domination where the "number of health care organizations in the United States would be reduced to as few as 1000 with each HMO serving from 5000 to several million persons" (38). Local HMOs are expected to "function either as autonomous units or branches of larger national or regional organizations with several subsidiaries . . ." (39). The historical significance of Ellwood lies not in his conceptualization of the HMO itself but in his ability to put the "idea whose time has come" into a strategy for eventual corporate control of health services delivery, to raise the profitability of the industry, and to contribute to increased worker productivity.

Prepaid group practice (a precursor of the HMO) existed even before the Committee on the Cost of Medical Care recommended it in 1933. The first plan originated in 1927 at Community Hospital in Elk City, Oklahoma, as a Farmers Cooperative (40). Subsequently, other prepaid group practices began. Among them were: Ross-Loos Medical Clinic in Los Angeles in 1929; Group Health Association, Inc., in Washington, D.C., in 1937; Kaiser-Permanente Medical Care Program in 1942; Health Insurance Plan of Greater New York in 1947; Group Health Cooperative of Puget Sound in 1947; Community Health Association in Cleveland in 1956 (41). These pioneer "not-for-profit" plans were generally progressive steps in their day. A closer examination of the Kaiser-Permanente example, however, sheds some light on why large corporations initially supported and continue to support the concept.

Henry D. Kaiser and Dr. Sidney Garfield, an industrial physician, created the Kaiser-Permanente Medical Care Program in the early 1930s for employees of

Kaiser Industries. The effort initially grew out of the need to provide medical care to workers at isolated construction sites. Maintaining the health of the workers through preventive care and providing early medical intervention to quickly return the worker to his job proved to be good business practice. Eventually, the prepaid medical care program was marketed to other industrial firms and today the Kaiser system remains the largest HMO. In fact, since 1957 the Kaiser-Permanente organization has itself been a multinational firm, servicing American nationals and other employees in several Third World nations where Kaiser Industries has investments (42, 43).

Prior to President Nixon's pronouncement of the HMO strategy, the Health Maintenance Organization Service (HMOS) had been established in the Health Services and Mental Health Administration in HEW (44). Without legislative mandate, funding for HMO stimulation was secured from the appropriations designated for the Regional Medical Program Service, Community Health Services, Social and Rehabilitation Services, and the Experimental Health Delivery Systems program for a total of $9.6 million in fiscal year 1971–1972 (45). Several key health provider interest groups were given contracts to promote the new delivery form as the industry responded with active discussion. Encouragement for enrollment came about through special Medicaid contacts and the dual-option for the HMO alternative for 20 million Medicare recipients under the Social Security Administration Amendments of 1970 and for the 2.5 million federal government workers under the Federal Employee Health Benefits Program. Additionally, the Office of Economic Opportunity revamped its health center program to form networks to become operational HMOs.

But amid this bureaucratic reshuffling, the Congressional rally of new legislation and hearings, and the action and reaction of health provider groups, HMOS was actively designing a program to attract finance capital. President Nixon's objective, as stated in his health message to Congress, was to attract a $300 million loan stimulus; consequently, three contracts for "private sector funding for HMOs" were given to the following consulting groups: Kappa Systems, Inc. (for venture capital and investment banking); Geomet, Inc. (for commercial insurance companies); and A. T. Kearney, Inc. (for banks). Their tasks were to develop a market among the HMOS grantees (traditional providers represented by physician groups, hospitals, medical schools, foundations for medical care, and consumer groups) by rendering "technical assistance;" to stimulate private investment interest by finance capital; and to bring the two together to entrench HMOs into private corporate hands. The general unavailability of large state financing for HMOs (alongside the Nixon Administration's policies of cutbacks and impoundments of HEW funds) created a situation of reliance on private capital for growth and expansion. In 1971, the same year as Nixon's pronouncement, HEW listed 14 major corporations, 21 "entrepreneurial organizations," and 15 insurance companies actively investigating HMOs for investment purposes (46).

HEW maintained "great flexibility" in the HMO concept to seduce present providers into this alternative delivery form. HMOs had sought to undermine opposition from organized medicine by promoting the Independent Practice Association, the fastest growing model; it requires lower start-up costs compared to the more centralized type of HMO. By bringing together solo and small-group practitioners, it allowed physicians to remain in private practice with their patients; however, physicians must submit to peer review and accept a prearranged fee schedule for HMO patients. Over time, the fee-for-service physician entrepreneur slowly becomes reduced to a salaried employee.

Likewise, hospitals, faced with conditions which control their costs of operation, also have an alternative in an HMO, the Health Care Corporation. The American Hospital Association proposed this HMO model (47). Most hospital efforts in HMOs have been directed to linking up with other HMO groups, however.

The passage of the Health Maintenance Organization Act of 1973 (Public Law 93-222) represented a dramatic change in state policy for the actual restructuring of the health delivery system from its previous thrusts in mere financing (48). By July 1974 Interstudy reported that there were 177 "operational" HMOs with 204 in the "formational" stage and 88 in the "planning" stage (49). The operational HMOs were estimated to serve over 7 million persons. This was not that impressive on the surface. Nevertheless, when economic conditions and the Watergate-disrupted state bureaucracy were taken into account, the HMO movement maintained some momentum. Furthermore, large corporations began viewing HMOs as profit-making ventures and as systems within which to improve productivity for their workers.

CORPORATE TAKEOVER MECHANISMS

Corporate ventures in HMOs came through (1) commercial insurance companies, (2) industrial corporations, and (3) workplace integration of industrial medicine with family medical care. These three major mechanisms are not mutually exclusive.

As was mentioned earlier, the Nixon Administration through the Health Maintenance Organization Service in DHEW took direct action to involve finance capital in the form of commercial insurance companies, banks, and venture capital firms. Finance capital has a concern for the economy as a whole; consequently, the direct action of these firms is highly dependent on economic conditions. Their involvement in HMOs depends upon the availability of capital in the economy and returns on alternative investments.

The insurance industry is interested in the lower reproduction costs of labor, especially since most of their life insurance policy holders come from the ranks of monopoly and state capital workers. Their traditional role in health insurance represents horizontal integration to the life insurance business. Better medical services, especially geared to prevention and early diagnosis and treatment, may tend to increase longevity to minimize outflows on life insurance. Further, a delivery system which efficiently coordinates a various range of health services may tend to reduce costs of workers' compensation.

In the 1970s the industry proceeded to cultivate a set of cooperative relations through HMOs to legitimate its continued existence in health care financing (50). Almost all larger insurance companies, such as Connecticut General, Equitable Life, Metropolitan, and Prudential, moved into the HMO arena, taking roles to assist in planning, administration, marketing, financial support, and underwriting (51). The insurance industry's present financial commitment to HMOs was estimated as $40 million by at least 55 companies in 1973 (52). Interlocks between commercial insurance companies and some Blue Cross plans began developing to utilize their commercial reserve capital combined with the special skills developed by the Blues in health financing (53). According to *Business Week* (25), 22 Blue Cross plans and 20 insurance companies back then were involved with 59 HMOs and "many more have plans on the drawing boards."

Industrial capital became involved in HMOs in less visible a manner than insurance companies. *Business Week* (25) maintains that corporations are

> . . . considering the feasibility of starting their own HMOs, either for their employees or as profit-making ventures. Scores of other corporations are exploring other possibilities—for example, providing start-up money for non-profit HMOs sponsored by unions, employer groups, consumer organizations, hospitals, or doctors themselves, with the HMOs committed to buy the corporation's products (computers perhaps).

A compilation of large corporations mentioned to be active in this "exploratory" stage read like the Fortune 500: North American Rockwell, Zenith, General Foods, duPont, Texas instrument, Goodyear, General Electric, IBM, Owens Illinois, Upjohn, Mobil Oil, General Mills, Inland Steel, Litton Industries, Brunswick, Standard Oil of Indiana, Eastman-Kodak, U.S. Steel, Sybron, and Whittaker Corporation, among others.

Much attention has been given to the proprietary HMOs in California (e.g., the HMO International subsidiary Consolidated Medical Services begun by Dr. Donald Kelly and Health Maintenance, Inc., begun by Dr. Harold Upjohn), primarily owing to their relationships with the Reagan Administration and their involvement with Medi-Cal funding. Exploitative financial tendencies in HMO operations clearly were present; *Business Week* (26) warned against the "fast-buck operators who are allowed to overexpand recklessly" because "the patients—and the employers that finance prepaid health care—will be the ones to suffer."

In the immediate future, these mercantile ventures faced numerous economic difficulties. HMO activity remained a speculative venture. Because state subsidization was insufficient, the avenue chosen for corporate influence came through existing health care providers, with corporations acting as conveners.

TOWARD AN INTEGRATION OF INDUSTRIAL MEDICINE WITH FAMILY MEDICAL CARE

One large corporate research and development effort appeared to be the major test marketing (54). Texas Instruments was given $99,963 in 1971 by the DHEW Health Maintenance Organization Service to "provide a detailed definitive guide for the establishment of an HMO anywhere in the nation" (45). In fiscal year 1972, HMOS awarded Texas Instruments $300,976 in additional contract monies (55) to continue to design a total HMO system in the Southwest. A HEW national policy statement (56) read:

> HEW will stimulate, create, and support a sociologic and economic environment through the judicious use of federal funds whereby optional enrollment in an HMO will be available to 2,400,000 people in DHEW Region VI by 1977 and 90% of the region's population by 1980.

A major defense contractor with a good track record in worker productivity boosts, Texas Instruments decided to "push into the consumer field" (57) to apply its business expertise to new ventures, health care services being one investment outlet. Texas Instruments worked with present providers of care, including a medical school.

Similarly, other HMOS technical assistance contracts to consulting firms (e.g., Macro Systems; Arthur Young and Company; Peat, Marwick, Mitchell and Company; and Litton Bionetics, Inc.) implicitly cultivated corporate interest in HMO development. The dependence on these consulting groups by the nonprofit HMOS grantees made up of traditional providers of care allowed for the formation of ties with the local corporate entities. What emerged in the organization form is described by Platou and Rice in *Harvard Business Review* (58) as "new corporate structures for the health field."

Eastman-Kodak and Xerox restructured the health delivery system in Rochester, New York. Three HMOs were begun in that area early in 1970, mainly initiated by the Rochester Community Advisory Committee to Study the Financing and Delivery of Health Care—a committee dominated by executives of the firms (59). To avoid the "company store" image, these firms have cajoled the Blue Cross–Blue Shield plans into responding to the "health care crisis."

Likewise, in Delaware County, Pennsylvania, eight major corporations began collaborating in late 1974 to devise an HMO for their 29,000 industrial workers despite the "uncertainty" of the HMO situation (60). Scott Paper, Sun Oil, Sun Shipbuilding and Dry Dock Company, Boeing-Vertol, Reynolds Metals, Westinghouse, Franklin Mint, and FMC paid for the feasibility study which enlisted the support of the area's providers and estimated that the Greater Delaware Valley Health Plan would be self-sustaining within two years. Marketing costs to the employees and their families were to be minimal, according to a Sun Oil medical director, since the companies' personnel departments were in a position to make it attractive.

The Conference Board Report on *Industry Roles in Health Care* (18, p. 83) mentioned other corporate ventures of a similar nature. Honeywell, General Mills, 3M, and Pillsbury, along with 20 other industrial and insurance companies, created the Twin-Cities Health Care Development Project for the Minneapolis–St. Paul area. Sandia Laboratories, a wholly owned subsidiary of Western Electric, attempted to restructure the health delivery system in Albuquerque, New Mexico by promoting the formation of two HMOs there (18, pp. 99; 38).

This corporate involvement in initiating HMOs for their workers took place amid a significant ideological call for the integration of industrial medicine, occupational health and safety programs, and family medical care. As was mentioned previously, Ellwood has attempted to entice corporations to take these steps by converting their in-plant medical facilities to ambulatory care units for HMOs. Dr. Jesse Steinfeld, former Surgeon General of the U.S. Public Health Service, has written that "for the employed population, the workplace represents an actual point of first contact, a portal of entry into the health care system, not only for the employee but for his family and his neighbor" (61). Edward N. Dolinsky, Director of Health Care Research for Metropolitan Life Insurance Company, wrote that the Occupational Safety and Health Act of 1970 and the HMO legislation offer opportunities to incorporate departments of occupational medicine as integrated services of an HMO (62). Robert O'Connor, an industrial medicine physician, maintains that occupational health services are the only concerted health maintenance programs (63), and Miles Colwell, in a presentation to the Industrial Health Foundation entitled "The Balance Sheet in Employee Health Conservation," stated that the industrial physician may be the primary physician of the future for the worker and the family when the integration is achieved (64).

Dr. William Jend Jr., Medical Director of the Michigan Bell Telephone Company, provided a more thoughtful rationale for health maintenance of the worker (65). He maintained that corporate concerns must be heightened for both physical and mental health since the worker on the job cannot be separated from the home. He commented that "the higher return on the total investment in employee health which accrues to industry when such services are promoted has received insufficient emphasis." Further he argued that the "workplace is probably the ideal locale to practice real preventive medicine on a wide and effective scale" and industrial health services "can be an important part of the total health delivery system." In realizing that it makes good sense to mobilize existing health resources, as corporate involvement in HMOs sought, he goes on to say:

> Even if the company preferred not to provide this care in its own facilities, it has an obligation to see that community health resources are operated efficiently and the best techniques are used. Many dedicated laymen serving on hospital, insurance or community health boards do not bring to this responsibility the same perceptiveness in demand for the use of new and imaginative techniques that they apply to their own business.

In short, a greater consciousness about the value of workers was urged by corporate leaders and industrial medicine physicians. A sweeping, costly reorganization carried out through a governmental program of national health insurance however, was to be precluded through this deliberate effort by corporations.

The experience of the Gates Rubber Company in providing a company health service patterned on the HMO sheds insight on how an individual firm comes to view investment in worker health (18, p. 80). Gates integrated industrial medicine and occupational health and safety programs with family medical care for its employees, offering a full range of medical services since 1963. Among the benefits the company purports to derive are not only the lower costs for employee benefit programs, but also the cost-efficient, quality care delivered under circumstances controlled by the company in addition to direct benefits from lower absenteeism, work loss, and sick benefit payouts.

Many corporations, like Gates, began to realize that the high cost of labor associated with worker "down time" required intervention. The HMO, placed in an industrial setting, could reduce absenteeism (66) through required sickness certification and affect work loss from disability. In other words, health services in the workplace should be viewed as a personnel function.

HEALTH SERVICES AS SOCIAL CONTROL

An examination of the subtle forces leading to a definition of health under capitalism sheds understanding on the workplace HMO plans. The long-term objectification of labor has been systematically developing with the capital accumulation process.

Large scale complex corporations have a profound need to dominate and control all the conditions that affect their viability (2). Given the absolute need in the economy to control conditions of labor, corporate and government workers have become the primary target of corporate programs for adjustment and adaptation to alienated work. The HEW report written by the Upjohn Institute for Employment Research, *Work in America* (67), attempted to address this issue of worker alienation. This much heralded report addressed the redesign of the workplace to reduce the crisis level of absenteeism, turnover rates, wildcat strikes, sabotage, poor quality products, and reluctance by workers to commit themselves to the worktask. These dysfunctionalities affect production and profits.

Today, the highly skilled nature of America's "human capital" has transformed it into a major part of the means of production itself. Nearly two-thirds of the civilian labor force is employed in the monopoly and state sectors, presenting a generally stable set of workers as opposed to those in the competitive capital sector. This bifurcation of the labor force presents an important structural characteristic to be considered for an optimal allocation of health resources in the economy. In the past, expenses related to workers' health tended, like pollution expenses, to be externalized; however, with the increasingly social character of production and the unplanned monopoly capital expansion, workers' health clearly affects the profits of capital. Under the HMO reorganization, social investment in human capital maintenance becomes more rational and precise. In operational terms one's wage level provides for the ability to purchase a benefit package. Unlike the traditional health insurance policies, the HMO benefit packages provide front-end money for lower cost ambulatory services and minimize the high cost tertiary medical services. These latter services become available as riders to the benefit packages of higher income groups. Class delineation of health care services thus engulfs the ideological structure that defends differences in wealth and income.

REFERENCES

1. Baran, P., and Seezy, P. *Monopoly Capital*. Modern Reader, New York, 1966.
2. Baran, P. *The Political Economy of Growth*. Monthly Review Press, New York, 1956.
3. Block, F., and Hirschhorn, L. The international monetary crisis. *Socialist Revolution* 11: 7–50, September–October, 1972.
4. Block, F. Contradictions of capitalism as a world system. *Insurgent Sociologist* 5(2): 3–21, 1975.
5. Miliband, R. *The State in Capitalist Society: An Analysis of the System of Power*. Weidenfeld and Nicholson, London, 1970.
6. O'Connor, J. *The Corporations and the State*. Harper Colophon, New York, 1974.
7. O'Connor, J. *The Fiscal Crisis of the State*. St. Martin's Press, New York, 1973.
8. Health Policy Advisory Council. *The American Health Empire: Power, Profits and Prestige*, pp. 95–123. Random House, New York, 1970.
9. Meyers, H. The medical-industrial complex. *Fortune* 81(1): 90–126, 1970.
10. Medicine in hot water. *Forbes*, p. 27, March 15, 1968.
11. Rogers, D. Medicine and change. *Johns Hopkins Med. J.* 133: 170–175, September 1973.
12. Robert Wood Johnson Foundation. *Annual Report 1973*. Princeton, 1973.
13. Committee on the Costs of Medical Care. *Medical Care for the American People*. University of Chicago Press, Chicago, 1932.
14. Elling, R., and Lee, O. Formal connections of community leadership to the health system. In *Patients, Physicians and Illness*, by E. Jaco. Free Press, New York, 1972.
15. *Building a National Health Care System*. Committee for Economic Development, New York, 1974.
16. Stewart, C., and Siddayao, C. *Increasing the Supply of Medical Personnel*. American Enterprise Institute, Washington, D.C., 1973.

17. *Washington Health Organization Conference on Health Care Legislation*. Business Round Table. Washington, D.C., June 20, 1974.
18. Lusterman, S. *Industry Roles in Health Care*. Conference Board, New York, 1974.
19. Changing the system of health care. *Morgan Guaranty Survey*, New York, December 1972.
20. Is there an HMO in your future? *Forbes*, p. 28. March 15, 1973.
21. Faltermayer, E. Better care at less cost without miracles. *Fortune* 81(1): 80–83, 1970.
22. It's time to operate. *Fortune* 81(1): 72, 1970.
23. Rothfeld, M. Sensible surgery for swelling medical costs. *Fortune* 88(4): 110–119, 1973.
24. Editorial: Health maintenance: No place to economize. *Fortune*, p. 162, September 1973.
25. A revolutionary plan to keep people healthy. *Business Week*, p. 58, January 12, 1974.
26. Editorial: A place for HMOs. *Business Week*, p. 80, January 12, 1974.
27. Still waiting for that revolutionary health plan. *Business Week*, p. 53, January 13, 1975.
28. Hospitals that heel themselves. *Newsweek*, pp. 72–73, May 28, 1973.
29. Inglehart, J. Health report/prepaid group medical practice emerges as likely federal approach to health care. *National Journal*, p. 1443, July 10, 1971.
30. Center For Political Research. Industrial Safety and Health Report, October 1–15, 1971. *CPR Research*, p. 6, Washington, D.C.
31. Nixon, R. Building a national health strategy. Special Message to Congress, Washington, D.C., February 18, 1971.
32. Ellwood, P. Health maintenance strategy. *Med. Care*, p. 291, May–June 1971.
33. Ellwood, P. Implications of recent health legislation. *Am. J. Public Health*, p. 20, January 1972.
34. Ellwood, P. Health Maintenance Organizations: Concept and strategy. *J.A.H.A.* 45(6): 53–55, 1971.
35. Ellwood, P. Big business blows the whistle on medical care costs. *Prism*, pp. 13–15, December 1974.
36. Alford, R. The political economy of health care: Dynamics without change. *Politics and Society*, p. 124, winter 1972.
37. Ellwood, P., and Herbert, M. Health care: Should industry buy it or sell it? *Harvard Business Review*, pp. 99–107, July–August 1973.
38. Ellwood, P. *Testimony before the Senate Subcommittee on Public Health and Environment*, Serial No. 97-90, Part II, p. 363. U.S. Government Printing Office, Washington, D.C.
39. Ellwood, P. Models for organizing health services and implications of legislative proposals. *Milbank Mem. Fund Q*. October 1972.
40. MacColl, W. *Group Practice and Prepayment of Medical Care*. Public Affairs Press, Washington, D.C., 1966.
41. MacLeod, G., and Prussin, J. The continuing evaluation of Health Maintenance Organizations, *New Engl. J. Med.* 288, p. 439, March 1, 1973.
42. *Health Service Experience and Capabilities*. Kaiser Foundation International. Oakland, California.
43. Hughes, J., editor. *Health Care for Remote Areas: An International Conference*. Kaiser Foundation International, Oakland, California, 1972.
44. Iglehart, J. Health report/Democrats cool to Nixon's health proposal, offer their own alternatives. *National Journal*, p. 2310, November 20, 1971.
45. HMO Program Management Status Report November 1971. Health Maintenance Organization Service, Department of Health, Education, and Welfare, Washington, D.C.
46. Industrial Safety and Health Report, August 1–15, 1971, p. 23. Center For Political Research, Washington, D.C.
47. *Ameriplan: A Proposal for the Delivery and Financing of Health Services in the United States*. American Hospital Association, Chicago, 1970.
48. Dorsey, J. The Health Maintenance Organization Act of 1973 (P.L. 93-222) and prepaid group practice plans. *Med. Care* 13(1): 1–8, 1975.

49. Wetherville, R., and Quale, J. A census of HMOS July 1974. *Interstudy*, Minneapolis, Minnesota.
50. Kelman, S. Toward political economy of medical care. *Inquiry* 8(3): 30–38, 1971.
51. Present Degree of Insurance Company Investment in HMO Development. Health Insurance Association of America. Correspondence, February 14, 1973.
52. HMO Program Status Report October 1974. Health Maintenance Organization Service, Department of Health, Education, and Welfare, Washington, D.C.
53. Insurers moving into health care delivery. *American Medical News*, pp. 13–14, August 20, 1973.
54. Texas Instruments, Inc. *Development of an Implementation Plan for the Establishment of a Health Maintenance Organization*. U.S. Department of Health, Education, and Welfare, Washington, D.C., 1971.
55. HMOS Management Status Report April 1–June 30, 1972. Health Maintenance Organization Service, Department of Health, Education, and Welfare, Washington, D.C.
56. Quoted in Texas Instruments Task Report 54004-002 Implement Texas Instruments OST (Objective-Strategy-Tactic) System For Region VI HMO Development, Dallas, Texas, undated.
57. Texas Instruments: Pushing hard into the consumer markets. *Business Week*, p. 39, April 24, 1974.
58. Platou, C., and Rice, J. Multi-hospital holding companies. *Harvard Business Review* 50(3), May–June 1972.
59. Rhein, R. HMO: Attacks continue but 14,500 physicians now offer prepaid health care in one form or another. *Medical World News*, pp. 53–60, January 27, 1975.
60. Shoemaker, J. Business/finance: Firms plan for health care revolution. *Philadelphia Inquirer*, p. 8-C. January 19, 1975.
61. Steinfeld, J. The workplace as a health care resource. *J. Occup. Med.* 12: 315–317, August 1970.
62. Dolinsky, E. Health Maintenance Organizations and occupational medicine. *Bull. N.Y. Acad. Med.* 50(10): 1122–1137, 1974.
63. O'Connor, R. The role of industry in the health of the nation. *J. Occup. Med.* 10: 379, 1968.
64. Colwell, M. The Balance Sheet in Employee Health Conservation. Presentation to Annual Meeting of the Industrial Health Foundation, October 13, 1970.
65. Jend, W. Where do we want to be in occupational medicine? *J. Occup. Med.* 15(7): 577–579, 1973.
66. Williamson, J., and van Nieuwenhuizen, M. Health benefit analysis: An application in industrial absenteeism. *J. Occup. Med.* 16(4): 229–233, 1974.
67. W. E. Upjohn Institute for Employment Research. *Work In America: Report of a Special Task Force to the Secretary of Health, Education and Welfare*. MIT Press, Cambridge, 1973.

CHAPTER 5

Proprietary Hospital Chains and Academic Medical Centers

Howard S. Berliner and Robb K. Burlage

After over 15 years of expanding operations as owners and managers of general care hospitals, why should the for-profit sector become interested in teaching hospitals? What are the implications—for the health system, for the Academic Medical Centers and for the proprietary chains—of such changes in ownership patterns?

Why AMCs have agreed to become involved with proprietary companies (such as stated needs for greater access to capital) is a question that has already been studied by others in detail (1-3).

Given general strategic interpretations of the recent corporate restructuring of academic medical centers, including joint ventures with proprietary chains, we focus our attention on the overall behavior of the chains themselves. Of particular interest are the potential integration strategies and locational consolidations of the investor-owned systems that include teaching hospital acquisitions, joint ventures, management contracts and other linkages.

As of mid-1985, there are 17 hospitals with academic affiliations that have some documented relationship with a proprietary hospital firm. Of these, 10 are simple management agreements, two are joint ventures with medical schools, one is a lease arrangement and only four are outright owned by a hospital chain (4). Negotiations underway might increase these totals by the end of 1986, but a major increase is not likely. Additionally, there are several arrangements in place under which proprietary hospital chains will construct and operate new teaching hospitals or participate in joint ventures to build new institutions, primarily psychiatric hospitals, with academic medical centers (5).

Today one-third of U.S. community hospital acute care beds are in teaching institutions which are part of affiliated academic medical center networks

(Figure 1). About one-sixth of U.S. beds are owned or managed by proprietary chains (70 percent in the big four chains—Hospital Corporation of America, Humana, National Medical Enterprises and American Medical International) (Figures 2-6). The intersection between the two at present is quite small as is detailed in Figure 7.

Many predominantly northern and northeastern metro-regions still reflect the dominance of academic medical center affiliated institutional networks as the primary imperative of health care organization. These are the "Sick Citadels" of Lewis and Sheps, some at fiscal bay but most alive and restructuring in 1986 (6).

A number of southern and western metro-regions are now being dominated by the proprietary chains. In a few places thus far (Louisville, Omaha, Wichita) a "core interpenetration process," has emerged to reflect the apparent dual strategies of major chains expansion and AMCs restructuring. In and around other, especially populous, metro-regions (LA, Chicago, Washington, D.C., Houston, Nashville, Tampa–St. Petersburg, Miami, Denver and New Orleans), either beginning movements of joint ventures and other forms of interpenetration are emerging. There we can observe a suggestively fecund pattern of AMCs and chains co-habiting, as it were, regional market and teaching/social responsibility space.

It should be noted that future projections of the growth of the proprietary chains may be premature and fatalistic as the dimensions of total nationwide overbedding and the financial market vulnerability of these corporations becomes more obvious. The sudden stock price massacre of Hospital Corporation of America and other major hospital chains in October, 1985 had an immediate cause in the unprecedented flattening of earnings projections for the final quarter of 1985. The Chief Executive Officer of HCA acknowledged that his company was not yet sufficiently integrated into the total health care business and too invested in acute care services (7). It is thus possible that hospital management companies will undergo a systematic devolution of their acute care orientation over the next several years.

In terms of the emerging overall configuration of the health system in the United States, the question can be asked: under what conditions will a larger number of AMCs interpenetrate with proprietary hospital management chains across the nation? Will a new uneven pattern combining the tendencies of each of these formations emerge—are we going from "medical empires" to "corporate medical empires" in these regions? Will the "Louisville" model—Humana, Humana Heart Institute, University of Louisville School of Medicine and Louisville (City) hospital—a corporate proprietary chain penetrated and integrated academic medical center complex, supported by a proprietary prepaid insurance and alternative services network, become the model for other regions around the country (8)?

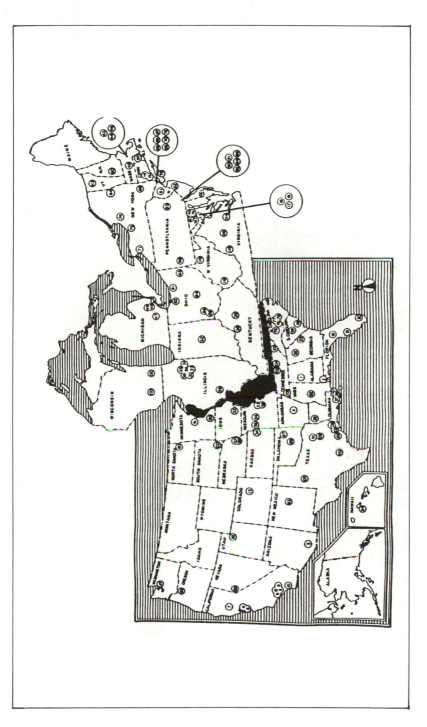

Figure 1. Distribution of academic medical centers in the United States, 1984.

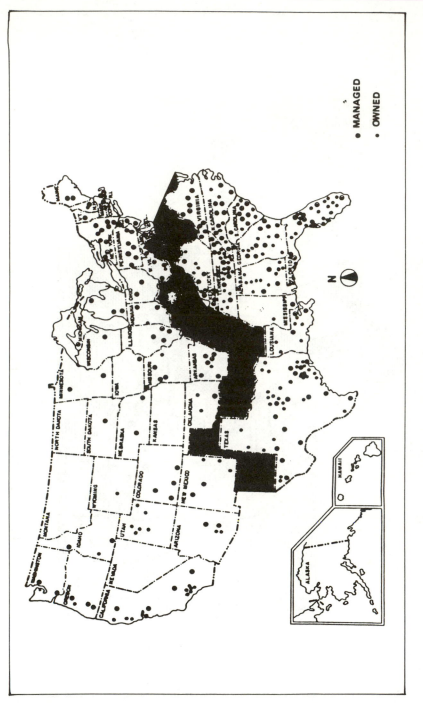

Figure 2. Distribution of Hospital Corporation of America hospitals, owned or managed, 1984.

● MANAGED

● OWNED

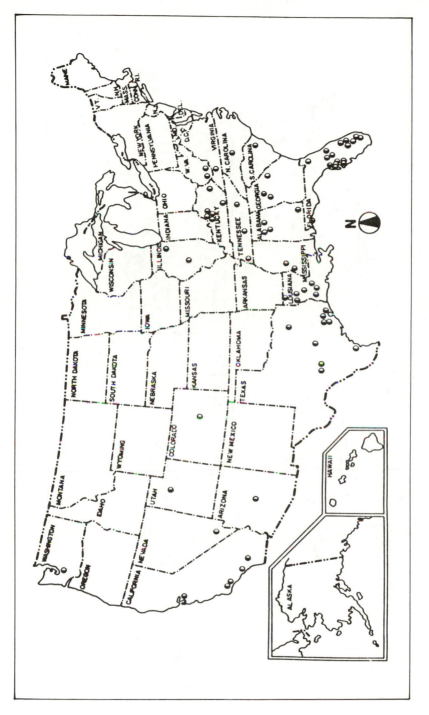

Figure 3. Distribution of Humana hospitals, 1984.

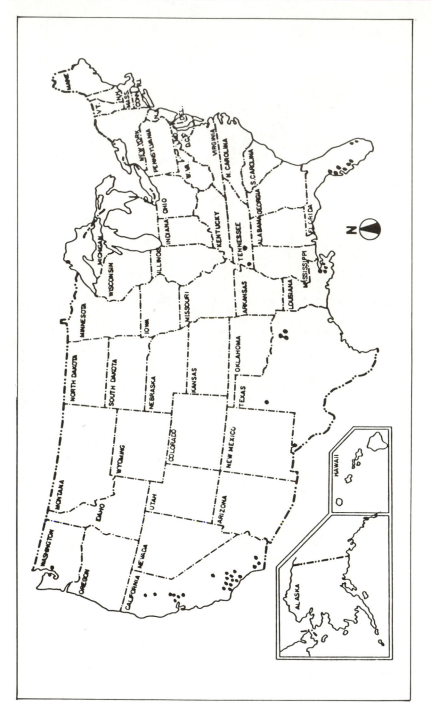

Figure 4. Distribution of National Medical Enterprises hospitals, 1984.

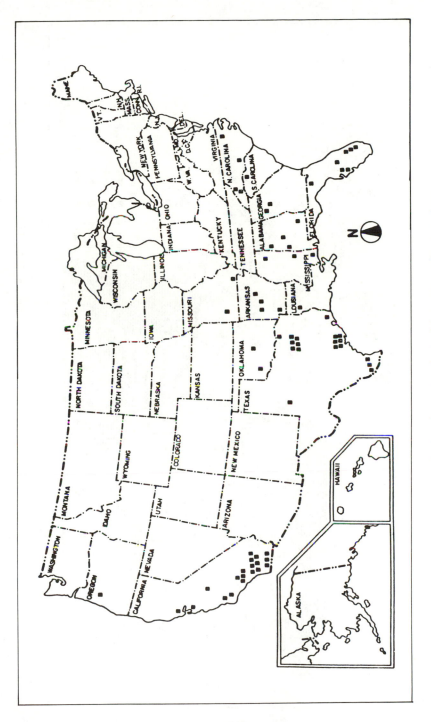

Figure 5. Distribution of American Medical International hospitals, 1984.

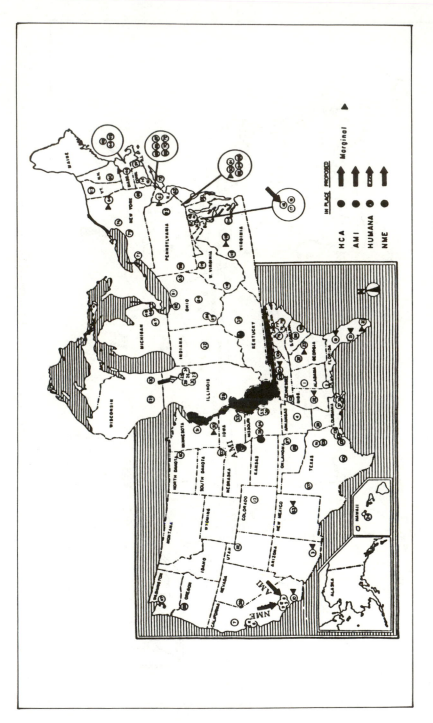

Figure 6. Interpenetration of proprietary chains and AMCs, 1985.

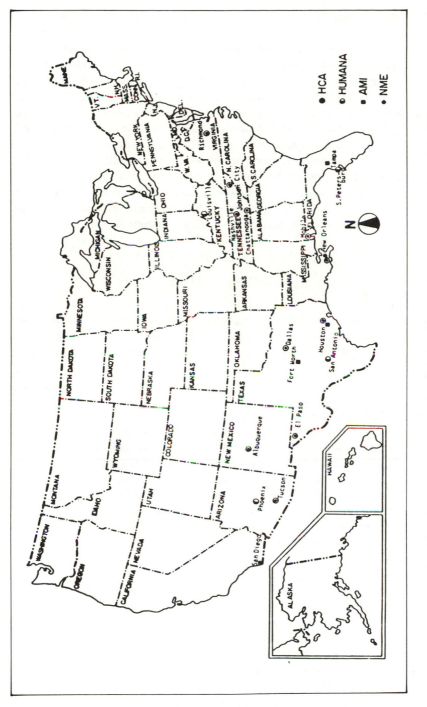

Figure 7. Cities with more than two acute hospitals owned/managed by the same proprietary chain, 1984.

105

Of the over 700 investor-owned hospitals in the United States, approximately 70 percent are owned or managed by four major hospital management firms—Hospital Corporation of America (HCA), Humana, American Medical International (AMI) and National Medical Enterprises (NME). While there are many similarities among the four companies there are also considerable differences in terms of corporate strategy, long-range plans and approach to the health field. To outline the distinctions between the companies and the effects of their individual approaches regarding relations with AMCs, we focus on general acute care hospitals, not on psychiatric and other specialized institutions, including nursing homes. However, acquisition or close linkages to such additional entities, while marginal to the overall academic medical center complex, if affiliated at all, may be of strategic interest to some proprietary chains.

REGIONAL ISSUES

Figure 1 depicts the location of the AMCs of the continental United States; Figures 2–5 geographically depict the location of the big four chain company hospitals, including the managed units in the United States. Figure 6 highlights those areas where particular hospital corporations have more than two institutions in close proximity. Figure 7 depicts those areas of the country where there are presently AMC-chain linkages.

While AMCs are spread throughout the country, proprietary hospital chains are concentrated in the southeast and southwest. A geographic analysis of hospital locations would indicate that HCA is the most geographically diverse company of the four, while Humana is most concentrated regionally.

If vertical integration and flagship status were major issues, one might expect close relations with AMCs in areas of geographic concentration or in areas where the firm had a major presence (the corporate offices, for example). With the exception of Humana's linkage with the University of Louisville, there does not seem to be any geographic linkage between the relations of the AMC and hospital companies.

Because these changes are only a few years old, and because there are long negotiations before the final culmination of an agreement, little basis exists from which to predict how these maps will change. There has been little movement to expand acute care facilities into the east and north central states, although this may change as the number of hospitals available for acquisition in the southeast and southwest becomes more limited, with Chicago and Washington, D.C. the most likely new areas.

If only a few national chains prevail and each can have only a few advertised centers of excellence, it would seem that a likely number of flagship facilities would be less than two dozen institutions nationwide.

HCA

The largest of the proprietary chains, Hospital Corporation of America, owns or manages over 400 institutions (9). It has the greatest experience with academic medical centers of the chains, managing 10 centers and owning three with several joint ventures that include teaching/research institutions. HCA purchased the Wesley Medical Center, a major teaching hospital of the University of Kansas, in Wichita, Kansas and the Lovelace Medical Center, a teaching hospital of the University of New Mexico in Albuquerque, New Mexico (10). The company has also signed an agreement to purchase a teaching hospital affiliated with the University of Oklahoma. HCA is the most diversified hospital company, with subsidiary ventures in hospital supply, pharmaceuticals, manufacture and high-tech R+D (11). Its recent aborted attempt to merge with American Hospital Supply Corporation received wide publicity (12). HCA has concluded arrangements with a number of pharmaceutical firms to utilize their network of institutions to perform clinical trials of drugs prior to FDA approval. HCA's attempt to buy the McLean Hospital, a psychiatric teaching affiliate of Harvard University, first broke the ice with respect to chains and AMCs (13). The publicity that accompanied this ultimately unsuccessful attempt may have helped to make future negotiations between AMCs and potential buyers less public. With the exception of specialty and psychiatric institutions, HCA has shown relatively little interest in areas other than the sunbelt states. It is rapidly moving to establish its insurance plan throughout the South and Southwest and has access to a considerable amount of capital for future acquisitions. Its size may pose a major barrier to its continued horizontal expansion as there remain relatively few markets where it can expand without creating anti-trust conditions. This may push it further in the direction of other types of hospitals (including AMCs) as well as other regions of the country. HCA has shown little interest in forming regionally integrated networks of its hospitals do date. HCA has not shown any interest in providing a "branded" health care. In fact, it is difficult to ascertain from the outside whether or not a hospital is an HCA institution. The company prefers to use a decentralized management style and in many cases leaves the original administrators or purchased facilities in place. This lack of national or even regional identity may pose problems for its insurance ventures and for its attempts to market on the basis of a flagship approach.

HUMANA

Humana is the second largest hospital company with 90 institutions (14). While it currently has only a long term lease arrangement to operate the University of Louisville Medical Center in Louisville, Kentucky (the corporate headquarters), it has agreed to erect a new teaching facility for the Chicago Medical

School in north Chicago. This proposal, however, has run into conflict with local health planning agencies. Humana is the most interesting of the chains because it has been the most direct in its marketing strategy.

Humana adds its name to most of the hospitals it owns (15). It has eschewed management contracts in favor of long term leases and direct ownership. It has sought regional and national visibility. The "Centers of Excellence" located in Humana hospitals around the sunbelt are programs of clinical research and new/high-technology diagnosis and therapy aimed at improving the public perception of the quality of the institution (16). The establishment of the Humana Heart Institute and its program of subsidized artificial heart operations have given company both wide name recognition and the potential to capitalize on a unique procedure that may in time become clinically effective with a huge market (17). The trade journals have reported that before the first Humana artificial heart operation, its name recognition was practically zero. Yet after the operation, almost 16 percent of the U.S. population knew what Humana was, including 23 percent of the college graduates and 34 percent of people with graduate degrees (18). The association of a proprietary corporation with the latest advances in medical technology may do much to counter the negative perception and criticisms of quality of care in investor-owned facilities (19). Humana also has been most dramatic in its efforts at vertical integration and linking finance and delivery systems. Humana has bunched many of its hospitals geographically in particular markets. The three community hospitals in Louisville serve as feeders for the teaching facility that Humana leases. In the Chicago area, Humana purchased a chain of freestanding ambulatory care centers to serve as feeders to its two community hospitals with its proposed new teaching hospital on top of the referral pyramid. In both cases the larger object is to introduce to employers the Humana Care Plus system, a comprehensive health insurance plan in which the use of Humana facilities is encouraged through lower or no deductibles.

NME

National Medical Enterprises owns or operates 90 acute care hospitals and over 350 nursing homes and psychiatric institutions (20). It has been active in building freestanding ambulatory care centers to serve as feeder systems for its community hospitals and in so doing has increased the proportion of private pay patients in its hospitals significantly (21). It operates PPOs in Tampa and Miami and HMOs in California and Texas. It has utilized TV advertising more than the other chains (22) venture in the AMC area has been an agreement to build a $100,000,000 teaching hospital on the University of Southern California campus along with an ambulatory care center, a Diagnostic and Treatment center, a hotel and a garage (23).

AMI

American Medical International has become an increasingly visible actor in the AMC business (24). It has been active in a series of ventures with not-for-profit institutions to expand its horizons. In affiliation with the St. Lukes–Episcopal Hospital in Houston, a major teaching affiliate to the Baylor College of Medicine, it plans to refer patients to St. Lukes from its Houston facilities for their tertiary care needs. AMI is marketing an insurance package in conjunction with St. Lukes to employers in the Houston area (25).

AMI has agreed to erect and operate a series of magnetic resonance imaging centers for AMCs including the University of California at Irvine and the University of Utah Hospitals (26). It has purchased the St. Joseph's Hospital in Omaha, Nebraska and the Presbyterian–St. Lukes Medical Center in Denver—both major teaching facilities. It is currently in negotiation with the George Washington University to purchase its hospital in Washington, D.C. and already operates the George Washington HMO.

Most recently AMI has agreed to build a small new teaching hospital for the University of California at Irvine (UCI), linking it to its three other hospitals in Orange County and as part of its AMICARE insurance plan there. The recently developing AMI-UCI venture involves one of America's largest local land and real estate companies, the Irvine company, owner of one-sixth of fabled Orange County's territory (home of the original Disneyland in Anaheim). The Irvine Company plans to make the new AMI hospital the centerpiece of a 400 acre biomedical research complex. AMI may also take over the management of UCI Medical Center, if the originally publicized plan is followed (27).

One can thus see a wide range of activities being carried out by the largest hospital chains, and many of these activities are increasingly focused around the AMC.

REASONS FOR PROPRIETARY CHAIN INVOLVEMENT

In general, there appear to be four major explanations for the involvement of proprietary chains with academic medical centers. These can be most simply described as: 1) vertical integration; 2) qualitative legitimation; 3) integration of finance and delivery systems; 4) short-term profit.

Vertical Integration

Proprietary chains have historically grown through horizontal integration, that is, by purchasing large numbers of small general hospitals (secondary care institutions). As there is increasing competition and hence increasing cost for the remaining desirable small hospitals, chains may be inclined to look for different types of hospitals. Tertiary care, largely though not exclusively found in teaching hospitals, presents a likely candidate. Until now, patients in chain institutions that need more intensive services or particular types of technology have had to be referred out of their system. The chains face the potential loss of those patients and they lose the associated revenues from the tertiary services. While many tertiary services are not profitable—many are. The chains may find that the ability to shift patients through the continuum of care is not only a convenient mechanism for locking patients into their overall systems, but also a useful way of keeping revenues within them. Proprietary chains may find that their mode of operation is more capable or selectively enhancing the profitability of selected tertiary care while avoiding or redirecting the costs of less profitable modalities.

While Medicare prospective payment is seen by the government as a mechanism for reducing costs or at least reducing cost acceleration, most teaching hospitals, particularly with the direct and indirect teaching adjustments included have thus far found PPS to be in the aggregate financially profitable. Even with proposed reductions to the indirect teaching add-on and freezes on the direct adjustments, efficiently and/or selectively operated teaching institutions may continue to do well under DRGs.

The chains may see in the ownership of teaching institutions, and their corresponding high technology services, a means of increasing the percentage of foreign patients who utilize their facilities in this country—that is those rich foreigners who come to the United States for their medical care. An institution offering a service that is unduplicated throughout the world may well find itself deluged with patients who can afford to pay top charges for such a service. The Humana artificial heart technology experiments are a potential case in point, should the clinical outcomes substantially improve.

The concept of vertical integration stresses that the system is more important than the particular institution. It is not the prestige of any particular hospital that is being marketed (though there is no reason why this cannot be) but rather the ability of the chain itself to fulfill all medical care needs well. Thus it is not necessary to own the most prestigious teaching hospital so much as to own a teaching hospital. To the extent that the proprietary chain is interested in revenues and retention of patients and market share, the best tertiary hospital need not be the one with the best research or educational programs so much as the one with the best local reputation for patient care, or the ability to market itself as such.

Qualitative Legitimation through Flagship Status

The proprietary chains started by building up their systems from the accretion of small hospital units in the south and southwest. While they have a somewhat more national scope at present, they are still heavily concentrated in the sunbelt. The quality of care offered by the hospitals that constitute the chains has been subject to a great deal of scrutiny and it has been surmised that the chains do not offer the highest quality care in general and certainly not the most technologically specialized or advanced. As they have grown in economic and political significance nationally, they have strategized to enhance their public image and reputation. The acquisition of a teaching hospital may lend a considerable boost to the public image of the chain. The mystique of the teaching hospital remains such that if they become integral components of the hospital chains, they will do much to legitimate the corporate images even perhaps in terms of public involvement and care for the indigent.

The concept of the flagship differs from that of vertical integration in the sense that the flagship institution is more important than the system itself. Too many flagships though, may destroy the myth that the institution is "special." Each of the chains could have one or more (if they were in different regions) and perhaps a national flagship. As the proprietary chains begin to penetrate the east and north central states, they may likely seek to establish connections with institutions which could become flagships in order to generate substantial national/regional publicity to directly aid its marketing. For such an institution, patient care reputation alone may not be sufficient to legitimate its continued growth. We would therefore expect such institutions to maintain teaching and research programs, though not as considerable as the premier academic medical centers. Such flagship institutions would also aid the chain in labor force recruitment as well as potentially becoming the corporate R+D headquarters.

Integration of Finance and Delivery

Each of the major hospital chains started a system-wide insurance business. The most well-known is the Humana Care Plus system.

By owning a teaching hospital within the region, the chains would be spared the expense of having to contract for specialty and high technology care. Moreover to the extent that people will join an HMO based as much on the tertiary hospital that provides their specialty care as on which primary care physicians they can choose, control of or connection to an academic medical center becomes critical (28).

Short-Term Profit

The above three explanations use theoretical arguments to attempt to understand why proprietary chains have attempted to buy up teaching hospitals. Another way of looking at this eschews formal organization and marketing theory: observe that the teaching institutions which have been purchased have all been profitable. Thus, Wesley Medical Center in Wichita, Kansas (purchased by HCA) was expected to have an operating surplus of $13 million in 1984 and Presbyterian–St. Lukes Medical Center in Denver Colorado (purchasd by AMI) was expected to show a surplus of $17 million (29). HCA has recently agreed to manage a teaching facility in Canada which has a well-known organ transplantation program and one of the largest *in-vitro* fertilization programs in Canada (30). It may very well be that immediate economic performance of the acquired institution makes certain teaching hospital of interest to the proprietary chains. Their teaching status may be secondary to their profitability. This only implies that short range financial benefits may take precedence in corporate decision making over long term strategic planning.

POLICY IMPLICATIONS AND ANALYSIS

Regional Variations

Humana, and to an increasing extent, AMI of the big four proprietary chains seems to have a consciously developed strategy of seeking linkages with AMCs in areas where a capacity exists to use them as referral institutions. Thus, the immediate prospect of vertically integrated networks of proprietary chains is limited to a few notable cases. The arrangement that AMI worked out—linkage with voluntary institutions rather than formal ownership or management agreement was another model. Figures 1–7 of current proprietary density of operations and on inter-penetration with AMC institutions, suggest leads for careful area case monitoring and a perspective on overall national developments.

Industry Maturation

The for-profit hospital chain has been around since 1968. In that relatively brief time it has grown enormously. While the concentration that exists in other industries and services has not yet come to the hospital sector, in some regions of the country it is close to being a dominant force. Yet it seems obvious that the acute hospital bed growth phase of the industry is slowing, if not ending. In the shift to related services development and the shoring up of market share, a more mature industry is apparent. Proprietary health care corporations now sponsor public interest projects and contribute to local charities and civic organizations; at the same time they still do not accept indigent patients to the extent that they can avoid them. One of the correlates of maturation is the change in self-perception on the part of the industry owners and workers. They no longer see themselves as newcomers and mavericks and therefore are somewhat more willing to take a part in industry-wide functions and responsibilities. In the hospital industry, this may include sponsoring medical research, taking some role in the training of health services workers, including physicians, and playing a more prominent national role in health policy formulation. Thus the movement to associate with AMCs may be a case of doing well by doing good, even if the motivation is primarily to do well.

Expansion

An increasing expansion of proprietary chains into subsidiary areas of health care out of the realm of personal health services delivery can be predicted. This includes insurance, medical supply, pharmaceutical, construction, real estate, and managerial, information and planning services. To date much of the associated development of the proprietary chains has been into long term care, home care and ambulatory services. This may broaden extensively given connections with tertiary medical centers which yield higher levels of expertise in management and a means of dealing with larger institutions.

Divestiture of Ownership

What little available public information about the terms of buyouts of teaching hospitals by the chains indicated that most agreements have escape clauses allowing for the resale of the institution back to its parent if certain conditions are not satisfied. Teaching hospitals may thus be in a substantially better position to maintain levels of service and prior commitments than smaller, isolated facilities. It would seem unlikely that an organization, be it a voluntary hospital board of trustees, a university or a religious group, having sold its hospital would be able to afford to ever buy it back. Conceivably, if hospital chain stocks were to fall, or the companies themselves were bought out by larger economic entities, companies may seek to divest themselves of AMCs to free up capital or because of a lack of interest in that market.

Downside Risks

Under this rubric may come a worst scenario if proprietary hospital chains make further inroads into the academic medical center. These could include lowering amounts of indigent care, neglecting basic research as more corporately-useful clinical research is pursued, and the rationalization of employment levels within AMCs to be more consistent with the patterns of proprietary community hospitals. Outcomes will depend upon a number of factors including:

1. the orientation of the for-profit parent firm;
2. the reason the firm related initially with the AMC. A company might well decide to abandon its quest for vertical integration, for example, and begin to "cut its losses" on the AMC. If the teaching hospital was originally purchased to become a flagship, additional funds might be given the institution as a gesture of good faith and public relations. If profit was the primary reason for the acquisition and the institution stopped making the desired profit level, dramatic changes would be expected;

3. the number of affiliations with AMCs—a few such acts might be for the public spotlight, but if there are many institutions, changes at one will seem less significant;
4. public reaction and organization—a well informed public and especially the larger AMC community will be able to spot trends and tendencies which may be inimical for the continuation of the comprehensive AMC mission. Early and vocal warning may be effective in mobilizing public reaction to negative changes in the teaching institutions.

CONCLUSIONS

In early 1986, the number of teaching institutions that have formal affiliations with proprietary hospital chains remains small. We foresee no significant increase in these numbers over the next few years. Given the most recent changes within the health care system, the acquisition of teaching hospitals seems to be epiphenomenal to other, more pervasive developments such as prepayment systems and insurance marketing.

Our mapping does not indicate any one clear national or even inter-regional institutional systems pattern. What we have found is best explained as uneven, short-run opportunism among financially healthy teaching hospitals seeking expansion and consolidation. We have found no activity among those "needy" teaching hospitals desperate for survival.

Historically, the attitude of medical schools and teaching hospitals regarding public service needs and commitments has ranged from indifference and specialty fragmentation to outright resistance. Public ownership of academic medical centers has not made the institutions any more responsive to community needs.

Both state and national monitoring of proprietary teaching hospital performance—and action regarding overall requirements and responsibilities—will be necessary to ensure that their missions are not substantially altered under new ownership. Local groups must continuously monitor the practices and behaviors of these institutions to achieve their social and scientific responsibilities for both their local areas and national interests.

The dual phenomena of proprietary chain expansion, penetration and mixed real estate development and of the parallel corporate restructuring and proprietarization of private voluntary and public teaching hospital complexes in the 1980s further confounds the focal planning issues of the 1970s of expansionary medical empire displacement of community housing and physical abandonment of neediest, low-income and minority communities.

A basic development affecting the chains is that market forces are pushing away from acute care hospital bed acquisition or capitalization, except insofar as they contribute to fuller systems integration for cost control or, especially, for more legitimation as part of long term marketing for prepayment activities.

The chains quick acquisition profits may be fast drying up including those from major teaching hospitals.

As academic medical center complexes become corporately restructured with or without direct interpenetration of major investor owned chains, whether their missions are further skewed from public services needs ultimately must be evaluated on a case by case basis. While this analysis has been restricted to the growing number of AMCs with reported proprietary linkage, serious consideration needed to be given to comparable evaluations of AMCs without outside proprietary intervention. Policy concerns about "healing" the academic medical center must concentrate on continuing debates about mission within these institutions, not simply on either opportunities or problems of proprietary chain interpenetration. For the forseeable future, both the problems and strengths of restructuring AMC complexes will likely be as important across the nation for health systems change as the spread of the chains.

REFERENCES

1. Anderson, G. et al. Investor-owned chains and teaching hospitals. *New Engl. J. Med.* 313: 201-204, 1985.
2. A corporate transfusion for teaching hospitals. *Business Week*, February 4, 1985, pp. 32-33.
3. Fiscally fit teaching hospitals eye sellouts to for-profit chains. *Modern Healthcare*, January 4, 1985, pp. 36-40.
4. Investor-related academic health center: An "uncertain courtship?" Medical News, *JAMA.*, June 7, 1985, pp. 3049-3056.
5. Shahoda, T. Multis courting teaching hospitals. *Multis*, February 1, 1985, pp. M18-19.
6. Lewis, I., and Sheps, C. *The Sick Citadel*. Oelgeschlager, Gunn and Hain, Cambridge, MA, 1983.
7. *Wall Street Journal*, October 7, 1985, p, 33.
8. *Wall Street Journal*, February, 1986, p. 1.
9. Hospital Corporation of America. *Annual Report, 1984*. Nashville, TN, 1984.
10. Wesley Trustees. Church approach sale. *Modern Healthcare* February 15, 1985, p. 35.
11. HCA unveils diversification plan. *Hospitals* 19, December 1, 1984.
12. Purdim, T. Hospital company and no. 1 supplier plan huge merger. *New York Times* April 1, 1985, p. A1.
13. Reading, A. Involvement of proprietary chains in academic health centers. *New Engl. J. Med.* 313: 194-197, 1985.
14. Humana Corporation. *Annual Report, 1984*, Louisville, KY.
15. Tatge, M. Humana's game plan for expansion includes exploiting its "Brand Name." *Modern Healthcare*, January 4, 1985, p. 48.
16. Shahoda, T. Humana's goal: Centers of excellence draw exceptional physicians, and their patients follow. *Multis*, December 1, 1984, p. M32.
17. Humana making the most of its place in the spotlight. *Business Week*, May 6, 1985, pp. 68-69.
18. Humana name recognition is 16%: Not household word. *Modern Healthcare*, January 11, 1985, p. 11.
19. Profitable American hospitals. *The Economist*, May 18, 1985, pp. 82-83.
20. National Medical Enterprises. *Annual Report, 1984*. Los Angeles, CA.
21. Fackelmann, K. NME selecting business strategies that help boost hospital admissions. *Modern Healthcare*, November 15, 1984, p. 24.

22. Vignola, M. National medical enterprises. *L. F. Rothschild, Unterberg, Towbin Research*, New York, May 7, 1984.
23. NME, USC plan tertiary care hospital. *Modern Healthcare*, March 1, 1985, p. 114.
24. American Medical International. *Annual Report, 1984*. Beverly Hills, CA.
25. Wallace, C. AMI, St. Lukes Episcopal discussing integrated delivery system for Houston. *Modern Healthcare*, February 15, 1985, p. 135; AMI enters joint venture with six Houston Hospitals; AUX [Hospitals], February 16, 1985, p. 29.
26. AMI diagnostic services to buy MRIs for two university hospitals. *Hospitals*, January 16, 1985, p. 32.
27. Irvine medical center's sale spurs teaching hospital debate. *Modern Healthcare*, October 25, 1985, p. 102.
28. Vignola, M. Hospital management industry: Health systems emerge. *L. F. Rothschild, Unterberg, Towbin Research*. New York, February 22, 1985.
29. Anderson et al. op cit.
30. HCA enters Canadian market via pact with Ontario hospital. *Modern Healthcare*, 5, 1985, p. 14.

CHAPTER 6

The Proprietarization of Health Care and the Underdevelopment of the Public Sector

David G. Whiteis and J. Warren Salmon

INTRODUCTION

Two major and interconnected issues confronting health care delivery in the United States today are hospital failure and the rapid encroachment by the for-profit sector. The operational influence on the entire delivery system can be seen by analyzing the dramatic growth of investor-owned hospital chains during the early years of this decade. The *Modern Health Care* survey shows a 15.0 percent increase in total beds owned, leased, or managed by investor-owned multi-hospital chains between 1982 and 1983 (1, p. 66), and a 15.1 percent increase between 1983 and 1984 (2, p. 76). During the latter time period, profits of the investor-owned chains responding to the survey rose 28.5 percent from $693.5 million to $89.1 million (2, p. 76), continuing a trend that had shown a 37.7 percent increase (from $530.5 million to $730.7 million) between 1982 and 1983 (1, p. 66). Alongside these corporate profit figures, however, have been huge losses by public hospital systems, which recorded a $360 million deficit for 1984, 57.2 percent greater than the $229 million deficit they suffered in 1983 (2, p. 76).

A closer examination of U.S. hospitals in the 1980s reveals a significant amount of financial crisis among those not blessed with ongoing capital reserves from the stock and bond markets, and well-paying privately-insured patients. The American Hospital Association (AHA) reported that 156 community hospitals closed between 1980 and 1984, with the greatest single concentration of closings (28.9 percent) being in large metropoolitan areas with populations over 1.5 million (3, p. 15). The great majority of failed hospitals during this

117

time (84.5 percent) were *not* members of multi-hospital systems (3, p. 17). Preliminary results from a study in progress at the University of Illinois at Chicago indicate that a similar pattern exists for hospital closures during the period 1985–87 (4). These findings reveal that, even in the current era of cost-cutting, retrenchment, and increased financial pressure, some hospitals continue to thrive while others are in jeopardy.

The relationship between the rampant growth of the proprietary sector (accompanied by an increasing corporatization of "not-for-profit" hospitals mimicking their for-profit counterparts), the deepening crisis in the public health sector, and the implications for the medical profession have been noted extensively (5). Corporate strategizing has encouraged such cost-saving techniques as "cream-skimming" of middle class clienteles on the part of many hospitals, leaving smaller voluntary and public hospitals more financially vulnerable and at a higher risk (6). The AHA's portrait of "the typical closed community hospital" between 1980 and 1984 is instructive in this regard (3, p. 1):

> . . . under 199 beds in size, investor-owned [but not, as noted above, owned by a large national chain] or nongovernment, not-for-profit; the provider of a small number of facilities and services . . . a non-teaching hospital; located in a metropolitan area; in existence for approximately 35 years; not a member of a multi-hospital system; and not the only community hospital in the county in which it was located.

Recent federal policy has encouraged and exacerbated the financial pressures on hospitals already most at risk. The American Hospital Association reports that annual unreimbursed care more than doubled to $5.7 billion between 1980 and 1984 (7). In the face of this pressure, many hospitals are increasingly unable, or unwilling, to care for the medically indigent. Management pressure has increased on emergency room officials to restrict access to Public Aid patients, resulting in well-documented and drastic increases in the "dumping" of patients on already-overburdened public institutions (8, 9).

This consolidation of health capital into concentrated markets and the incessant push toward a for-profit health care industry at the expense of public medicine represents a condition of development and underdevelopment (10). As such it reflects the economic system of capitalism as a whole. As Navarro points out (11, p. 41):

> We cannot understand the maldistribution of resources in the health sector without analyzing the distribution of economic and political power in these societies, i.e., the question of who controls what and whom, or, as it is usually phrased in political economy, who controls the means of production and reproduction?

In the wake of this push toward corporate consolidation, those left behind—the working poor, the unemployed, racial minorities, many elderly women and children—are gradually being denied access to the vital resources needed to participate actively in their own health and the health of their communities. As we will show, the structure of the health care industry, its long history of technology-intensive intervention, and the current trends toward for-profit care with removal of services to those left behind in the wake of the corporate siphoning of public resources, are all of a piece. They are signs and symptoms of the larger illness, the underdevelopment of public resources under corporate development. To quote Navarro again, "the way to break with the under-development of health is to break with the sickness of underdevelopment" (11, p. 33).

SCIENTIFIC MEDICINE, TECHNOLOGY, AND CORPORATE SELF-INTEREST

The long history of the alliance between the medical establishment—including medical education, research and development, and the establishment of medical professionals as an elite within society—and the corporate sector has been well-documented (12-14). Seen in this context, it is obviously no accident that the course of medical research in the United States has been largely dictated by an emphasis on disease-focused, individual-based, physician-centered intervention. Social, economic, and environmental origins of disease have been largely ignored by modern biomedicine, despite increasing epidemiological evidence linking disease and illness to poverty, occupation, unemployment, and political powerlessness.

The history of U.S. medicine throughout the 20th century has been characterized by the joining of spectacular technological advances with a hospital-dominated system to promote both research and the technology it has spurred. By original intent the medical training system has focused upon in-hospital, postgraduate education at university-affiliated (and often corporately endowed) teaching institutions, thus providing a ready labor supply to fill hospital beds. Since the implementation of Hill-Burton in 1946, many of these beds have been constructed with massive federal subsidies, further cementing the alliance between corporate medicine and federal policy.

This alliance has been strengthened through reimbursement mechanisms, as well. The fee-for-service payment system, buttressed strongly by the intro-duction of Blue Cross and Blue Shield in the late 1930s, was finally solidified by the introduction of Medicare and Medicaid in the mid-1960s. Such a payment structure encouraged dependent care-seeking behaviors and disease-focused, technological interventions propelled by the profit motive (15), as befitted an industry under ever-increasing corporate influence. A rational investigation of more thorough preventive care and more effective, community-based models to meet human health needs, focusing as it necessarily would on social and environmental causes of illness, continued to be downplayed. Such an alternative focus may have given the United States an entirely different urban health care system.

The interconnection of the medical industry with the larger economic system is clear: the emphasis on a "technological fix" to fix human health problems created ready "markets" for an entire array of medical services and products, ranging from hospital lawyers equipment and construction, pharmaceutical and medical supplies to consultants, lawyers, financial advisors, and most recently, computer systems and software. Large-scale corporate suppliers quickly realized that the medical industry had several desirable features: a large and available market of people who have traditionally considered health a priority in their lives; access to a ready labor market and a large supply of valuable technology through close associations with medical facilities and schools; and state and federal programs to financially bolster the health care industry (16). With these recommending characteristics, it is no wonder that the health care "market" soon attracted corporate suppliers who established their power and gained a monopoly over a burgeoning range of goods and services for which technological interventions created increasing demand. Not to be ignored is the fact that this medical model of care was the result of findings gathered over years of scientific research conducted largely under corporate sponsorship, either directly or through major universities (14).

A major step in furthering corporate inroads in health care delivery came with the Health Maintenance Organization (HMO) strategy of the Nixon administration. Designed to increase private sector involvement in health care, it did not accomplish the hoped-for results for several reasons: consumer and professional misgivings about HMO's, the mid-70s recession, chaos inflicted on the federal bureaucracy by Watergate and its aftermath, and, ironically, insufficient funding of HMO's because of Nixon administration cutbacks and impoundments. However, propelling forces toward proprietarization were set in place for the investor-owned hospital firms and health maintenance organizations (17).

As health care costs skyrocketed through the 1970s, largely spurred by the upward spiral of new capital investment and the resultant expenditures as more sophisticated equipment and methods became *de rigueur* for hospitals competing for their market share, business purchasers found that employee health benefit costs were cutting into their profit levels. The corporate class, encouraged by its policy organizations' studies and recommendations, expanded its own health-related activities to provide preventive programs for employees and began to muscle health providers and insurers on cost containment. The motivation was stated explicitly: to encourage employees to "enjoy healthy lifestyles while affording the employer the ability to stabilize costs," in the words of one corporate position paper (18, p. 18).

Large business purchasers also sought to influence public policy through lobbying by the U.S. Chamber of Commerce and the Washington Business Group on Health (19) and through formation of local business health care coalitions. An overall thrust began toward health care as an investment in human capital, rather than as a human need for everyone in society. Worker productivity, reduced absenteeism, higher morale, and lower health benefit outlays were seen as advantageous to labor and management alike since, as another corporate policy paper put it, "they are footing much of the bill" (20, p. 1).

More insidious has been the Reagan administration emphasis on "market-place competition" and its resultant pressure on all providers, including private "not-for-profit" hospitals that formerly shared community responsibility for caring for the indigent, to ". . . either get out of the starting block first or do a better job than the pioneers and end up dominating the market . . ." as recommended by *Modern Healthcare* (21, p. 2). To do this, the hospital industry has been pressured by third party payers, HMO's, and local business coalitions to reduce excess bed capacity and length of stay, amidst a shrinking hospital sector resulting from federal reimbursement cuts and the adoption of Medicare's Diagnostic Related Groups (DRGs). Avoiding the estimated 35–40 million Americans without health insurance or other means to contribute to hospital profits has become in some cases an organizational survival strategy.

The effect of growing corporatization of health care goes far beyond strategies to affect financial security. An ever-growing fixation on a bottom-line approach can be seen throughout the literature in exhortations to find, as *Hospitals*, the journal of the American Hospital Association, recommended as far back as 1978, "a method for capacity reduction that gives priority to corporate consolidations and unilateral closure of entire hospitals which is . . . likely to result in the greatest cost savings (22, p. 63). Tinged with fear of financial disaster and a preoccupation with "trying to capture as much of the health care market as possible" (20, p. 2), hospital strategies have evolved that perceive even the "legitimate concerns and interests" of those fearing the repercussions of closure as "obstacles to effective action" to be "addressed and resolved from a balanced perspective"(22, p. 66). This "balance" between human need and economic interest may be ultimately defined, of course, by local business coalition participants in the debate.

In several cities, entire neighborhood areas are losing most or all of their hospital services (23, 24). This has resulted in diminution or complete elimination of emergency and outpatient services and a loss of economic enterprises "that employ a large number of people that contribute to the economic well-being of their communities . . . and the quality of life in the community"(22, p. 66). Thus, patients are denied access, health worker jobs are lost, and neighborhoods disintegrate even further.

The relationship between this community deterioration and the further withdrawal of health services is a dialectical one. Since the mid-70s, data have shown a growing phenomenon of economic crisis and hospital closure among institutions serving the poor and minority populations of major U.S. cities (25). Obscured as these figures have been in analyses of the alleged "health" of the industry, they nonetheless paint a very different picture when viewed in the light of the historical perspective given here. They must also be examined along with the trends they portend—trends toward an increasing stratification between the availability of health care for the affluent and the dismantling of the delivery system that has traditionally served the underserved segments of the population.

Attention must also be given to the overall phenomenon of increased disinvestment in public goods as a necessity of the current economic crisis, both in the United States and abroad. The global move toward privatization, in health care as in other services, is characteristic of an overall historic direction to remove many state-guaranteed or provided services from the general population. This contextual development has given rise to the emerging multi-tiered health care system in the United States. The system is thus an outcome of larger historical processes which, we maintain, result from increasing corporate power and economic consolidation. It signifies an accompanying decrease in the provision of health, human services, and economic support to "unproductive" segments of the population and to their communities.

PRIVATIZATION AND CAPITALISM: LET THE BUYER BE WELL

As we have seen, corporatization and proprietarization trends in health care, and the submission to corporate class restructuring, did not begin with the current economic crisis. Nor did they originate the commodification of health needs to be purchased by those who have the means to afford care for the benefit of those who sell it. However, it is clear that closures of urban hospitals and the present restructuring of the health sector are part of a larger move toward removal of public goods and services from certain population segments: the "unproductive" poor working class, aged, and disabled.

Placed in the context of the late 20th century capitalist development, this dismantling of health care institutions to exclude the "unproductive" population comes at a time when there is a rerouting throughout the international economic order of substantial amounts of formerly public monies into private accumulation, in an effort to shore up sagging profit levels. Navarro outlines the situation confronting the major industrial countries (26, p. 108):

> (1) Extremely high levels of unemployment; (2) unprecedented levels of inflation; (3) an economic slump [indicated by continual declines in the GNP of the major Organization for Economic Cooperation and Development (OECD) countries during the past year and a half]; (4) a dramatic decline . . . of world trade with substantial balance of payments deficits in most OECD countries; and (5) an alarming growth of public debt in most of the western core states.

Navarro goes on to analyze this crisis as being largely precipitated by strengthening working-class movements in Western capitalist nations; the challenge of newer economic powers ranging from West Germany and Japan to Taiwan, Korea, and Brazil, among others; the emergence of anti-imperialist and anti-colonialist movements in peripheral countries, which make it more difficult for continued exploitation there; and the rise, through greater areas of the world, of socialist forces offering alternatives to world capitalism (26, p. 109). These factors have all precipitated serious curtailment of public spending to cut collective consumption throughout the United States, the United Kingdom, West Germany, and France.

More specifically, in the United States we have seen a dramatic drive to privatize a wide range of formerly public goods. The criminal justice system shows signs of an incipient corporate encroachment: Corrections Corp., a for-profit prison management firm, cofounded by Kentucky Fried Chicken mogul Jack Massey (who was also instrumental in beginning Hospital Corporation of America), is being considered by the Tennessee legislature as manager for that state's penal system (27). Likewise, corporate inroads on public education (28) and both the storage and dissemination of a wide range of information and knowledge (29) are being noted. *The Nation* has reported that corporate predictions for the growth of the information industry show as much as 90 percent of all communications facilities in the United States under the control of 15 large companies by 1995 (29, p. 710).

This prediction is strikingly similar to some that have been made about the consolidation of health care. Ellwood has estimated that by the mid-1990s "there will be ten giant national firms providing 50 percent of the medical care in this country" (30, p. 1). In 1985, four companies—Hospital Corporation of America, American Medical International, Humana, and National Medical Enterprises—owned or managed 12 percent of all U.S. hospitals (30).

In recent years, this unlimited expansion has slowed somewhat. Pressures brought on by over enthusiastic corporate expansion have forced the corporate giants to retrench, slow down their acquisition schemes, and slough off some of their less profitable hospitals. Overall profits fell 47.1 percent between 1985 and 1986 (31), and by a far smaller 4.8% between 1986 and 1987 (32).

However, such strategies as diversification into ambulatory and long-term care continure to reap enormous benefits for large-scale health entrepreneurs. Profits for corporate chains which cleared $105 million in 1987, Humana ($192 million) and NME ($81 million) continue at a healthy pace (33). More significantly, the success of corporate medicine has hastened the adoption, throughout the health care system, of a business approach toward the production and distribution of what was formerly considered a public good. This process of corporatization has transformed the nature of U.S. health care delivery in the late 20th century, and is itself a part of a larger effort on the part of the corporate class to divert formerly public resources into profit-making enterprises.

HOSPITAL FAILURE AND THE DISINVESTMENT IN
THE PUBLIC GOODS

The stark contrast between recent corporate growth and the underdevelopment of public sector health care for the uninsured and poor has already been noted. Especially revealing are studies by McLafferty in New York City, which show a strong positive correlation between closure and the percentage of minority population in a hospital's service area, especially for voluntary and municipal hospitals (25). Proprietary hospitals were found less vulnerable to neighborhood change and socioethnic composition because many serve populations primarily from areas outside their specific neighborhoods, do not provide outpatient or emergency care for the uninsured, and draw most of their patients from physician referrals, which do not necessarily reflect the immediate area's demographic makeup (25). It should be noted here that proprietary hospitals in McLafferty's study were not owned or managed by large corporate chains but rather by smaller, local concerns. It is possible to expect that this contrast between proprietary and the public and voluntary institutions will become even greater as large-scale proprietarization takes place and local hospitals become managed by investor-owned firms with little or no local involvement. Thus, the increasingly corporate approach toward bottom-line business portends an exacerbation of urban hospital closures.

Numerous other studies and surveys have identified additional causes and predisposing factors that put hospitals at high risk of closure. A survey in 1982, conducted by the American Hospital Association, found five primary reasons: (1) financial (26.8 percent of all closures), (2) replacement by a new facility (23.4 percent), (3) low occupancy (14.3 percent) (4) an outdated facility (13.4 percent), and (5) lack of medical staff (10 percent) (34). As noted above, hospital size is also an important variable. AHA data and evidence from ongoing investigations show that no closure has occurred among community hospitals with 500 or more beds between 1980 and 1987, while the great majority closures have been suffered by hospitals with under 199 beds (3, p. 4; 15).

The success of multi-hospital, for-profit chains and the accompanying high-risk status of smaller community "not-for-profit" and public hospitals must be seen in the context of overall social policy redirection (35). The trend toward emphasizing private development over the redistribution of public goods did not begin, as some liberal theorists would have us believe, with the Reagan administration. The number of persons covered by Medicaid, for instance, declined by 1.5 million even before Reagan took office (between 1977 and 1979) (36, p. 13).

Cutbacks under Reagan have surely exacerbated this, creating new barriers to equity in the receipt of health services. Since 1980, with deep federal cuts in social welfare programs, Medicaid roles have been reduced more drastically than ever before. In 1981, Medicaid cuts were proposed or enacted in 28 states, and six dropped Medicaid entirely for families with unemployed parents; in

1982, federal cuts in Aid to Families with Dependent Children (AFDC) resulted in loss of coverage for approximately 661,000 children and 181,000 adults. The end result has been that less than half of the country's poor are now covered by Medicaid. In some states, such as Mississippi and Texas, as many as 75 percent of all indigents are excluded (36, p. 13).

These cuts, along with the Medicare DRG reimbursement strategy, have had a devastating effect on urban hospitals with older facilities, serving large numbers of minority and elderly patients. Such hospitals, already at high risk of closure, often have less capital to invest in high-technology equipment and thus lose out in attracting or maintaining medical specialty services. While private for-profit institutions perceive the uninsured and poor as pariahs, often refusing them care outright, certain voluntary and municipal hospitals have patient loads with increasing numbers of the uninsured and poor. More and more voluntary institutions are following the example of their proprietary counterparts by denying admission to unprofitable patients. A survey of 23 large urban public hospitals in 1983 revealed that they received an average of 13 percent of their revenues from private insurers. Grady Memorial in Atlanta received 8 percent, Chicago's Cook County Hospital received 7 percent, D. C. General only 3 percent, and Bellevue in New York received none (37, p. 594). These figures may even have decreased by now.

Reductions in Medicaid reimbursement have a dual effect; filling public hospital beds with more patients needing intense, complex care, for which the hospital will not be sufficiently reimbursed; and denying hospital care to an ever-growing number who find themselves without the "safety-net" of Medicaid. These people are increasingly refused care by other than public hospitals, which now continue to treat patients only at a financial loss (7–9).

Meanwhile, economically strapped inner city hospitals with patient loads consisting almost entirely of publicly funded patients depend on these revenues to keep operating. As public, as well as private, reimbursement becomes more restricted, these institutions—the most dependent upon recipients of public monies to remain in operation—lose proportionately more patients than other hospitals (24). Thus the clarion cry of competitionists, concerned about revenue loss from unfilled beds, has become elimination of "excess capacity" in for-profit and "not-for-profit" hospitals alike (22), meaning more closures of marginal hospitals, many of which are located in city neighborhoods and small towns of most need.

The growing ranks of the uninsured and underinsured, as well as Medicaid recipients and some Medicare beneficiaries without private supplemental insurance, are facing the erosion of the delivery system upon which they previously relied. Alternative sources of care will continue to become more limited in the absence of a new infusion of funds, such as in a national health program or even state health insurance schemes. Meanwhile, the corporate sector rushes to take advantage of current technological and policy developments to further consolidate its hold on the entire spectrum of health care delivery.

EXPANSION AND DIVERSIFICATION: SURGICENTERS, EMERGICENTERS, FRANCHISING, AND ACADEMIC MEDICINE

As corporate hospital profits grew, the logic of capitalist expansion demanded that these firms move into other related areas of care. Proprietary chain ventures into the insurance business had promise, during the early 1980s, to capture patients from "not-for-profit" institutions. These diversifications sought to engage national contracts from corporate purchasers for their nationwide system operations (38). In practice, this strategy was overambitious (39); the chains have largely withdrawn from the insurance business, although close corporate ties still exist, such as those between Hospital Corporation of America and the Equitable Life Insurance Company (40).

Other ventures have proven far more lucrative. Major investor-owned nursing home companies increased their number of beds by 17.1 percent to 153,655 in 1984. Industry experts predict that by the end of the decade, the majority of chain-operated beds will be controlled by 10 to 20 firms (3, p. 126).

Predictably, corporate inroads into other areas of health care are giving patients fewer places of "last resort" when hospitals will not accept them. The nursing home industry is solidly corporate-owned; the option of transfer for patients whose hospital care is uncovered under Medicare's Prospective Payment System (PPS) will be less certain for the poor unless Medicare, which does not pay for nursing home services, shifts funds to catastrophic or long-term care coverage. Observers predict a growing push on the part of for-profit nursing homes to attain a greater percentage of privately insured patients, even to the point at which "if payments to nursing homes are cut too much, nursing homes will stop accepting Medicare and Medicaid patients" (41, p. 132).

This problem will likely by exacerbated by increased growth and competitive pressure from the corporate multi-national chains. Observers predict an eventual takeover of nursing home companies by the corporate health giants (41) as "more 'ma and pa' operations . . . [are] falling by the wayside" in the face of drastic increases in beds owned and constructed by corporate multi-institutional chains (42, p. 137–138).

The rapid proliferation of freestanding health care centers and home health care agencies can be seen as symptomatic of the tendency of U.S. medicine to focus on intervention-oriented, disease-specific techniques, instead of a preventive approach to address the larger social and environmental origins of disease. Home health care agencies posted the greatest growth in the nonhospital arena between 1983 and 1984, with an 80 percent increase; other leaders included urgent care centers (a 65 percent jump); primary care centers (27 percent); and durable medical equipment dealers (72 percent) (43, p. 144), furthering the strategic corporate link between technology and medicine. Again, predictions show the freestanding centers, currently suffering some financial difficulties, being used more and more as feeders into already existing corporate-owned hospitals, and eventually also becoming absorbed by the multi-system chains (44).

Corporate control has also extended into the proliferating surgicenter industry, taking advantage of new technology and also of regulations that exempt outpatient care from the payment restrictions of PPS. Although independent centers continue to outnumber chain-owned facilities, corporate-owned surgicenters are growing in strength and number, and conduct a disproportionate share of the procedures performed (45, pp. 148, 150). As in the hospital business, a few powerful entities are becoming dominant. Especially notable is the geographic distribution of the facilities, which appear to be following the migratory pattern of U.S. economic development. The Sun Belt hosts the preponderance of freestanding surgicenters: the largest are Medical Care International (Houston), AMI (Beverly Hills), Surgical Care Affiliates (Nashville), and Alternacare (Los Angeles) (45).

Similar growth has been experienced in other areas of health service. The number of retail store dental centers rose 160 percent between 1980 and 1982, although non-traditional settings still provide a small percentage of dental services nationwide—2 to 5 percent (46, p. 160). The leading retailer in housing dental clinics is Sears, Roebuck & Company, which operated 43 dental facilities in 19 states in 1985 (47, p. 152). This growth is described by industry spokespersons as "explosive" and is expected to continue "as part of a trend affecting all professions" (46, pp. 160, 163). Privatization of health care to for-profit auspices has pervaded all aspects of health care delivery. Ambulance service, for example, was once a local government service. It is now under private contract in over 55 percent of the nation's towns and cities; another 15 areas are reportedly ready to switch. The proprietary trade association, American Ambulance Association in Sacramento, California, represents 800 companies whose revenues total more than $1.5 billion (48).

Eye care, foot care, weight loss, dermatology, and liposuction and other cosmetic surgery are other profitable areas of commodified health needs fit for corporate production, found increasingly in freestanding centers. It should be noted that this for-profit surge in the ambulatory arena maintains its opposite in the underdevelopment of public health clinics and other community-based agencies. Such out-of-hospital ventures to insured persons with disposable incomes siphon away more patients and income, reinforcing a survival mentality among local public and "not-for-profit" institutions. Closures and cutbacks have been spreading through federally-funded community health centers and local public health departments across the nation.

Finally, there is evidence that academic medical centers, the health care venue of last resort for many poor and uninsured patients, are being targeted for corporate takeover. Teaching hospitals, like public hospitals, rely disproportionately on Medicare and Medicaid, and they also bear a great burden of bad debt, giving more "free care" than nonteaching hospitals (49). Several teaching institutions, beginning with the University of Florida Hospital in 1982, have entered into contractual arrangements with corporate chains to construct new facilities or manage existing ones (49). It should be noted that specific details of these contractual arrangements differ from case to case, and not all observers think that this constitutes a major trend at present. However given the history of corporate involvement in U.S. medical care from the earliest days to the present, these nascent trends bear careful examination. Berliner and Burlage (50) point out that ownership or leasing of a major academic medical facility can be an important component of corporate marketing and public relations strategy. This strengthened emphasis on marketing of health care as a commodity is a vital component of overall corporatization and proprietarization trends, and portends an intensification of corporate strategies to consolidate and seize formerly public goods for corporate profit.

HEALTH AS A COMMODITY: INDIVIDUALIZATION, SEGMENTATION, AND NON-HOLISTIC HEALTH

The concept of health as an individual concern, disassociated from the political, economic, social, and environmental contexts in which we live, certainly did not begin with present corporatization trends. Isolated, intervention-oriented, high-technology services for separate conditions in different offices, all for different individual bodies, is a non-holistic approach to the human body and the wellbeing of the person, analogous to the preferred capitalist perspective of society as consisting of isolated individuals, joined together only by market forces and competing self-interests. Such a push toward procedural interventions in a profit-driven health system only serves to increase this fragmentation and limit health achievements.

This individualization of the concepts of health and illness, and the isolation of these concepts from an overall picture of today's social reality, has been further imbedded in our consciousness by the models of medical intervention favoring the profit drives of major corporations. Americans are being told that large-scale, more efficient corporate-run health organizations promise an improved state for health care delivery. Thus, people are distracted from conceptualizing the larger social context in which human health is primarily decided (16).

As inner city and remote rural hospitals close and retrench in the face of massive disinvestment, and as under-supported public hospitals and strapped teaching institutions struggle more with the burden of taking on the public responsibility for health, many communities are left behind with little or no access to care. These people are at high risk for major diseases. They are also the uninsured, lacking sufficient public goods such as housing, education, nutrition, social support, and employment. The emphasis on a "technological fix" to a whole array of political, cultural, and personal conditions leading to chronic degenerative illness further alienates people from their day-to-day health necessities. The class nature of this condition for poor and working people is apparent.

Meanwhile, the more affluent are enticed to consider their health a consumer good to be provided like a movie or a hamburger; entertainment, nourishment, even pre-packaged beauty and social acceptance can be obtained from health spas and fitness centers. Faddish, often pseudo-scientific health products, lines of cosmetics, and diet and vitamin regimens proliferate throughout the private sector. Such methods of individual health groping may do little to alleviate problems created by high-stress, competitive, and overly consumptive lifestyles in which the upper-middle class is compelled to participate to climb the corporate ladder of success. Ultimately it may be shown that the emergent corporate health care model is unhealthy for the more affluent, as its attendant underdevelopment is for the poor. The collective nature of society and the class nature of illness is obscured in the face of the myth that an individual's own behavior is the sole source of his or her illness or well-being.

In summary, for-profit health care in the United States and the resultant corporatization of the "not-for-profit" firms is removing health care from those Americans most in need. The exclusion of this population from necessary services appears to be related to a systematic attempt to curtail public consumption of health and other formerly public resources. The implications of this corporate transformation portend further breakdown of family and community caring networks, which may harm all "consumers" of health care, not only the poor. Seen in the light of current efforts on the part of international capital to shore up profits by diverting public goods into private control, urban slums exist as the United States' domestic Third World. In this perspective, development and underdevelopment are again seen to go hand-in-hand.

REFERENCES

1. Johnson, D. E. Multi-unit providers: Survey plots 457 chains' growth. *Modern Healthcare* 14(5): 65–84, 1984.
2. Johnson, D. E. Investor-owned chains continue expansion, 1985 survey shows. *Modern Healthcare* 15(2): 75–90, 1985.
3. Mullner, R., McNeil, D., and Andes, S. National trends in hospital closure 1980–1984. American Hospital Association, Office of Policy Analysis Publication no. 59, pp. 1–32, Chicago, 1985.
4. Mullner, R., Rydman, R., Whiteis, D., and Rich, R. "U.S. Hospital Closures 1980–87: An Epidemiologic Case Control Study." Center for Health Services Research, University of Illinois School of Public Health, Chicago. Unpublished manuscript, 1988.
5. Rhein, R. W. Hospitals in trouble: Crisis for doctors. *Medical World News* 21: 58–68, 1980.
6. Relman, A. S. The new medical-industrial complex. *New Engl. J. Med.* 303: 963–970, 1980.
7. Reinhold, R. Treating an outbreak of patient dumping in Texas. *New York Times*, May 25, 1980, p. 4.

8. Chicago's private hospitals deny care to the poor. *All-Chicago City News*. July 23, 1983, p. 6.
9. Schiff, R. L. et al. Transfers to a public hospital: A prospective study of 467 patients. *New Engl. J. Med.* 314(9): 552–559, 1986.
10. Dowd, D. F. *The Twisted Dream: Capitalist Development in the United States Since 1776*. Winthrop Publishers, Cambridge, Mass., 1974.
11. Navarro, V. *Medicine Under Capitalism*. Prodist, New York, 1976.
12. Starr, P. *The Social Transformation of American Medicine*. Basic Books, New York, 1982.
13. Brown, E. R. He who pays the piper: Foundations, the medical profession, and medical educational reform. *Int. J. Health Serv.* 10(1): 71–88, 1980.
14. Markowitz, G. E. and Rosen, D. N. Doctors in crisis: A study of the use of medical education reform to establish modern professional elitism in medicine. *Am. Q.* 25(1): 83–107, 1973.
15. Salmon, J. W. The competitive health strategy: Fighting for your health. *Health and Medicine* 1(2): 21–30, 1982.
16. McKinlay, J. B. (ed.). *Issues in the Political Economy of Health Care*. Tavistock Publications, New York, 1984.
17. Salmon, J. W. *Corporate Attempts to Reorganize the American Health Care System*. Doctoral dissertation, Cornell University, 1978 (unpublished).
18. *Highlight of an Effective Employee Benefit Management System*. Position paper, BPI, Inc., Westmont, Ill., 1980.
19. *The Formation of a Medicine and Business Coalition*. American Medical Association, Office of Corporation Liaison, Medical Practice and Professional Relations Group, 1981.
20. *Health Care Horizons '77*. Touche Ross & Co., New York, 1977.
21. John, D. E. Chains integrate health care services into local networks. *Modern Healthcare* 15(12): 2, 1985.
22. Gottlieb, S. R. Reducing excess capacity is a tough but necessary job. *Hospitals* 52: 63–68, 1978.
23. *The Killing of Philadelphia General Hospital*. Health Information and Action Group, Philadelphia, 1976.
24. Sager, A. Why urban voluntary hospitals close. *Health Services Research* 18(3): 450–475, 1983.
25. McLafferty, S. Neighborhood characteristics and hospital closure. *Soc. Sci. and Med.* 16: 1667–1674, 1982.
26. Navarro, V. The crisis of the international capitalist order and its implications on the welfare state. In *Issues in the Political Economy of Health Care*, edited by J. B. McKinlay. Methuen/Tavistock Publications, New York, 1984.
27. Montgomery, J. Corrections Corp. seeks lease to run Tennessee's prisons. *The Wall Street Journal*, September 13, 1985, p. 8.
28. Kraft, S. Corporations enter the classroom: Private companies fill the gap left by dwindling government funding. *Valley Advocate*, Springfield, Mass., January 1, 1986, pp. 1–6.
29. Shiller, H. Information: A shrinking resource. *The Nation*, December 28, 1985/January 4, 1986, pp. 708–710.
30. Hull, J. B. Medical turmoil: Four hospital chains facing lower profits, adopt new strategies. *The Wall Street Journal*, October 10, 1985, p. 1.
31. Bell, C. W. Hospital systems report 47.1% drop in profits last year. *Modern Healthcare* 17(12): 37–90, 1987.
32. Multi-unit providers survey. *Modern Healthcare*, June 3, 1988.
33. *Forbes 500 Annual Directory* 41(9), April 25, 1988.
34. Hernandez, S. R. and Kaluzny, A. D. Hospital closure: A review of current and proposed research. *Health Serv. Res.* 18(3): 419–436, 1983.
35. Weiss, K. Corporate medicine: What's the bottom line for physicians and patients? *New Physician* 9: 1–25, 1982.
36. *Health Care Financing Program Statistics/The Medicare Medicaid Data Book* 13, p. 111. Health Care Financing Administration, 1981.

37. Dallek, G. The loss of hospitals serving the poor. *Health Serv. Res.* 18(3): 593–597, 1983.
38. Koenig, R. Humana earnings increased by 15% in fourth period. *The Wall Street Journal*, October 9, 1985, p. 2.
39. M. D. behavior seen as cause of losses. *American Medical News*, May 1, 1986, p. 2.
40. Kenkel, P. J. Managed-care crowth continued in 1987 despite companies' poor operating results. *Modern Healthcare*, June 3, 1988, pp. 20–38.
41. Punch, L. Investor-owned chains lead increase in beds. *Modern Healthcare* 15(2): 126–136, 1985.
42. Punch, L. Chains expand their operations, expecting prospective pay boom. *Modern Healthcare* 14(5): 131–140, 1984.
43. Wallace, C. Ambulatory care facilities multiply. *Modern Healthcare* 15(2): 142–146, 1985.
44. Punch, L. Freestanding units lose money, but that doesn't stunt growth. *Modern Healthcare* 14(5): 150–153, 1984.
45. Henderson, J. Surgery centers double: Consultant. *Modern Healthcare* 15(12): 148–150.
46. Gondela, E. Franchise, retail dental operations record major gains. *Modern Healthcare* 14(5): 160–163, 1984.
47. Gondela, E. More clinics opening, but growth rate falls. *Modern Healthcare* 15(12): 152–154, 1985.
48. Hollie, P. G. Ambulances go private. *New York Times*, May 25, 1986, Section 3, p. 1.
49. Reading, A. Involvement of proprietary chains in academic health centers. *New Engl. J. Med.* 313(3): 194–197, 1985.
50. Berliner, H. S. and Burlage, R. K. Proprietary hospital chains and academic medical centers. *Int. J. Health Serv.* 17(1): 27–45, 1987.

CHAPTER 7

Corporatization and the Social Transformation of Doctoring

John B. McKinlay and John D. Stoeckle

We are witnessing a transformation of the health care systems of developed countries that is without parallel in modern times (1, 2). This dramatic change has implications for patients and, without exception, affects the entire division of labor in health care. What are some of these changes and how are they manifesting themselves with respect to doctoring?

THE CHANGES

Over the last few years especially, many multi-national corporations, with highly diverse activities, have become involved in all facets of the generally profitable business of medical care from medical manufacturing and the ownership of treatment institutions to the financing as purchase of services in PPO's and HMO's (3, 4). Conglomerates like General Electric, AT&T, and IBM, among many others, now have large medical manufacturing enterprises within their corporate divisions. Aerospace companies are involved in everything from computerized medical information systems to life support systems. Even tobacco companies and transportation enterprises have moved into the medical care arena. In addition to this industrial or manufacturing capital, even larger financial capital institutions (e.g., commercial banks, life insurance companies, mutual and pension funds and diversified financial organizations) are also stepping up their involvement in medical care and experiencing phenomenal success (5, 6).

Besides corporate investments in health care, corporate mergers of treatment organizations and industrial corporations are also taking place. Privately owned hospital chains, controlled by larger corporations, evidence continuing rapid growth. Much of this growth comes from buying up local, municipal and voluntary community hospitals, many of which were going under as a result of cutbacks in government programs and regulations on hospital use and payment. By 1990, about 30 percent of general hospital beds will be managed by investor hospital chains (5, 7-9). Because the purpose of an investor owned organization is to make money, there is understandable concern over the willingness of such organizations to provide care to the 35 million people who lack adequate insurance coverage and who are not eligible for public programs (10-15).

RESPONSES

Regulations

Confronted with an ever deepening fiscal crisis, the state continues to cast around for regulatory solutions—one of the latest of which is DRGs for Medicare patients which reimburse hospitals by diagnosis with rates determined by government. If the actual cost of treatment is less than the allowable payment, then the hospital makes a profit; if treatment costs are more, then the hospital faces a loss, even bankruptcy, especially since an average of 40 percent of hospital revenues come from Medicare patients. This probably ineffective measure follows many well-documented policy failures (e.g., PSROs) and its consequences for the health professions are profound. These regulatory efforts, corporate mergers, investor-owned hospital chains, federally mandated cost containment measures, among many other changes, are transforming the shape, content and even the moral basis of health care (16-19). How are these institutional changes affecting the everyday work of the doctor?

New Management

By all accounts, hospitals are being managed by a new breed of physician administrators (20-22) whom Alford aptly terms "corporate rationalizers" (23). While some have medical qualifications, most are trained in the field of hospital administration, which emphasizes, among other things, rationalization, productivity, and cost efficiency. Doctors used to occupy a privileged position at the top of the medical hierarchy. Displaced by administrators, doctors have slipped down to the position of middle management where their prerogatives are also challenged or encroached upon by other health workers. Clearly, managerial imperatives often compete or conflict with physicians' usual mode of practice. Increasingly, it seems, administrators, while permitting medical staff to retain ever narrower control of technical aspects of care, are organizing the necessary coordination for collaborative work, the work schedules of staff, the recruitment of patients to the practice, the contacts with third party purchasers and determining the fiscal rewards.

Some argue that many administrators are medically qualified, so they act so as to protect the traditional professional prerogatives. This view confuses the usual distinction between status and role. As many hospital and HMO doctors will attest, when a physician is a full-time administrator, he is understandably concerned to protect the bottom line, not the prerogatives of the profession. When these interests diverge, as they increasingly must, it becomes clear where the physician/administrator's divided loyalty really resides. One recent survey of doctors shows that a majority do not believe that their medical directors represent the interests of the medical staff. As a result, the AMA has concluded that "as hospital employees . . . medical directors may align their loyalty more with hospitals than with medical staff interests" (24). To counteract these trends, it has been seriously suggested that "physicians should be trained in organization theory . . . to act as liaisons among all those with an interest in medicine, including patients, health care providers, insurers, politicians, economists, and administrators."

Specialization-Deskilling

Specialization in medicine, while deepening knowledge in a particular area, is also circumscribing the work that doctors may legitimately perform. Specialization can—with task delegation—reduce hospitals' dependence on its highly trained medical staff. Other health workers (e.g., Physicians Assistants and Nurse Practitioners) with less training, more narrowly skilled, and obviously cheaper can be hired. Doctors, while believing that specialization is invariably a good thing, are being "deskilled"—a term employed by Braverman to describe the transfer of skills from highly trained personnel to more narrowly qualified specialists (25). Many new health occupations (PA's, NP's, CN's) have emerged over the last several decades to assume some of the work which doctors used to perform. Not only is work deskilled but it is increasingly conducted without MD's control as other professional groups and workers seek their own autonomy. These processes receive support from administrators constantly searching for cheaper labor, quite apart from the controlled trials which revealed that "allied health professionals" can, in many circumstances, do the same work just as effectively and efficiently for those patients who must use them. Preference for the term "allied health professional" rather than "physician extender" or "physician assistant" reflects the promotion of this occupational division of labor.

Just over a decade ago, Victor Fuchs (26) viewed the physician as "captain of the team." Around that time, doctors (usually males) were the unquestioned masters and other health workers (usually female), especially nurses, worked "under the doctor" to carry out his orders. That subordination is disappearing. Nowadays, physicians are required to work alongside other professionals on the "health care team." The ideology of *team work* is a leveler in the hierarchical division of healthcare labor. Other health workers—for example, physiotherapists, pharmacists, medical social workers, inhalation therapists, podiatrists, and even nurses in general—may have more knowledge of specific fields than physicians, who are increasingly required to defer to other workers, now providing some of the technical and humane tasks of doctoring. While some MD's continue to resist these trends, and have publicly complained about "the progressive exclusion of doctors from nursing affairs" (27-29); still others have accommodated to the changing scene captured in the title of a recent article: "At This Hospital, the 'Captain of the Ship' is Dead" (27).

Commentators have identified the "gatekeeping" function performed by doctors (to determine and legitimate access to generally scarce resources: e.g., certain medications and highly specialized personnel) as a special characteristic that distinguishes them from other health occupations and reinforces their central position in the division of labor. But even this gatekeeping function appears to be changing. For example, in some 21 states, nurses are now able to prescribe a wide range of medications. Despite opposition from doctors, pharmacists in Florida may now prescribe drugs for many minor ailments (30). Physician organization and resistance has been unable to curtail the introduction and growth of midwifery in some areas of the country.

Specialization has also weakened the political position of doctors because they now tend to affiliate only with disparate professional societies relevant to their own field of practice, rather than the generic and increasingly distant AMA. AMA membership continues to decline annually and there are estimates that less than half of all doctors now belong. Fragmentation of the profession through sub-specialty societies severely curtails the influence of the AMA representing all the profession. One recalls the power of the AMA only a decade ago when it successfully delayed and then shaped Medicare and Medicaid legislation. In contrast, the AMA is now losing significant battles in the courts over issues which affect the position and status of doctors. Antitrust rulings (permitting doctors to advertise), and decisions prohibiting any charges over and above the federally determined DRG rates, are major examples. In Chicago this year (1987) a federal judge issued an injunction ordering the AMA to immediately end its professional boycott of chiropractors on the grounds that it violated the Sherman Act with "systematic, long-term wrongdoing and the longer-term intent to destroy a licensed profession" (31). Responding to recent proposals to introduce a flat, all inclusive payment for doctors' services associated with each type of hospital case, Dr. Coury (Chairman of the AMA's Board of Trustee) claims doctors are becoming "indentured servants of the government" (32).

Doctor Oversupply

The growing oversupply of doctors in developed countries reinforces these trends in medical work and professional power by intensifying intraprofessional competition and devaluing their position in the job market. During the 1970s, the supply of physicians increased 36 percent, while the population grew only 8 percent. U.S. medical schools continue to pump 17,000 physicians into the system annually. One report projected an oversupply of 70,000 physicians in the United States by 1990 and an excess of 150,000 by 2000. The ratio of doctors to the general population is expected to reach one in 300 by 1990 (33, 34). This level of intensity, obviously much higher in the northeast and west coast, renders fee for service solo practice economically less feasible. Again, the changes that are occurring are captured in the title of a recent article "Doctor, the Patient Will See You Now" (33). There are reliable reports that doctors are unemployed in a number of countries and increasingly underemployed in quite a few others (34). Doctors have apparently received unemployment payments in Scandinavian countries, Canada and Australia. Official recognition of physician oversupply exists in Belgium, which is restricting specialty training, and the Netherlands, which is reducing both medical school intake and specialty training (35).

The oversupply of doctors is thought to be a major reason for the recent shift to a salaried medical staff, which has been so dramatic as to be termed "the salary revolution" (36). There are estimates that over a half of all U.S. doctors are now in salaried arrangements, either part- or full-time (36). By the year 2000 it is projected that the proportion of doctors in solo or independent fee for service practice will have declined to about one quarter (36-40). Young medical graduates are especially affected by the trends described and often prepared to accept a limited job (and role) for a guaranteed fixed income (without heavy initial investment in setting up a practice and obtaining liability protection from astronomical malpractice insurance premiums) with the promise of certain perks (regular hours, paid vacation, retirement plan, etc.). The division of labor in health care is increasingly stratified by age and gender, with females and younger doctors disproportionately in salaried positions. Forty-seven percent of physicians under thirty-six years of age were salaried in 1985, while only 19.4 percent of their colleagues over 55 were employees. The percentage increase for this youngest category of physicians between 1983 and 1985 was significantly larger than for the other age groups, increasing 5.3 percentage points. Female physicians were nearly twice as likely to be employees as their male colleagues. Only 23.5 percent of males were salaried in 1985 versus 45.5 percent of females. Again, the percentage increase for female employee physicians was larger than for males over the years 1983-85. While self-employed physicians consistently earned nearly $38,000 more per year than salaried physicians, ($118,600 versus $80,400 respectively for 1985), self-employed doctors worked an average of one and a half weeks more in 1985 (47.4 weeks versus 45.9), spent an average of six more hours per week on patient care activities (52.6 hours per week versus 46.6) and saw an average of 19 more patients per week (122.6 visits per week versus 103.9) (42). One survey of over 2,000 hospitals found that the trend to a salaried medical staff was most marked in areas with high ratios of doctors to population. Physician oversupply and their associated economic vulnerability may force doctors to accept lower incomes and the increasingly alienating work conditions practicing in HMO's, clinics and hospitals of "today's corporate health factors," just as 19th century craftsmen accepted the factory floor forced on them by their move to the industrial plant (43).

Anecdotal reports from older doctors indicate that medicine today is not like "the good old days" (44). The malpractice crisis, DRGs, the likelihood of fixed fees, and shrinking incomes (projected at a 30 percent decline over the next decade) all combine to remove whatever "fun" there was in medical practice. Some wonder aloud whether they would choose medicine if, with the benefit of hindsight, they had to do it all over again (45). While doctors used to want their children to follow in their footsteps, many report that they would not recommend medicine today. Recent graduates have doubts of other kinds. They fear their debts will force them into specialties on the basis of anticipated earnings, rather than intrinsic interest (46). College advisors may dissuade the highly talented students they counsel from choosing medicine because its job market looks so bleak. The number of medical school applicants dropped 4.8 percent in 1986 and is expected to decline 9 percent more in 1987, according to the AMA and the Association of American Medical Colleges. First-time enrollments in medical schools in 1986 were down for the fifth straight year. Although it is difficult to identify a single factor responsible for these declines, it appears students fear a glutted market, concern over an average debt of $33,499 (1 117.2 percent increase since 1980), alarm over soaring malpractice insurance rates and a perception that the practice of medicine is becoming less individualistic, with more government regulation and more doctors working in "managed care" systems that have corporate-like structures (47). These professional concerns are expressed in the urban academic medical centers (where physicians with international reputations presumably enjoy a privileged status) as well as local community hospitals throughout the country.

Unionization—A Harbinger of a Trend?

There are reports from across the United States that physicians are rebelling against the continuing challenges to their authority and attempts to cut their incomes by Health Maintenance Organization (HMO's) and other corporate-like means of organizing the profitable production of medical care (34, 48, 49). One recent manifestation of doctors' frustration with the profound changes already described is increased interest in unionization. Several unions have been or are being formed in different areas of the country to represent doctors working as full-time employees of state and local government, and in HMO's. The largest is the Union of American Physicians and Dentists, based in Oakland, California, with a membership of around 43,000 in 17 states. Some unions (e.g., the Group Health Association in Washington, D.C.) have even staged strikes. The HMO organizational structure and that of other similar prepaid health-care plans appear to generate disgruntlement among its salaried physician employees who were socialized to expect considerably more status and professional autonomy than the HMO permits. There are now 625 of these medical factories in the United States serving some 25.8 million people, up from 260 with 9.1 million subscribers in 1980. There are legal obstacles to physician unionization because antitrust laws prohibit independent businessmen, including doctors in private practice, from organizing to fix prices. Recognizing this Minnesota Medical Society recently passed a resolution asking the AMA to seek government permission to form a union. National attention has recently focussed on a struggle in Minneapolis where salaried physician employees of the Physician's Health Plan of Minnesota (the largest HMO in the state) are organizing to unionize (50). According to Dr. Paul Ellwood (a leading health services researcher who first coined the term "health maintenance organization") the Minneapolis dispute portends "a critical turning point. . . . There are very few places where it's gone as far as it has here, but it's moving in that general direction everywhere" (50).

For understandable reasons, many physicians and the lay public recoil at the thought of and disparage unionized doctors. Only a decade ago unionization among physicians was unthinkable, the movement commonly considered to be working class. Aaron Nathensen, an ophthalmologist with the Minneapolis Physician's Health Plan expresses a widely held view as follows: "When I entered the practice 15 years ago, unionization was thought of as totally unprofessional, unmedical and unAmerican. But there's a growing feeling that we're losing control—losing control of patients, losing control of the health industry" (50).

Theories of Change

Some of the forces transforming medical care and the work of doctors have been described. How does one *explain* what is occurring? *Why* is it happening?

Probably the best account of the stage by stage transformation of the labor process under capitalism is provided by Karl Marx. Although not concerned with health care (51) his thesis is applicable. During the precapitalist period, small-scale independent craftsmen (solo practitioners) operated domestic workshops, sold their products on the free market, and controlled the production of goods. Over time, capitalists steered many of these skilled workers into their factories (hospitals) where they were able to continue traditional crafts semi-autonomously in exchange for wages. Eventually, the owners of production (investors) began to rationalize the production process in their factories by encouraging specialization, allocating certain tasks to cheaper workers, and enlisting managers to coordinate the increasingly complex division of labor which developed. Rationalization was completed during the final stage when production was largely performed by engineering systems and machines, with the assistance of unskilled human machine minders (52). The worker's autonomy and control over work and the workplace diminished, while the rate of exploitation increased with each successive stage in the transformation of production.

Weber's account of the same process (bureaucratization) is strikingly similar (53). According to Weber, bureaucracy is characterized by: 1) a hierarchical organization, 2) a strict chain of command from top to bottom; 3) an elaborate division of labor; 4) assigning specialized tasks to qualified individuals; 5) detailed rules and regulations governing work; 6) personnel are hired based on competence, specialized training and qualifications (as opposed to family ties, political power, or tradition); 7) a life-time career from officials is expected (54). He described how workers were increasingly "separated from ownership of the means of production or administration." Bureaucratic workers became specialists performing circumscribed duties within a hierarchical structure subject to the authority of superiors and to established rules and procedures. According to Weber, bureaucratic employees are "subject to strict and systematic discipline and control in the conduct of the office" they occupy. For Weber, the bureaucratic form of work was present not only in the area of manufacturing but also in churches, schools and government organizations. It is noteworthy that he also included hospitals: ". . . this type of bureaucracy is found in private clinics, as well as in endowed hospitals or the hospitals maintained by religious orders." While Weber viewed bureaucracy as the most rational and efficient mode of organizing work, he also saw the accompanying degradation of working life as inevitable (27, 54).

It is argued that the process outlined by Marx and Weber with respect to a different group of workers, during a different historical era, is directly applicable to the changing situation of doctors today, now that the "industrial revolution has finally caught up with medicine" (George Rosen). Whereas, generally speaking, most other workers have been quickly and easily corporatized, physicians have been able to postpone or minimize this process in their own case. Now, primarily as a result of the bureaucratization that has been forced on medical practice, physicians are being severely reduced in function and their formally self-interested activities subordinated to the requirements of the highly profitable production of medical care.

While Marx offers a most complete and theoretically well-grounded explanation of the social transformation of work (including doctoring), other commentators have described threats to professional autonomy. C. Wright Mills (55) warned of a "managerial demiurge" suffusing all the professions, including doctoring. In 1951, he wrote:

> Most professionals are now salaried employees; much professional work has become divided and standardized and fitted into the new hierarchical organizations of educated skill and service; intensive and narrow specialization has replaced self cultivation and wide knowledge; assistants and subprofessionals perform routine, although often intricate, tasks, while successful professional men become more and more the managerial type. So decisive have such shifts been, in some areas, that it is as if rationality itself had been

expropriated from the individual and been located as a new form of brain power in the ingenuous bureaucracy itself (55, p. 112).

Describing "The Physicians' Changing Hospital Role" over 20 years ago, Wilson (56) saw the growth of specialization in medicine producing diminished perceptions of doctors' expertise and a routinization of charisma. This theme was developed by Myerhoff and Larson (57) when they argued that doctors were losing their charisma and becoming culture heroes: a major difference between the charismatic and culture hero is that the former is a force for social change, while the latter is the embodiment of tradition. The culture hero appears to serve as an agent of social control (58).

During the 1970s, Haug (59, 60) detected a trend towards deprofessionalization which had its origin in the changing relations between professionals and consumers. The unquestioned trust which a client has in a professional is often thought to distinguish professionals from other "ordinary" workers. According to Hughes (61) relations with professionals are embodied in the motto *credat emptor*, "let the taker believe in us," rather than *caveat emptor*, "let the buyer beware," which exists in most other areas of commerce. According to Haug, (59, 60) consumers' unquestioning trust in professionals is diminishing as the knowledge gap between the medical profession and the consumer diminishes. She regarded the modern consumer as better educated and more likely to comprehend medical subjects, which results in a narrowing of the knowledge gap. She also viewed the computerization of knowledge as making it more accessible to all. New specialized occupations have arisen around new bodies of knowledge and skills that physicians themselves are, understandably, no longer competent to employ. These and related trends have, in her view, deprofessionalized medicine, a consequence of which is to reduce physicians to mere specialists dependent on rational, well-informed consumers who approach their service with the same skepticism (caveat emptor) that they bring to other commodity purchases. As a result of deprofessionalization, doctors are becoming just another health occupation.

Margarli Larson (62) provides a penetrating systematic description of the progressive loss of autonomy and control over work among professionals. She distinguishes three areas in which the loss of autonomy (or alienation) is occurring: economic, organizational, and technical. According to her formulation, doctors experience *economic* alienation when they become salaried employees of hospitals or when, in common with most other workers, they must place hospital interests above their own. *Organizational* alienation occurs when cost conscious hospital administrators, or managers, create systems and procedures to increase doctors' productivity and efficiency, and coordinate their work with others in the division of medical labor. *Technical* alienation refers to the process of curtailing or removing the actual decisions involved in diagnosing and treating patients. From what has been described above, it appears that doctors are experiencing loss of autonomy on all three of these dimensions, albeit at different rates depending on where they work and what specialty they practice.

IS THE PROFESSION STILL DOMINANT?

During the late 1960s, Freidson developed a view of professionalism (articulated in two influential books published in 1970, *Profession of Medicine* and *Professional Dominance*) which asserted that the medical profession (doctors) dominated other health care occupations in the division of labor. Nearly two decades after his original work and while conceding profound organizational changes and a transitional status (63, 64), he still views the medical profession as:

> Dominant in a division of labor in which other occupations were obligated to work under the supervision of physicians and take orders from, with its exclusive license to practice medicine, prescribe controlled drugs, admit patients to hospitals, and perform other critical gatekeeping functions, the medical profession is portrayed as having a monopoly over the provision of health services" (64, p. 13).

Attention is focussed here on Freidson's view of professional dominance solely because it remains the dominant view of professionalism. However, it is increasingly subject to challenge (1, 48, 52, 62, 65, 66). In one of his more recent contributions (64), Freidson tests the adequacy of alternative explanations of the changing position of doctors (especially deprofessionalization and proletarianization) against the "standard" of his own view of professional dominance.

While perhaps an adequate description of the situation of doctors back in the 1960s, much water has passed under the bridge since that time. Indeed, Freidson seems to overlook the period that has elapsed since his original important contributions. Defending his position in 1985 (64), he refers to the position that he "asserted not long ago" (1970). A great deal of change has occurred over the intervening 15 years however, some of which has been described above. There is nothing wrong with modifying, refining or evolving a position on the basis of intervening change, or new data and experience (67).

Quite apart from the fact that it is now necessarily somewhat dated, Freidson's description and approach has additional limitations:

(a) Grounded in the social constructionist perspective (68), it *raises more questions than it is able to answer*. Its ability to accommodate the macrostructural changes that have occurred in health care has been described elsewhere (48).

(b) The professional dominance perspective is a *description of an earlier state of affairs*—a snapshot of the position of doctors back in the 1960s—*not an explanation or theory* which sustains close scrutiny today. Practicing physicians familiar with Freidson's work, view it as a fairly accurate account of an earlier and much preferred golden age (69). Freidson bases his work in the past (1960's) and attempts to explain the present. The thesis of corporatization, or proletarianization, looks towards the future and argues, on the basis of what is presently occurring and has already occurred in other sectors of the economy, that this is also likely to happen to doctors in the future.

(c) Freidson (64, 70) bemoans the absence of evidence to support the rival theories of deprofessionalization and proletarianization. One should note that apart from the observational work reported in *Doctoring Together* (1975), Freidson has *never gathered or reported primary data to support his own viewpoint* (only secondary sources are ever used). Moreover, it is extraordinarily difficult to obtain information from, say, the AMA, or to gain access to medical institutions. The evidence for professional dominance is no stronger, or weaker, than that used to advance the rival theories of deprofessionalization and proletarianization. The point is we are all groping under the same light, which is often kept deliberately dim. Moreover, it is very difficult, if not inappropriate, to apply traditional positivistic techniques to the study of change of the order captured by the notion of proletarianization. Imagine asking Yeoman farmers and artisans in Elizabethan England, through questionnaires and interviews, if they appreciated the long-term consequences of the enclosure movement! Quite the same limitation is present in the modern study of the historically changing relation of doctors to the means of medical care production.

(d) Freidson (64) has often depicted competing theorists as political visionaries—their work being "too grand and sweeping to have much more than a rhetorical and possibly political value"—". . . proletarianization is not a concept as much as a slogan," and "it would be a mistake to regard such literature (proletarianization) as evidence of actual change instead of desire for change" (64). One should note that concern over the changing situation of doctors and the worrisome direction of health care is also coming from conservative circles—from Harry Schwarz, in the *New York Times* (30), who writes that, "MD's are getting a raw deal" to Arnold Relman, editor of *The New England Journal of Medicine* (18), who warns of the danger of the medical industrial complex—a work that bears a resemblance to earlier work on the medical industrial complex in *Monthly Review* in 1978 (71).

TOWARDS PROLETARIANIZATION

The healthy debate over the changing position of doctors within the rapidly changing health care system is likely to continue for some time. Along with others in Britain (72, 73), Australia (74), Canada (52, 64, 72, 75, 76), Scandinavia

(77), and the U.S. (24, 33, 43, 66, 76) we have elaborated one viewpoint (proletarianization), and have presented as much data as can be easily mustered. Although Freidson views it as "equivocation," several clarifying caveats have been deliberately introduced in an attempt to minimize misunderstandings associated with the notion of proletarianization. The theory of proletarianization seeks to explain *the process by which an occupational category is divested of control over certain prerogatives relating to the location, content, and essentiality of its task activities, thereby subordinating it to the broader requirements of production under advanced capitalism.* That is admittedly and necessarily a general definition. However, in order to provide operational specificity, and to facilitate the collection of the evidence which everyone desires, seven specific professional prerogatives which are lost or curtailed through the process of proletarianization are identified as follows: 1) *The criteria for entrance* (e.g., the credentialing system and membership requirements; 2) *The content of training* (e.g., the scope and content of the medical curriculum); 3) *Autonomy regarding the terms and content of work* (e.g., the ways in which what must be done is accomplished); 4) *The objects of labor* (e.g., commodities produced or the clients served); 5) *The tools of labor* (e.g., machinery, biotechnology, chemical apparatus); 6) *The means of labor* (e.g., hospital buildings, clinic facilities, lab services); and 7) *The amount and rate of remuneration for labor* (e.g., wage and salary levels, fee schedules) (34).

Which of these prerogatives is lost, or curtailed, through proletarianization, is associated with the relative power of any occupation and is a function of the degree of unity or cohesiveness within an occupational group, the stage of production associated with the sector in which the occupation is located, and the extent to which the tasks of the occupation can be technologized.

Table 1 lists these important prerogatives and contrasts the situation in the United States of small-scale fee-for-service doctors in the past (say, around the turn of the 20th century) with the situation of bureaucratically employed doctors today. Every single prerogative listed has changed, many occurring over the last decade. The net affect of the erosion of these prerogatives is the reduction of the members of a professional group to some common level in the service of the broader interests of capital accumulation. One of the difficulties for the proponents of proletarianization is that the process is very difficult to recognize. Indeed, it is occurring at such a level and so slowly in some cases that it may only be amenable to historical analysis some time in the future. It would be a mistake to view this as a cop out.

With regard to doctors who are increasingly subject to it, the process is masked both by their false consciousness concerning the significance of their everyday activities and also by an elitist conception of their role, so that even if recognized, doctors are quite reluctant to admit it.

While experiencing, on a daily basis, what has been described above, many physicians do not comprehend the historical magnitude of the process we have

Table 1

Some differences between the working conditions of doctors in the United States around 1900 and today

Key prerogatives of an occupational group	Physicians in small-scale, fee-for-service practice (1900)	Physicians in bureaucratic practice today (1988)
1. Criteria for entrance	Almost exclusively upper- and middle-class white male students.	Medical schools forced to recruit proportion of minorities and women.
2. Content of training	Largely dictated by the AMA through local medical societies.	Federal government and other "outside" interests affect the content and scope of curriculum through training programs, student loans, etc.
3. Autonomy over the terms and content of work	Work typically more generalized and controlled by the individual practitioner himself.	Work typically segmentalized and directed by administrators in accordance with organizational constraints (profit).
4. The object of labor	Patients usually regarded as the physician's "own patients."	Patients are technically clients, or members of the organization, whom physicians share with other specialists.
5. The tools of labor	Equipment typically owned or leased by the practitioner, and employees are hired by the practitioner.	Technology typically owned by the employing organization and operated by other bureaucratic employees.
6. The means of labor	The physical plant is typically owned or rented and operated by physicians themselves.	The physical plant typically owned by and operated in the interests of the organization (profit).
7. Remuneration for labor	The hours worked, the level of utilization, and the fees charged are pretty much determined by the individual practitioner.	Work schedule and salary level determined by organization. Sometimes limitations on "outside practice."

been describing. To capture the level of our analysis of what is occurring, it may be useful to parallel it with early industrial developments in cottage industry based Elizabethan England or, closer to home, changes in American agriculture—in both of which situations industrialization and corporatization slowly shunted aside small scale production, eroding the market situation of independent workers. A major effect of the enclosure movement in England was to slowly drive many small growers and grazers off the land into the cities where factories were developing and where they would become wage earners. These factories, in turn, eventually penetrated the countryside, destroying the yeoman-based agriculture and cottage industry in much the same way that large scale agricultural interests in the United States have been squeezing out small farmers.

It is our argument then that the industrial revolution has fully caught up with medicine. We are beginning to see the same phenomena in this sphere of work. From the preceding description, it is clear that we view the theory of proletarianization as a useful explanation of a process under development, *not* a state that has been or is just about to be achieved. The process described will most likely continue for a considerable period of time. An earlier article, on the social transformation of doctoring, was entitled, "Towards the Proletarianization of Physicians," not "The Proletarianized Physician" (34). The term "proletarianization" denoted a *process*. Use of the preposition "towards" was intended to indicate that the process was still continuing. Roemer (78) has recently offered a critique of the notion of proletarianization. He raises serious points and no doubt the thesis could benefit from some fine tuning (79). No one can have the final word on this subject, especially when we are attempting to explain a trend of which we are in the midst. Only time will tell who is most correct in assessing the historical trends discussed. Perhaps, this work should be put aside until the turn of the century. If what occurs in the next 17 years is anything like the dramatic transformation we have witnessed over the last 17 years (since 1970), doctoring then will bear little resemblance to that which is being discussed today.

REFERENCES

1. Starr, P. *The Social Transformation of American Medicine*. Basic Books, New York, 1982.
2. Light, D. W. Corporate medicine for profit. *Scien. Am.* 255: 38–54, 1986.
3. McKinlay, J. B. (ed.). *Issues in The Political Economy of Health Care*. Tavistock Publications, London, 1984.
4. Institute of Medicine. *For-Profit Enterprise in Health Care*. National Academy Press, Washington, D.C., 1986.
5. Salmon, J. W. Organizing medical care for profit. In: *Issues in the Political Economy of Health Care*, edited by John B. McKinlay, pp. 143–186. Tavistock, New York, 1984.
6. Navarro, J. *Crisis, Health, Medicine*. Tavistock Publishers, London, 1986.
7. Salmon, J. W. Profit and health care: Trends in corporatization and proprietization. *Int. J. Health Serv.* 15(3): 1985.

8. Kennedy, L. The proprietarization of voluntary hospitals. *Bull. NY Acad. Med.* 61: 81–89, 1985.
9. Eisenberg, C. It is still a privilege to be a doctor. *New Engl. J. Med.*, April 1986, p. 1114.
10. Robert Wood Johnson Foundation. *Updated Report on Access to Health Care for the American People*. Princeton, N.J., 1983.
11. U.S. Bureau of the Census. Economic characteristics of households in the United States: Fourth quarter 1983. In *Current Population Reports*, p. 70–84. Government Printing Office, Washington, D.C., 1985.
12. Farley, P. J. Who are the underinsured? *Milbank Mem. Fund Q.* 63: 476–503, 1985.
13. Iglehart, J. K. Medical care of the poor—a growing problem. *New Engl. J. Med.* 313: 59–63, 1985.
14. Sloan, F. A., Valvona, J., and Mullner, R. Identifying the issues: A statistical profile. In *Uncompensated Hospital Care: Rights and Responsibilities*, edited by F. A. Sloan, J. F. Blumstein, and J. M. Perrins, pp. 16-53. Johns Hopkins University Press, Baltimore, 1986.
15. Himmelstein, D. U., Woolhandler, S., Harnly, M., et al. Patient transfers: Medical practice as social triage. *Am. J. Pub. Health* 74: 494–496, 1984.
16. Daniels, N. Why saying no to patients in the United States is so hard. *New Engl. J. Med.* May 22: 1380–1383, 1986.
17. Cunningham, R. M., Jr. Entrepreneurialism in medicine. *New Engl. J. Med.* 309: 1313–1314, 1983.
18. Relman, A. S. The new medical industrial complex. *New Engl. J. Med.* 303: 963–970, 1980.
19. Relman, A. S. The future of medical practice. *Health Affairs* 2: 5–19, 1983.
20. Eisenberg, L., and Virchow, R. L. K. Where are you now that we need you? *Am. J. Med.* 77: 524–532, 1984.
21. Freedman, S. A. Megacorporate health care: A choice for the future. *New Engl. J. Med.* 312: 579–582, 1985.
22. Himmelstein, D. U., and Woolhandler, S. Cost without benefit: Administrative waste in U.S. health care. *New Engl. J. Med.* 314: 441–445, 1986.
23. Alford, R. *Health Care Politics: Ideological and Interest Group Barriers to Reform.* University of Chicago Press, Chicago, 1975.
24. American Medical Association. Effects of competition in medicine. *JAMA* 249: 1864–1868, 1983.
25. Braverman, H. *Labor and Monopoly Capital.* Monthly Review Press, New York, 1974.
26. Fuchs, V. *Who Shall Live?* Basic Books, New York, 1975.
27. Blackwood, S. A. At this hospital 'the captain of the ship' is dead. *RN* 42: 77–80, 1979.
28. Garvey, J. L., and Rottet, S. Expanding the hospital nursing role: An administrative account. *J. Nurs. Admin.* 12: 30–34, 1982.
29. Alspach, J., et al. Joint physician-nurse committee ensures safe transfer of tasks. *Hospitals* 56: 54-55, 1982.
30. Florida says pharmacists may prescribe drugs. *New York Times*, April 12, 1986.
31. AMA ordered to end chiropractic boycott. *Boston Globe*, August 29, 1987.
32. Plan would alter doctors' payment under Medicare. *New York Times*, November 14, 1984.
33. Friedman, E. Doctor, the patient will see you now. *Hospitals* 55: 117–118, 1981.
34. McKinlay, J. B., and Arches, J. Towards the proletarianization of physicians. *Int. J. Health Serv.* 15(2), 1985.
35. Berube, B. Italian health care: Who's minding the clinic? *Can. Med. Assoc. J.* 130: 1625–1627, 1984.
36. Anderson, A. *Health Care in the 1990's: Trends and Strategies.* American College of Hospital Administrators, Chicago, 1987.
37. Freshnock, L. J. *Physician and Public Attitudes on Health Care Issues.* AMA, Chicago, 1984.

38. Glandon, G. L., and Werner, J. L. Physicians' practice experience during the decade of the 1970's. *JAMA* 244: 2514–2518, 1980.
39. Taylor, H. *Medical Practice in the 1990's: Physicians Look at Their Changing Profession.* H. J. Kaiser Family Foundation, Menlo Park, California, 1981.
40. Iglehart, J. K. The future supply of physicians. *New Engl. J. Med.* 314: 850–854, 1986.
41. Schroeder, S. A. Western European responses to physician oversupply. *JAMA* 252: 373–384, 1984.
42. Socioeconomic Monitoring System Survey. Center for Health Policy Research. American Medical Association, Chicago, 1986.
43. Berrien, R. What future for primary care private practice? *New Engl. J. Med.* 316: 6, 334–337, 1987.
44. Friedman, E. Declaration of interdependence. *Hospitals* 57: 73–80, 1983.
45. Freidson, E. Review essay: Health factories, the new industrial sociology, 1967.
46. McCarty, D. J. Why are today's medical students choosing high-technology specialties over internal medicine? *New Engl. J. Med.* 317: 567–568, 1987.
47. *New York Times,* August 30, 1987.
48. McKinlay, J. B. The business of good doctoring or doctoring as good business: Reflections on Freidson's view of the medical game. *Int. J. Health Serv.* 8: 459–488, 1977.
49. Marcus, S. Unions for physicians. *New Engl. J. Med.* 311: 1508–1511, 1984.
50. Doctor's dilemma: Unionizing. *New York Times,* July 13, 1987.
51. Marx, K. *Capital,* Vol. I. Random House, New York, 1977.
52. Wahn, M. The Decline of Medical Dominance in Hospitals. University of Manitoba, Winnipeg (Canada), unpublished manuscript (1985).
53. Weber, M. *Economy and Society.* Bedminster Press, New York, 1968.
54. Gerth, H. and Mills, W. C. *From Max Weber.* Oxford University Press, New York, 1968.
55. Mills, C. W. *White Collar.* Oxford University Press, New York, 1953.
56. Wilson, R. The physician's changing hospital role. In *Medical Care,* edited by W. R. Scott and E. H. Volkart, pp. 408–420. Wiley and Sons, New York, 1966.
57. Myerhoff, B. G., and Larson, W. R. The doctor as cultural hero: The routinization of charisma. *Hum. Org.* 17, 1958.
58. Zola, I. K. Medicine as an institution of social control. *The Soc. Rev.* 20(4): 487–504, 1972.
59. Haug, M. Deprofessionalization: An alternate hypothesis for the future. In *Professionalization and Social Change,* edited by P. Halmos, pp. 195–211. Sociological Review Monographs (20), Keele, 1973.
60. Haug, M. The erosion of professional authority: A cross-cultural inquiry in the case of the physician. *Milbank Mem. Fund Q.* 54: 83–106, 1976.
61. Hughes, E. C. *The Sociological Eye.* Aldine, New York, 1971.
62. Larson, M. S. Proletarianization and educated labor. *Theory and Soc.* 9: 131–175, 1980.
63. Freidson, E. The medical profession in transition. In *Applications of Social Science to Clinical Medicine,* edited by L. H. Aiken and D. Mechanic, pp. 63–79. Rutgers University Press, New Brunswick, N.J., 1986.
64. Freidson, E. The reorganization of the medical profession. *Med. Care Rev.* 42: 11–33, 1985.
65. Coburn, D., Torrance, G. M., and Kaufert, J. M. Medical dominance in Canada in historical perspective: The rise and fall of medicine? *Int. J. Health Serv.* 13: 407–432, 1983.
66. Oppenheimer, M. The proletarianization of the professional. In *Professionalization and Social Change,* edited by P. J. Halmos, pp. 213–227. Sociological Review Monograph 20, Keele, 1978.
67. McKinlay, J. B. On the professional regulation of change. *Soc. Rev. Monog.* 20: 61–84, 1973.
68. Bucher, R., and Stelling, J. Characteristics of professional organizations. *J. Health Soc. Behav.* 10: 3–15, 1969.

69. Burnham, J. C. American medicine's golden age: What happened to it? *Science* 215: 1474–1479, 1982.
70. Freidson, E. The future of professionalization. In *Health and the Division of Labour*, edited by M. Stacey, et al., pp. 140–144. Croom Helm, London, 1977.
71. McKinlay, J. B. On the medical-industrial complex. *Monthly Rev.* 30(75), 1978.
72. Armstrong, D. The decline of medical hegemony: A review of government reports during the NHS. *Soc. Sci. and Med.* 10: 157–163, 1976.
73. Parry, N., and Parry, J. Professionals and unionism: Aspects of class conflict in the national health service. *Soc. Rev.* 25: 823–841, 1977.
74. Willis, E. *Medical Dominance: The Division of Labor in Australian Health Care.* Allen and Unwin, Sydney, Australia, 1983.
75. Esland, G. Professionalism. In *The Politics of Work and Occupations*, edited by G. Esland, pp. 213–250. University of Toronto Press, Toronto, 1980.
76. Crichton, A. The shift from entrepreneurial to political power in the Canadian health system. *Soc. Sci. and Med.* 10: 59–66, 1976.
77. Riska, Elianne. *Power, Politics and Health: Forces Changing American Medicine.* Societies Scientiarum Fennica, Commentationes Scientiarum Socidium 27, 1985.
78. Roemer, M. Proletarianization of physicians or organization of health services. *Int. J. Health Serv.* 16(3): 469–471, 1986.
79. McKinlay, J. B., and Arches, J. Historical changes in doctoring: A reply to Milton Roemer. *Int. J. Health Serv.* 15(3), 1986.

PART 3

International Experiences

Observers of the international health scene recognize the deteriorating conditions facing many health care systems around the globe. Desperate to address their climbing costs and organizational difficulties, and enamored by American medical advances and technology, many nations look to the United States for solutions, and many in the United States are eager to share both our dominant ideology along with, of course, sales of U.S. products and services. The fascination with health maintenance organizations, prospective payment under diagnosis-related groups, private insurance programs and the like by conservative governments abroad has ballooned. This U.S. export has not been limited just to ideas on market strategies in health care, but has also included the operations of the largest hospital and certain other proprietary providers.

In this section's first chapter, "Multinational Operations of U.S. For-Profit Hospital Chains: Trends and Implications," Berliner and Regan provide data as of 1985 on the outward extension of the American corporate health phenomenon. The presence of the U.S.-based proprietary hospital chains abroad has diminished somewhat, notably with hospital sales by National Medical Enterprises and Hospital Corporation of America. As with other U.S. multinational investment, the presence of these health care firms profoundly influence national policies toward greater privatization. As Berliner and Regan note, there has been a competitive stimulation of other private health companies in most of these nations. As mentioned here, the NME acute care facilities in England were sold to the British United Provident Association. NME still operates 18 long-term care facilities in a subsidiary, Westminster Health Care, which is building ten others (1). As in the states, these firms have diversified to reap the higher profits found in the out-of-hospital ownership area, including management services which do not require substantial capital investment under unstable conditions.

In Canada a quite different situation has been in place. Its system of health care has been shaped by political, cultural and social forces which place constraints on both corporatization and proprietarization. In certain provinces, significant changes are occurring but more to the order of what Fried, Deber, and Leatt term "deprivatization," i.e., where the scope of government involvement actually is expanding to include a more comprehensive definition of health care. These trends differ from those found in their southern neighbor, mainly due to universal coverage for the population and its behavioral impact on their health care institutions. The authors in their chapter, "Corporatization and Deprivatization of Health Services in Canada," find U.S. models, if introduced there, leading to both higher costs and lower quality.

Rayner's "Lessons from America? Commercialization and Growth of Private Medicine in Britain" provides a detailed case study of how the forty year old National Health System (NHS) is fighting off privatization attempts in the context of the challenge from both foreign and domestic firms. It is a particularly important discussion now that Prime Minister Margaret Thatcher's government seeks to spin off hospitals to be "self-governing" and to institute an insurance mechanism for the British citizenry. While Rayner argues here that private medicine has been in a state of flux and is still vulnerable to attacks from opposition parties, these new policy directions for the NHS support the point of Berliner and Regan that for-profit health care developments across the world hold many larger social implications for public policies.

REFERENCE

1. NME sells acute-care hospitals in England. *Mod. Healthcare*: 16, Dec. 9, 1988.

CHAPTER 8

Multi-national Operations of U.S. For-Profit Hospital Chains: Trends and Implications

Howard S. Berliner and Carol Regan

Over the past several years, numerous reports and studies have examined the increasing vertical and horizontal integration occurring within the American health care system (1). The diversification of major hospital chains—not-for-profit as well as proprietary—into such fields as medical supply, insurance, management information systems, long-term care, ambulatory care, managed care and home care has been well documented (2). This expansion of the domain of the hospital industry has drawn praise from a wide variety of analysts as a more efficient approach to health care delivery (3).

One element of horizontal integration that has not been previously examined is the movement of for-profit hospital chains into foreign countries, a facet of health systems growth neglected even by the recently published Institute of Medicine study on For-Profit Enterprise in Health Care (4). At the end of 1985, nine U.S.-based hospital companies operated 95 hospitals in 17 countries and one foreign hospital corporation operated 26 hospitals in the United States (see Table 1). This multi-national growth seems to be on the increase at the same time that the domestic policies of these companies seems to be in a state of flux.

The four largest U.S. for-profit hospital chains—Hospital Corporation of America (HCA), Humana, National Medical Enterprises (NME), and American Medical International (AMI)—currently operate almost 70 percent of domestic proprietary acute care beds and almost 15 percent of total domestic acute care beds (5). These same firms also operate 2/3 of the foreign hospitals owned by U.S. companies.

Our data are derived from the Annual Reports and 10K statements of the companies as well as from the Federation of American Health Systems (the

155

Table 1

Total number of hospitals operated by multi-national hospital corporations
1978–85

Company	Year				
	1978	1979	1981	1983	1985
American Medical Int. (AMI)	8	15	20	25	33
Charter Medical Corp.	—	—	1	3	4
Community Psychiatric Centers	—	—	2	3	7
Hospital Affiliates Int.	1	6	—	—	—
Hospital Corporation of America (HCA)	5	10	17	27	31
Humana Corp.	3	1	3	4	4
Hyatt Medical Enterprises[a]	2	2	—	—	1
National Medical Enterprises (NME)	—	—	3	3	5
Paracelsus[b]	—	—	—	13	26
Ramsay Hospital Corp.	—	—	—	—	9
Universal Health Services	—	—	—	—	1
Whittaker Corp.	—	—	5	8	—
TOTAL	16	34	51	86	121

[a]Hyatt Medical Enterprises became Nu-Med. Inc.
[b]Paracelsus Corporation is a West German-based corporation with hospitals in Austria, France, Switzerland, United States and West Germany.
Source: Federation of American Hospitals Directories, 1979–1986.

trade organization of the proprietary chains). It is important to note that serious discrepancies exist between these data sources which in some cases, but not all, may be due to differing reporting periods.

INTERNATIONAL INVESTMENTS OF THE LARGE
FOR-PROFIT U.S. HOSPITAL CHAINS

Basic statistics on the domestic operations of the major chains is provided in Table 2. We summarize in Tables 3 and 4 what is known about the international hospital operations of these firms. Several additional points are worth noting:

1. Hospital Corporation of America has made a major investment in Latin American hospitals. The six hospitals that it operates in Brazil are part of AMICO, an HMO with over 750,000 enrollees from 1400 employers. HCA has also recently started an insurance plan (PayMed) which covers the health care costs of Canadians traveling in the United States and it is marketing medical and psychiatric diagnostic packages in Latin and Central America to bring people to their U.S. hospitals.

Table 2

Domestic operations of four major U.S. hospital companies.

	Hospitals			
	Owned	Operated	Beds	1985 revenues
Hospital Corporation of America	190	196	68,097	4,997,978,000
National Medical Enterprises	121		13,668	3,034,000,000
Humana Corp.	87		17,696	2,875,145,000
American Medical Int.	118		18,130	2,655,800,000

Source: 1985 Annual Reports.

Table 3

Total number of hospitals operated by multi-national hospital corporations by country[a] 1978–85

	Year				
Country	1978	1979	1981	1983	1985
United Kingdom	4	8	12	24	38
Australia	1	14	10	13	23
United States	–	–	–	12	21
Switzerland	1	–	3	3	7
Brazil	–	–	7	7	7
France	3	2	2	3	5
Saudi Arabia	1	3	9	14	5
Austria	–	–	–	1	2
Canada	–	–	–	1	2
Spain	–	–	2	2	2
Singapore	2	–	–	1	2
Other—total[b]	4	8	6	5	7
TOTAL	16	34	51	86	121

[a]Only those hospitals operated by corporations outside of country of origin are listed. Numbers include those under construction.

[b]Includes countries with only one hospital. Since 1978 this has included Egypt, Panama, United Arab Emirates, Venezuela, Yemen, Greece, Mexico, Ecuador, Hong Kong, Malaysia and Guam.

Source: Federation of American Hospitals Directories, 1979–1986.

Table 4

Foreign market activity of multi-national hospital corporations outside of country of origin, 1985

Country	Company: OWNED/MANAGED										
	AMI	Charter Medical Corp.	Community Psych. Centers	HCA	Humana	NME	Nu-Med	Paracelsus	Ramsey Hospital Corp.	Universal Health Services	TOTAL
EUROPE											
Austria								2/0			2/0
England	12/0	2/0	7/0	8/1	2/0	3/0	1/0			1/0	36/1
France	0/2							3/0			3/2
Greece	0/1										0/1
Scotland	0/1										0/1
Spain	0/2										0/2
Switzerland	5/0	1/0			1/0						7/0
MIDDLE EAST											
Saudi Arabia	0/3			0/2							0/5
United Arab Emirates		0/1									0/1
AMERICAS											
Brazil	0/1			6/0							6/1
Canada	0/1			0/1							0/2
Ecuador	0/1										0/1
Mexico					1/0						1/0
Panama				1/0							1/0
United States								21/0			21/0
PACIFIC AREA											
Australia	3/0			11/1					8/0		22/1
Hong Kong									1/0		1/0
Malaysia						0/1					0/1
Singapore	1/0					1/0					2/0
TOTAL	21/12	3/1	7/0	26/5	4/0	4/1	1/0	26/0	9/0	1/0	102/19

Source: Federation of American Hospitals, 1986 Directory [6].

2. National Medical Enterprises has only recently started to exhibit an interest in international hospital ownership and it has moved to create a niche for itself in the Pacific rim. It has recently entered into an agreement with the C.Itoh Corporation of Japan to pursue potential joint ventures in the third world.
3. The Humana Corporation operates a hospital in Mexico City and has attempted to bring Central American patients to its domestic hospitals.

American Medical International has the most extensive foreign operations of the major chain companies. Its 13 hospitals in the United Kingdom (including the famous Harley Street Clinic) make it the largest independent health group in that country. It also operates psychiatric care centers, alcohol treatment centers, head injury clinic and primary care centers in the United Kingdom.

Some smaller domestic hospital chains have also invested in foreign institutions. In some cases (e.g., Community Psychiatric Centers) this has been solely specialty hospitals, whereas Ramsay Hospital Corporation operates general acute care institutions.

Very little is known about the profit dimensions of this international business. Of the four big chains, only HCA provides data specifically on its international operations in its annual report. In 1982, HCA earned $94,109,000 in gross revenues from its international ventures, but lost $1,733,000 on them. In 1983, it earned $3,939,000 in profits on over $108,000,000 in revenues. In 1984, its profits jumped to $10,045,000 on over $113,000,000 in revenues. For the first three months of 1985, HCA reported $3,091,000 in profits on $26,430,000 in revenues from its international operations. Given the size of HCA, these profits contribute only a marginal amount to their aggregate bottom line. Nevertheless the steady increase in both revenues and profits is suggestive that growth will continue in this sphere. It should be noted that we cannot determine from the data provided to what extent overhead and development costs have been loaded onto the international units and thus cannot assess the true nature of the profit picture.

ANALYSIS

The penetration of international markets by American proprietary hospital chains is a small but growing movement. For many of the chains, contracts for building and later operating hospitals, particularly in the Middle East, were the starting point for their international operations.

The movement from management contracts to hospital ownership was spurred on by several common factors based on the geographic location, nature of the health system, and the economy of the area involved.

Middle East

With the rapid growth of the oil economies of the Middle East in the early 1970s, some "petro-dollars" were invested in building up the infrastructure of the oil-producing countries in an effort to improve the standard of living for the population. Since these countries had little experience with modern hospitals and medical care, they awarded construction contracts to get the institutions built and management contracts to operate the facilities once they were erected. Many of these contracts were given to American proprietary hospital companies.

As the Middle Eastern countries generated their own cadres of hospital managers (many trained in U.S. hospital administration programs), the services of the contractors were no longer necessary. Political instability in that region has led to the abrogation of contracts with U.S. firms by countries no longer friendly (e.g., Iran) and the recent declines in oil revenues has led to the termination of hospital management contracts for lack of funds. As Table 4 documents, the Middle East is no longer a major source of income for American hospital firms. Nevertheless, the experience that the companies acquired in building and managing hospitals in foreign countries was certainly a positive incentive to expand such operations.

Western Europe

The majority of international investment by U.S. hospital chains has been in Western Europe, largely in England. The major factors leading to hospital ownership and construction in England (and these are largely true for other European countries as well) are: 1) political receptivity to foreign capital; 2) good growth potential; 3) lack of indigenous competition; 4) ability to establish a distinct "niche."

Political Receptivity

In Britain, the conservative government of Margaret Thatcher has been eager to introduce a private sector into the country to compete with the National Health Service, as part of its attempt to reprivatize the domestic economy. The Thatcher administration was highly receptive to American hospital firms for they were seen both as an alternative to the NHS and as a source of new health care capital and services (7). Many of the American-owned hospitals are newly constructed and the vast majority of the others have been extensively renovated and equipped. Thus, the health system has been modernized without the need to invest scarce domestic capital on the National Health Service.

Growth Potential

An executive of AMI noted in 1981: "In every country where we have studied national health programs (and I think we have studied them all), we have found that those programs have created their own problems as populations grew. The national health system became strained and overburdened as citizens developed a higher sense of entitlement to more advanced health care. The way to relieve that strain is to encourage the emergence of a strong private health system" (8). Because the Western European countries have some form of universal health insurance or health service, the American companies found no indigent care problem to arouse domestic opposition. The proprietary chain hospitals were seen as responding to the growing use of private health insurance as an executive level perquisite in many of the European countries with a national health service. A vicious cycle was generated in which the growth of private insurance spurred the introduction of private hospitals which ignited further growth of private insurance. The American hospitals both created and satisfied the demand for an alternative health system to the National Health Service (9).

Lack of Indigenous Competition

Because Britain has had a National Health Service for almost 40 years, its hospitals were unprepared to meet the challenge of American firms introducing new facilities with modern equipment and using high-powered marketing techniques and management styles unknown in the British health sector. Reports in the British and international press about the success of the American hospital corporations in the United States, along with the European interest in all things American, gave them a certain cachet among sectors of the population with private insurance or the income to allow their use. Moreover, the U.S. hospital companies were flush with cash and riding high on Wall Street giving them a distinct advantage over potential local competitors. To date, there is only one non-American proprietary hospital firm, The West Germany-based Paracelsus Corporation, and all of its hospitals are located in the United States.

Nichemanship

The American hospital chains have been able to establish a distinct niche within the European market. In some cases, as in England, they have been able to develop several discrete niches—high technology services, high amenity hospitals, and novelty services.

One of the major weaknesses of the National Health Service has been the ability to obtain quick and elective access to high technology services. The ability of NHS patients to schedule elective surgery or to obtain such procedures and operations as CAT scans and other diagnostic imaging, total hip replacement, lithotripsy, cardiac bypass surgery, etc. has been extremely constrained through rationing and by financial factors. Cutbacks in the NHS budget and the general domestic economic crisis in the United Kingdom either delayed or substantially reduced the acquisition and availability of new advances in medical technology. While the proprietary chain hospitals in the United States for the most part do not provide these services, they became major purveyors of high tech medicine in the United Kingdom.

Because of its centrality to world commerce, a large volume of international business is conducted in England and many foreign businesspeople receive their health care while in Britain. Wealthy foreigners who desire luxury accommodations and amenities and personalized services have long been a factor in British health care. The American chain hospitals had little trouble establishing or buying and renovating existing ultra-luxury hospitals to cater to this clientele.

The American firms also began to promote the utilization of generally low-tech but largely novelty services in the U.K. market—alcohol and drug abuse centers, bulimia and anorexia nervosa clinics, rehabilitation and sports medicine facilities, women's health care clinics, reconstructive surgery centers, *in-vitro* fertilization programs, etc. These programs, which have a growing popularity in the United States have also found a receptive audience in the United Kingdom. Here again, the American companies faced no competition and appealed to an exclusive population of private insurance holders.

PACIFIC AREA

The movement of the American chain hospitals into the Pacific area reflects the growing economic strength of that region as well as its increasing importance in world commerce and manufacture. The relatively recent growth of an affluent population able to support a domestic tertiary care hospital, rather than require travel to Britain or the United States, is the major reason that the chains have become involved. Growth has been particularly strong in areas with expanding wealth or international tourism and commerce (e.g., Singapore and Malaysia). The reasons for the substantial movement into Australia are closely related to the reasons for investment in Western Europe presented above.

The Americas

There are three major reasons for locating hospitals in Central and Latin America: 1) to provide services to the wealthy elite; 2) to establish facilities for the referral of patients to the domestic hospitals of the chain; 3) the efforts of the international banking and finance community to expand the private sector in health services delivery in countries with large western-bloc loans.

Many of the U.S. chains which have facilities in the Southeast and Southwest of the United States have established ventures to woo wealthy Latin and Central Americans to their U.S. hospitals through packages which combine family vacations with medical care. The establishment of a facility in one of the countries may also serve to give the American hospital a brand name recognition with the local elite.

IMPLICATIONS

The foreign operations of the American chain hospitals do not constitute a significant challenge to the health systems of the countries in which they operate. The penetration of the United Kingdom is the greatest, but even in that country the American firms represent less than 5 percent of total acute care beds. Despite this limited direct impact, the firms have a much greater indirect effect by providing alternatives to socialized medical systems and by diverting potential income-generating patients away from NHS institutions. Because the British National Health Service is the most directly affected by American hospital chains, the discussion of the implications of this phenomenon will be centered around it.

There are, of course, two ways of viewing the impact of the growth of private medicine in countries with a national health system: 1) they serve to reduce consumer pressure on the system by siphoning off a portion of the unmet demand—by shortening the waiting lists through people opting out of the system; 2) they serve to deprive the system of the political and economic clout of those people who, rather than fight for more resources being given to the NHS, opt out of the system entirely. To some extent, both are true.

The ideological challenge that private medicine poses for national health systems is a significant one. Throughout Western Europe the role of private medicine is being extensively debated. Professional and popular dissatisfaction with publicly provided care has been exacerbated by the example of modern, high tech, private hospitals. While national health systems still retain the overwhelming support of the population, the appeal of the private sector cannot be denied. As publicly run hospital care is retrenched for financial reasons, the private sector serves as both a reason for reduction in publicly provided services and an increasingly attractive replacement.

The export of American management techniques and health system concepts is another implication of the growth of the hospital chains. While the United States has chosen to reject such European concepts as regionalization of health services and universal health insurance coverage, we are presently exporting new techniques of cost-accounting, efficient management and health systems design. Recently, for example, considerable controversy was generated in Britain by the proposal from Alain Enthoven to create internal markets within the NHS to improve efficiency and to modernize service delivery through the use of HMOs

(10). There has also been discussion of DRG type case reimbursement systems in a number of European countries.

As noted above, private hospitals have grown in Europe in tandem with private insurance. The growth of private insurance not only ensures more business for the hospitals, but it also fragments popular support for the NHS and other similar national health systems by providing alternative structures for those able to buy their way out and by creating the impression, if not the reality, of a two-class system of care. If national health systems become perceived as systems for the poor alone, rather than as truly national systems, the demands they will be able to make on the national budget will be substantially diminished.

Raynor and colleagues argue that a major impact of the growth of private hospitals in the United Kingdom has been the draining away of staff (nurses, physicians, allied workers) who were trained at public expense. This not only lowers the costs of the private hospitals (but not their charges), but also leads to staff shortages in public facilities (11). To the extent that physicians can earn substantially higher incomes from the private facilities than they can from their NHS work, their commitment to the public sector may wane and their public patients may suffer inattention.

The success of the American private hospitals in the United Kingdom, and elsewhere, has led to the emergence of other private hospital companies, giving further impetus to privatization. Beyond this, the rapid growth of private corporations which contract-out specific hospital services—laundry, food service, laboratory services, cleaning, etc.—also has an impact on the development of private hospitals and on the remaining publicly supported system. Contractors such as Pritchards and the Hawley Group, for example, are themselves major transnational corporations. The effects of contracting-out of service work on employment, quality of care, and actual cost saving has been the subject of much recent debate and discussion (12).

A final implication of the growth of private hospital corporations is in the ability to provide American style medicine in a European location and a European price. Hospital care in the United Kingdom, for example, is easily 1/3 or 1/4 the price for the same care in the United States. Wealthy foreigners who might have come to the United States to get their tech care can now get the same care at virtually bargain basement rates. Moreover, the level of service and amenity in European private hospitals is far higher than that offered in America.

CONCLUSIONS

The movement of American proprietary hospital firms abroad is not a major shift in policy nor is it a major event *per se*. It is however, a potentially important development in terms of its effect on public medical care programs and perhaps more important for its effects on promoting the privatization of health care in other countries (13).

This movement raises many questions which cannot be answered or even appropriately addressed at this time due to lack of data about the extent of corporate penetration and its costs and profits. A number of labor unions, along with international labor federations, have been active in trying to gather such data, but to date little has been published (14). It is possible that learning more about the international operations of the proprietary firms will yield more insight into their domestic operations and strategies as well.

Among the questions that must be answered are the following:

- Are profits being drained from the United States to support the international operations; and vice versa?
- Is the movement described in this chapter the full extent of involvement or is the spread of multi-national health care still in its nascent stages?
- What is the effect of transnational provision of health care on the quality and standards of care provided and what is its impact on labor practices regarding health care workers?
- What are the impacts on the host country of the development of transnational chains?
- Can publicly run health systems compete with the private chains?

REFERENCES

1. Brown, M. and McCool, B. P. Vertical integration: Exploration of a popular strategic concept. *Health Care Man. Rev.* 11(4): 7–19, 1986.
2. Goldsmith, J. C. The healthcare market: Can hospitals survive? *Harvard Bus. Rev.*: 100–112, Sept.–Oct. 1980.
3. The New Entrepreneurialism in Health Care. 1984 Annual Health Conference. *Bull. N.Y. Acad. Med.* 61(1): 1985, 1985.
4. Institute of Medicine. *For-Profit Enterprise in Health Care.* National Academy Press, Washington, D.C., 1986.
5. Light, D. W. Corporate medicine for profit. *Scien. Am.* 255(6): 38–45, 1986.
6. *Federation of American Hospitals: 1985 Directory of Investor-Owned Hospitals.* FAH, Little Rock, 1986.
7. Raynor, G. Lessons from America: Commercialism and the growth of private medicine in Britain. *Int. J. Health Serv.* 17(2): 197–216, 1987.
8. Diener, R. *Federation of American Hospitals Review*, July–August, 1981.
9. Borrus, A. U.S. hospital chains move in on socialized medicine. *Bus. Week*, October 21, 1985, p. 56.
10. Enthoven, A. C. Reflections on Management of the National Health Service. Occasional Papers #5. Nuffield Provincial Hospitals Trust, London, 1985.
11. Raynor, G, Griffith, B., and Mohan, J. *Commercial Medicine in London.* Greater London Council, London, 1985.
12. *Contracting Out and Privatisation of NHS Services.* Confederation of Health Service Employees, Surrey, England, January, 1984.
13. Britain's Hospitals: A suitable case for treatment. *The Economist*, December 6, 1986, pp. 69–74.
14. International Healthcare Union Conference on Privatization. Service Employees International Union, Washington, D.C., April, 1986.

CHAPTER 9

Corporatization and Deprivatization of Health Services in Canada

Bruce J. Fried, Raisa B. Deber, and Peggy Leatt

National health insurance, the pride of Canadian social policy, has come under increasing scrutiny as costs increase. We here examine two private-sector borrowings—corporatization and privatization—and analyze the implications of current forces and trends for the manner in which hospitals and other health services organizations are structured and financed. Specifically, we suggest that the political economy of Canada has shaped the current health services system, and that these forces continue to place constraints on substantive changes within that system. We note the influence of a countervailing trend which we term "deprivatization," the extension of the scope of government involvement in financing and regulating health services.

THE RATIONALE FOR CORPORATIZATION AND PRIVATIZATION

In discussing possible changes in the Canadian health services system, it is important to define our terms. We use *corporatization* to mean an organizational restructuring in the direction of an organizational form typically found in industrial corporations, characterized by clearly articulated corporate objectives and a division between corporate and operational levels. The role of corporate staff is to advise and counsel the operational portions of the organization and to provide overall coordination. Corporate structure may also involve the presence on the board of "inside" executives, the compensation of board members, and changes in title and function of the top executives (1, 2). In the health care sector, corporate organization is most evident in the emergence of both multi-institutional systems and highly diversified corporate entities, which

167

may include both health and non-health divisions. As described below, Canadian hospitals have become increasingly corporatized without losing their non-for-profit status.

We use *privatization* to refer to the involvement of nongovernment actors (and dollars) in funding and managing health care services. In the health care sector, this category would include private philanthropy, the provision of services by noninsured professional and institutional providers, and entry into the system by private insurers. Most arguments in favor of privatization are rooted in the same ideological premises (3, 4). Most also begin with the proposition that government-funded programs are inefficient, and that the private sector, because of its historical experience with "bottom lines," is better able to contain costs. Economic theory implies that competition breeds efficiency, and that privatization enables government to deregulate, with order presumably being kept by the "invisible hand."

Another rationale for private sector involvement, especially for providers, is the fear of restrictions on the services the public is willing to pay for, and the resulting desire for an escape hatch. As Evans (5) has noted, one person's health care costs are another's health care incomes. Privatization thus represents an additional source of money, within a publicly-financed system, when public willingness to pay has reached its limits.

Advocates of privatization attack the premise that government is responsible for the individual's health or personal well-being and pay little attention to values such as "equity" or "distribution." They have not tended to focus on comprehensiveness of health insurance or oppose multi-tiered systems of care. At present, the furthest such arguments have been taken is a rejection of "Cadillac care" for all at public expense; the Reagan revolution attacks on entitlements have been repulsed north of the border. There are few proponents in Canada of a completely competitive system.

DE-PRIVATIZATION

Theories of incrementalism predict that it is very difficult to eliminate services once they have been provided (6). Particularly since health care is seen by Canadian policy makers as a right (7), and health programs are enormously popular, there is an impetus to increase the range of services funded by provincial health insurance plans. Acceptance of the well known WHO definition of health as encompassing "a state of complete physical, mental and social well being and not merely the absence of disease or infirmity" (8) has implications for the scope of health services to be made available at public expense. Canada has at least formally accepted this broader definition of health as extending beyond health services; the Canadian federal government, in the Lalonde Report, introduced the Health Field Concept as incorporating human biology, environment, lifestyle, and health care organization (9) and has continued to pay at least lip service to the importance of health promotion and "healthy public policy" (10). Governments face frequent demands to provide care for the "total human." A commendable desire to make health services available in the home, at presumably lower cost, thus evolves from short-term nursing (e.g., changing dressings) for acute conditions, through chronic care, adding physiotherapy, social work and, finally, homemaking and similar social supports, all at public expense. Drug plans are expanding, dental care is suggested, foot care is advocated, assistive devices are covered, and the range of public involvement steadily expands. The Ontario government is currently under enormous pressure to incorporate formerly private nursing homes into its continuum of care. This expansion of government's role into what was previously a private or community responsibility is what we have termed *deprivatization*. It is an important element in Canada's health services system, and is likely to have a major impact on cost projections.

AN OVERVIEW OF THE CANADIAN HEALTH SERVICES SYSTEM

Canada is the second largest country in the world, but its population is only 26 million, most of it concentrated in urban centers within 150 km of the United States border. Politically, Canada is a loose confederation of 10 provinces and two (virtually unpopulated) northern territories. The political system is modelled on British parliamentary tradition, with considerable power resting with the executive. The division of powers between federal (national) and provincial (state) levels of government was specified in the Canadian constitution; attempting to accommodate changing times to this rather rigid document has allowed federal-provincial relations to become a national obsession. Health care, however, is clearly a provincial responsibility, and Canada accordingly does not have a "national health care system." The disparities between provincial wealth involved the federal government in financing and influencing the provincial health plans, but management issues are clearly the responsibility of provincial governments.

Because Canada and the United States have similar demographic profiles, disease patterns, language, and culture, the last two decades have seen a number of comparisons between the two health care systems (3, 4, 11-13). The systems, however, are markedly different, and are becoming more so. Among the differences in their current situations are:

1. a volume driven competitive system in the United States compared with a government funded and regulated system in Canada;
2. a mixed prospective-payment DRG-based and per diem system for funding hospitals in the United States, compared with a prospective global budgeting formula in most Canadian provinces;

3. increasingly low hospital occupancy rates in many U.S. hospitals, compared with near 100 percent occupancy rates in most Canadian hospitals;
4. universal government-run health insurance in Canada, covering the entire population;
5. Canadian public acceptance, and even active encouragement, of government involvement in the economy and public programs;
6. Canadian requirements for meeting the national standards of universality, public administration, comprehensiveness, and portability specified in the Canada Health Act;
7. a single-party payer (government) in Canada, with greater efficiencies in administration costs. Canada has spent just over 8 percent of GNP to achieve better health status results than the United States, with expenditures of over 10 percent of a larger base.

The roles of the business community and organized labor in shaping health policy also differ markedly. In the United States, the business community, because of its role as the major private purchaser of health care, has been referred to as the "fourth party" (14). In Canada, government is by far the largest purchaser of health and physician services, and hospital budgets are almost completely funded through the provincial health insurance plans.

THE DEVELOPMENT OF THE CANADIAN HEALTH CARE SYSTEM

At the core of Canadian health services is a series of provincially-run insurance plans, which use public funds to finance and regulate, but not to manage, health services. Canada's system is thus quite distinct from a British-style national health service. The federal government has only limited powers over health care (in such areas of national interest as quarantine of immigrants; food and drug safety; and services for the north, natives, and the armed forces), although, through its spending power, it could (and did) assume a role in encouraging financing and setting the terms and conditions of provincial health insurance plans (15-18).

Particularly in contrast with the United States, the Canadian political and cultural environment has traditionally been not only accepting, but actively encouraging, of government involvement in the economy and public programs (19-21). In addition, a parliamentary system provides fewer "blocking points;" once a government is determined to introduce a policy, it is difficult for interest groups to stop or alter it (22). Analysis of Canadian health policy is thus more a function of institutional factors (including the relationships between national and sub-national units of government) than of interest group politics, particularly given the absence of federal constitutional authority over this policy area.

Each level of government in Canada has traditionally been jealous of its prerogatives, and "federal-provincial relations" has been a Canadian obsession.

The evolution from 1919, when health insurance was first proposed, has been well-described elsewhere (15-18, 23, 24). The earliest attempts to bring in a national plan were defeated by the provinces' opposition to federal incursions into their jurisdiction. The desire for availability of a uniform level of coverage was thus constrained by both the absence of federal constitutional authority, and the existence of economic disparities among regions, preventing the provinces from progressing without federal aid. Accordingly, programs were introduced piecemeal and incrementally. In the 1950s, the federal government helped with hospital building costs. It next introduced a program that would cost-share hospital-based services with provinces that chose to participate (the Hospital Insurance and Diagnostic Services Act in 1957); within four years, all provinces had chosen to join the program. In 1968, the Medical Care Act covered physician services; all provinces were included by 1971. These initiatives largely removed financial barriers to care, but did not change the basic structure of the health care delivery system. Instead, they entrenched the most costly forms of treatment (17), and have hindered efforts to introduce more cost-effective services (such as nurse practitioners). With respect to the privatization debate, however, the Canadian system now presents formidable barriers to the importation of a class-based model of health services delivery and the sorts of skimming behavior said to be characteristic of U.S. corporate chains (25-31).

To qualify for Federal cost-sharing, provincial health insurance programs were and are required to fulfill four conditions:

1. *universal* coverage on uniform terms and conditions "that does not impede, or preclude, either directly or indirectly whether by charges made to insured persons or otherwise, reasonable *access* to insured services by insured persons" (95 percent of the population, without exclusions, had to be covered within two years of provincial adoption of the plan; the Canada Health Act has expanded this to 100 percent coverage of residents);
2. *portability* of benefits from province to province;
3. *comprehensive* insurance for all medically necessary services; and
4. a *publicly administered* non-profit program.

Because of the structure of the cost-sharing formula, the Federal government had no control over the total amounts expended by the provinces, and the provinces had little flexibility in providing alternative forms of services. After considerable negotiation, Bill C-37 (Federal-Provincial Fiscal Arrangements and Established Programs Financing Act), covering health and post-secondary education (another cost-shared provincial responsibility) was passed in 1977. The new formula replaced cost-sharing with a combination of block-funding and tax points. Federal contributions for health and post-secondary education were no longer categorically earmarked, but became part of general revenues; these programs thus had to compete with other provincial priorities. The Canada Health Act (1984) reaffirmed the terms and conditions under which the provincial governments could receive federal contributions, and also instituted financial penalties for provinces that permitted physician extra-billing or hospital user charges. Following the (at times acrimonious) disputes within each province, including a physicians' strike in Ontario, all provinces have now complied with the federal terms (32).

Health care costs have been affected in a number of ways by the evolution of the health services system. In general, expenditures on health care rose rapidly, both in dollar terms and as a percentage of national expenditure, between 1946 and 1971 in both Canada and the United States, with both nations spending similar proportions of national income on health care. Personal health care costs—hospitals, physician and dental services, and prescribed drugs—rose from 300 million dollars (2.5 percent of GNP) in 1946 to 935 (2.9 percent) in 1956, and, with the introduction of hospital insurance, to 2.7 billion (4.3 percent) in 1966 and 5.1 billion (5.4 percent) in 1971. Total health care costs rose from 6.0 percent of GNP in 1961 to 7.5 percent in 1971; actual expenditures rose from 2.4 billion to 7.1 billion dollars (5). Complete nation-wide public coverage, however, stabilized health care expenditures at a roughly consistent proportion of national income. In contrast to the experience of the United States, where costs continued to increase as a proportion of gross national product, Canada's national health care expenditures fluctuated around 7.5 percent between 1971 and 1981, although total spending, reflecting the inflation of that period, showed what looked like a dramatic increase (from 2.6 billion in 1971 to 7.1 billion a decade later). This stability may or may not be persisting; the recent increase in health care costs to 8.4 percent of GNP in 1982 may be largely related to the slow growth of the economy (the denominator) rather than to out-of-control health care spending (the numerator). The public sector component of health care, however, has changed dramatically, rising from 43 percent of health care costs in 1960, to about 75 percent in 1975, and maintaining that level into the 1980s (5). As Detsky, et al. (33) have shown, hospital cost containment efforts during this period were quite effective, largely because government retained regulatory levers by which overall spending could be controlled. Nonetheless, the movement of health care spending into the public purse made it more visible, and a more direct target for cost control efforts (16).

THE PUBLIC/PRIVATE MIX IN CANADIAN HEALTH SERVICES

As Evans (5) has noted, the for-profit sector of health services is greatly limited in Canada, accounting for a mere 15 percent of health care expenditures, primarily for nursing home care, laboratories, and health care products (drugs and supplies, medical equipment, eyeglasses, and prostheses). Almost all hospitals are publicly owned, governed by community boards, and funded by a "single-party" payer—the provincial governments. Hospitals are highly regulated by the provincial government, and treatment of capital costs varies from province to province. For example, the precise terms of board structure in a given hospital are determined by the guidelines in that province's Public Hospitals Act. Changes in services offered often must be approved by provincial ministries of health. Certain special hospitals, most notably psychiatric hospitals, have been directly administered by the province, although there is a trend towards phasing out direct management and giving such hospitals local community boards. Most other community-based health services, including public health, ambulatory care, home care, and many institutional care facilities are included in the public sector, although, depending on the province, they may be regulated and funded through ministries of health, ministries of community and social services, or combinations thereof. A small but growing segment, ambulatory care and special purpose clinics (e.g., abortion, day surgery), represent a challenge to government policy. To date, they have usually been funded through the volume-driven fee-for-service portions of provincial health insurance plans, which rarely cover their capital and facility management costs. As another illustration of deprivatization, governments have recently indicated some desire to place them under global budgets.

Since the introduction of the national health insurance scheme in 1967, investor-owned hospitals have, in general, been prohibited, and private insurance companies restricted to the fringe markets (e.g., private and semi-private room supplements, dental plans, drug plans, and supplementary out-of-Canada coverage, especially for travel to the United States). Some provincial governments have also chosen to offer extended coverage, often to target groups (such as the elderly or the poor) for such services as prescription drugs, dental services, or long-term care. There has also been a growth in private insurance coverage for these services (5). Unlike their U.S. counterparts, employers do not directly pay health care costs for other than these "expanded" programs, except through taxes and premiums, and therefore have had little reason to push for changes in hospital or medical services delivery, and little desire to play such a role (34). Co-insurance and deductibles for insured medical services are rare (and discouraged by the Canada Health Act penalties). Pre-paid HMO-type organizations account for a very small fraction of health services.

Until recently, physicians were clearly on the private side of the health care system, even though their practices were essentially entrepreneurial firms funded by provincial governments. Most physicians are reimbursed on a fee-for-service basis, the payments based on fee schedules usually negotiated between the provincial medical associations and the provincial governments. Although most have accepted "full assignment," until recently, physicians retained the theoretical right to bill patients above and beyond the amount specified by the plan; these payments, called extra-billing, were out-of-pocket costs to patients and could not be covered by private insurance. The extent of this practice, although small in aggregate terms, varied widely by geographic region and medical specialty (32). As provinces try to control and be accountable for costs, there are strong indications that physicians are becoming increasingly "de-privatized;" provincial governments have attempted to control physician numbers, distribution, and fee levels, as well as the terms on which physicians can practice outside the provincial insurance plans. In 1986, the Canadian Supreme Court upheld the controversial British Columbia law allowing the government to restrict issuance of billing numbers in geographic areas of physician over-supply (35, 36). This ruling represents a major erosion of physician autonomy, and may have significant implications for future attempts by other provinces to control costs by restricting physicians' freedom to set up practice. Similar attempts to control physician costs are detectable in most Canadian provinces.

The end of extra-billing, assured by the passage of the Canada Health Act in 1984, has contributed to the deprivatization of physicians' practices. Although provinces vary in their interpretation of the ban, "private" contributions to physicians' incomes are now highly restricted. For example, Ontario's ban on extra-billing, which became law in 1986, forces even physicians who have opted out of the system entirely to charge no more than the Ontario Health Insurance Plan fee schedule amount, but allows their patients to be reimbursed directly by the government plan; Ontario patients are thus insulated from net out-of-pocket costs. Quebec, on the other hand, allows opted-out physicians to charge patients any fee they wish, but does not permit reimbursement from the plan; opting-out is thus a theoretically permissible, but economically unfeasible option for Quebec physicians. Two key features of privatization—the ability for hospitals to charge user fees, and the right of physicians to extra-bill—now incur financial penalties under the terms of the Canada Health Act and have been theoretically eliminated. Nonetheless, the sorts of controls over physicians' clinical practice characteristic of corporate medicine (37) are not a current feature of the Canadian health care scene.

Physicians are not happy with this trend towards deprivatization of their practice, and have increasingly advocated privatization as a perceived way of eliminating government regulation. There has been an ironic contrast between physicians' tendency to view themselves as private entrepreneurs and the reality of their government-supported practices (38, 39).

The provincial health insurance systems, by legislation, are publicly funded and administered. Even here, where the law is presumably unambiguous, there have been (unsuccessful) proposals by the right wing fringe to turn over certain functions of the health insurance system to private management. Comparisons between the low administrative costs characteristic of the Canadian system and the higher costs incurred in the United States, however, have diminished enthusiasm for such "reforms," and it is unlikely that they will be given much attention.

Also on the private side of the system are the producers and suppliers of drugs, medical equipment, and technology and, to a limited extent, the private health insurance companies that primarily provide supplemental benefits. To the extent that such industries deal primarily with government as a "guaranteed payer," deprivatization of their activities should increase. Nursing homes are in transition; once private, they are now subsidized by government and coming under increasing regulatory control. Although some representatives of insurance companies and the nursing home industry favor private sector involvement, most are instead clamoring for more public funds.

Canada's incremental journey to national health insurance led to the view that health care was a public service, or even a human "right" (7), and to a public service orientation among hospital boards and managers that was seemingly unconcerned with issues of efficiency. There was little incentive, for example, for a hospital to stay within its budget if the provincial government routinely absorbed both profits and losses. It is only in the last five years that hospitals have experienced significant pressures to be more "business-like" and to adopt many of the technologies and organizational arrangements characteristic of the private sector. The enormous popularity of health care has often made it feasible for hospitals to resist budgetary constraints through political appeals (e.g., running of deficits knowing that the government would be unable to resist pressures to pick them up). It is important to realize, however, that the existence of prospective global budgets theoretically gave provincial governments direct cost-control, without the necessity of the convoluted regulatory approaches required in the U.S. system. As noted earlier, Ontario has been very successful in achieving cost control; although improvement is always desirable, we are beginning with a reasonably efficient base.

THE LIMITS OF BUSINESS-LIKE APPROACHES TO HEALTH CARE

Although good management of human and fiscal resources is a necessary objective of any public or private organization, many recent pronouncements have tended to adopt a narrower definition, whereby the well-managed institution is one with the most favorable financial bottom line, regardless of other goals and values. It is this perspective that we have termed "business-like approaches." Although superficially appealing to many, we argue that this ideology has only limited applicability to health systems. As one illustration, in any calculation of economic effectiveness, one must decide *whose* bottom line will be evaluated. One can, for example, analyze from the viewpoint of the patient, the provider, the hospital, the insurer, the government, or society as a whole (40). To the extent that costs are shifted, the optimal outcome will differ. As Evans noted:

> In the United States the client for managerial services is the hospital board, and its objectives are increased revenues, growth of operations, or in some cases sheer survival. "Successful" management has meant primarily elimination of deficits, and increases in occupancy and throughput. These have been achieved by better control of bad debts, improved "marketing" of the hospital

in the community, and expansion of high mark-up ancillary services. But of course all such activities, while they improve the financial position of the individual hospital, *add* to the costs of hospital care as experienced by the community as a whole. No provincial reimbursing agency in its right mind would pay a private team for aggravating its problems (5).

The increase in revenue (from the viewpoint of the administrator) must equal the increase in expenditures (from the viewpoint of those paying for the health services); a government guarantee that bills will be paid becomes a prescription for increased costs. There is also little guarantee that the most marketable services are those most "needed." As one example, there are far more healthy people than sick ones, and thus a potential mass market in offering lifestyle services such as nutrition and fitness to basically healthy people. Duplication of services should be encouraged by bottom line-oriented administrators as long as the services can be marketed; private companies should not concern themselves with the benefit of the competition.

Serious attention to the bottom line would dictate practices contrary to both overall cost control and quality of care. In Canada, the insurer is the government and, idealistically, should also take into account the best interests of society. Consider what the response of a stereotypical "good businessman" would be to the U.S. DRG reimbursement system. These implications would extend far beyond the well-publicized tendency for private U.S. hospitals to turn away patients with insufficient insurance coverage (28). Any payment system generates incentives to act in particular ways. The old system paid hospitals on a *per diem* basis; our "good businessman" would respond to the incentives to over-service patients. The DRG method pays institutions a fixed rate based on diagnosis. Although no two patients will cost the hospital exactly the same amount, the designers of the system evidently assumed that high and low cost patients would balance each other. What new strategies could be followed to maximize hospital revenues under this system? Since no extra payment will be received, there is a clear incentive to discharge patients early, and preliminary data suggest that length of stay has indeed decreased. Readmission can be profitable as long as a new billing can be made; effectively used, the same patient can generate repeated visits (and accompanying revenue). If any non-reimbursable complications develop, the patient should be transferred to a new institution (which can then collect for the new DRG). Hospitals should invest in management information systems to analyze patient and disease characteristics, and then admit only the low-cost, high-profit patients in a diagnostic category. The high-cost ones can be left for the teaching and public hospitals; if those hospitals get into financial trouble, this is a problem for others. Physicians dealing with expensive patients should be denied hospital privileges, and patients with expensive diseases should be avoided. A profit-maximizing hospital should do the minimum possible for each patient, subject only to the limitations of potential lawsuits or loss of market share. If a new treatment is discovered for a formerly fatal disease, one should not use it unless it is cost-saving—dead patients are often more profitable, particularly if they die quickly (41).

If this portrait is disquieting, perhaps the business analogy has only limited usefulness. In Canada, there has been a societal consensus that health care should be received on the basis of need. In effect, Canadians have viewed health as a public good rather than as an individual consumer good. It is believed unethical to give unnecessary treatment just because the patient can afford to pay for it, and equally unethical to withhold treatment just because the patient cannot afford to pay. Under such circumstances, how reliable a guide can traditional economics be? As long as society will guarantee payment for "needed" services, people cannot be priced out of the market. Supply and demand is thus irrelevant as a means of controlling the volume of services provided. A "free market" guarantees only that no ceiling on prices exists. Efforts to market services guarantee only increased health care costs. Efforts to cut services become political hot potatoes (16, 42). A pure business ideology, however superficially appealing, appears to fit poorly with a well running health care system, a view that Canada's leading health economists have vigorously upheld (3, 5).

THE CORPORATIZATION/PRIVATIZATION DEBATE IN CANADA

The debate over corporatization and privatization of health services in Canada has taken a form distinct from that occurring elsewhere. In the U.S. context, privatization implies ownership by individual investors, who are primarily profit-oriented. The growth of for-profit medicine in the United States has been accompanied by a search for foreign markets, and Canada has certainly been viewed as an opportunity for expansion. In addition, Canadian companies have looked south for lessons. The public insurance system has presented a formidable barrier to such activities. However, the expansion in for-profit corporate chains has been visible among the noninsured services (e.g., dental clinics, nursing homes), as well as in the area of private laboratories. In Canada, there is little likelihood that hospitals will move or be permitted to move in the direction of actual private ownership, although there is in some jurisdictions constrained encouragement of public sector organizations, predominantly hospitals, raising funds from nongovernmental sources. There is tremendous sensitivity to any proposed changes in the Canadian health care system, and, while suggested alterations may seem trivial to outsiders, they are treated in Canada with the extreme skepticism and caution characteristic of sacred policy cows, such as the U.S. Social Security Program. Debate about privatization instead focuses on: 1) whether the private sector should be allowed into particular components of the health care system and 2) the extent to which the operations (including private fund-raising activities) of health care organizations should be regulated by government.

Canadians (with the exception of some physicians who perceive a greater earning potential south of the border) tend to be skeptical of trends in the U.S. health care system, and have strongly resisted attempts to emulate the United States or any other country, including Great Britain. Although Canada is not a country known for xenophobic nationalism, Canadians are reluctant to alter the uniquely Canadian methods of health care financing and delivery. Unlike the United States and Great Britain, no federal political party threatens the present public/private mix, although certain provincial political parties would like to encourage greater privatization (4). Among the professional associations and organizations, physicians represent the only group supporting some forms of privatization (43). In 1982, The National Council of Welfare described the Canadian Medical Association as the "harshest critic" of the Canadian health services system (44).

Because of the widespread suspicion of for-profit organizations, proprietary providers are highly scrutinized by Canadian governmental agencies. In Ontario, for example, some private nursing homes and representatives of the proprietary nursing home industry have vigorously complained that the provincial government imposes far more stringent guidelines on them than on similar organizations in the private sector. Private sector involvement in Canadian health services is viewed as aberrant, and thus in need of careful supervision. As a result, there are few proponents in Canada of a completely competitive system with unlimited entry by entrepreneurs. In addition, the trend towards deprivatization implies that markets may be unstable; there is a persistent risk that government might choose to expand coverage to previously uninsured services, with accompanying regulatory controls over volume and pricing. For example, proposals for provincially-sponsored dental plans, which tend to be based on the services of dental hygienists, would imply far fewer work opportunities for private dentists. The growth of private laboratories is largely dependent upon government regulations. In Ontario, for example, the current reimbursement system encourages the use of outpatient testing; inpatient laboratory work must be encompassed in the hospital's global budget, whereas outpatient work can be billed to the health insurance plan. Rumored changes in regulations to "get a handle on lab costs" could as easily alter the profitability. In addition, government retains the right to specify the services to be reimbursed and the settings in which they can be provided. In Ontario, CT scanning outside hospitals is not reimbursable, and the problem of diffusion in private offices or clinics has therefore not arisen (42).

Elements of Corporatization and Privatization

Debate about corporatization involves the right of health care organizations to alter their organizational arrangements by, for example, entering into some types of formal arrangements with other institutions. There has been considerable movement, although varying by province, towards increased consolidation, sharing of services, contract management, and mergers.

In discussions of corporatization of health services in the Canadian context, three central themes have been dominant:

1. increased used of alternative organizational arrangements, including corporate organization, mergers, and for-profit outside management of hospitals (contract management);
2. changes in financial arrangements, including increased private funding of institutions through philanthropy, commercial activities, or contracts with other corporations for purposes of capital replacement for facility or program replacement; and
3. increased use of out-of-pocket fees, including extra-billing by physicians and hospital user charges.

1. Alternative Organizational Arrangements. Of the many dramatic changes in health service organization in the United States, the most significant has been the move towards multi-institutional arrangements. In 1982, one-third of U.S. hospitals, with nearly 36 percent of the nation's hospital beds, belonged to a multi-hospital system (45). In addition, a large number of hospitals were involved in less intensive forms of multi-institutional relationships, such as management contracts, shared service arrangements, and joint ventures. The presumed benefits and problems of such arrangements in the U.S. have been well discussed and, to some extent, empirically documented (45–47).

Current research suggests that increased efficiencies result from such organizational changes, rather than from a difference between for-profit and not-for-profit organizations (48, 49). Indeed, some evidence suggests that for-profit institutions have higher costs than not-for-profit institutions, with the greater profitability coming from increased revenues, management of bad debts, and control over case mix (45, 47, 50). Investor-owned system hospitals have been found to provide statistically fewer "unprofitable" services (for example, outpatient, day care, screening, and occupational health services; home meal delivery; charity care for uninsured patients) than not-for-profit system hospitals (49).

It would thus seem that there is considerable scope within the current system for realizing efficiency gains from such organizational changes. Movement in this direction has thus far been limited in Canada, in part because of government commitment to preserving current arrangements. Ontario, more than any other province, has opened the door to carefully-controlled alternative methods of organization and financing. Since the early 1970s, the Ontario Ministry of Health has been attempting to cut back on, or at least contain, hospital costs (16). The Ministry was unable to fully maintain control over operating costs, partially because of labor and political disputes resulting from proposed bed closures, but the severe restrictions on hospital capital funding were retained. Until the recent allocation of capital funding announced in the 1987 Speech from the Throne, there had been little real growth in the institutional sector in Ontario in the past 10 years except in areas in which incentives were provided by the B.O.N.D. (Business Oriented New Development) program.

The B.O.N.D. program, introduced in 1982 in Ontario, attempted to encourage the public sector to benefit from private sector management practices. The program encouraged hospitals to increase revenues and contain costs through private sector approaches and better utilization of resources, and allowed hospitals greater freedom to allocate resources within their institution. Savings obtained by hospitals could be retained for hospital operations. The program also indicated to hospitals that the Ministry would no longer absorb operational deficits. A number of ways were suggested for hospitals to decrease costs or increase revenues, including multi-unit management and other joint and shared service arrangements.

Although the B.O.N.D. program may not be the direct cause, multi-hospital arrangements have increased since its inception. After implementation of the program, hospitals in some communities merged, amalgamated, or relocated services to take advantage of program incentives (51).

Contract management has been seen by some as an ideal method of obtaining additional capital and capturing the purported benefits of private sector management expertise while still retaining public control; possible benefits include improved management systems, economies of scale, and greater efficiency. As in the United States, the major argument against contract management is the fear that, by "skimming" or "channeling" patients, hospitals will concentrate on more profitable services at the expense of higher-cost, more labor-intensive services. The Ontario government has carefully controlled these efforts.

There are currently only three examples of hospital contract management in Canada. The management of the Hawkesbury and District General Hospital in eastern Ontario by American Medical International (Canada) Ltd., a subsidiary of the U.S.-based AMI Corporation, has improved both the hospital's financial position and the relations between its board and management (52). Because of the particularly idiosyncratic and difficult situation in the community before AMI's entry, however, the generalizability of this example is probably limited, and AMI has not been hired to run any other Ontario hospitals. Another U.S. firm, Comprehensive Care Corporation (Canada), a subsidiary of CompCare Ltd. management firm, has contracted with an Alberta hospital to provide a 15-bed alcohol and drug treatment program; other such contracts are being explored. Extendicare Hospital Management and Development Ltd., a subsidiary of Canada's largest nursing home chain, received a 20-year management contract in exchange for financing approximately 72 percent of the cost of managing a 120-bed chronic care wing of a Toronto hospital. However, the government pays operating costs, and the facility is clearly run by a community board.

Currently, Extendicare has management contracts for two health care facilities in Alberta, and one in Newfoundland. Although hospitals and provincial governments are pursuing the possibility of a limited role for private sector organizations in the financing and management of health service organizations, such developments have been slow, restricted to unusual situations, and carefully monitored.

2. Changes in Financial Arrangements. The charges of underfunding of health services in Canada sounded by the medical profession (53), hospitals (54), and politicians have been highly publicized and have generated considerable disagreement (55-57). Debate has focused on two questions: 1) If health services are underfunded, would private fundraising be more effective than using existing tax mechanisms? (58) and 2) Is the debate itself actually a guise for physician pressure for higher incomes (5, 56, 57)?

A 1984 Canadian Hospital Association (CHA) survey to determine the state of Canadian hospital capital and estimate future financial requirements predicted that hospitals would incur a significant shortfall of at least $770 million each year simply to maintain their current status (59, 60).

As a result of these perceived deficiencies, Canadian hospitals have become increasingly involved in fundraising through campaigns, revenue generation, special project funding, and the development of hospital foundations (61, 62). As indications of a trend towards privatization, however, these developments should be viewed with caution. New government funded capital projects must still be approved by the provincial government, which retains responsibility for operating costs. Thus, while hospitals are encouraged to raise funds, the manner in which government provided resources are used is regulated.

3. Increased Out-of-Pocket Fees. With the passage of the Canada Health Act in 1984 and subsequent actions by provincial governments, there is little likelihood that extra-billing and user fees will be relied upon in Canada in the near future, particularly given the strong popular support for the provisions of the Canada Health Act evident from public opinion polls. For example, a 1984 Gallup poll found 83 percent of Canadians opposed to extra-billing, and only 13 percent in favor; only 24 percent of those opposed to extra-billing supported increased taxation to increase physician compensation (32). The courts have already upheld certain provincial provisions that physicians had challenged as restrictions on their autonomy, and it is likely that even successful court challenges, would lead to changes in methods of implementation rather than policy goals. The major scope for patient payment would thus occur through government's decision to "deinsure" certain services and move them totally into the private sector. Although a few moves have occurred in this direction (e.g., the province of Alberta recently deinsured certain types of cosmetic surgery), any such initiatives would not only be very unpopular, but would have to be reconciled with the Canada Health Act requirement that all "medically necessary services" be fully covered. The scope for supplementary insurance coverage for elective procedures is, by definition, limited, since insurers recognize a classic example of moral hazard. In addition, the Canada Health Act penalties do not permit "coinsurance"—coverage must be "all or nothing." Under such circumstances, although the potential for deinsurance warrants close monitoring, the scope for major efforts in this direction is severely limited.

CONCLUSIONS

As a result of continuing pressures to operate more efficiently, Canadian health care organizations will likely continue on their course towards greater degrees of corporatization and borrowing of "business-like" approaches from the private sector. In particular, there will be a growth in the number and types of multi-institutional arrangements. Management technologies, such as automated management information systems, will continue to grow in use in Canadian health care organizations. Health administration education programs will continue to incorporate selected "business school" techniques into their curricula.

Reprivatization, however, is unlikely to accompany these efficiency moves. Although there will likely be some experimentation with private sector involvement, such as private management contracts, provincial governments will closely monitor and strongly limit the extent of private sector involvement. Most such developments will occur in areas which are not included in the national health insurance plans.

We see the U.S. trends as having been buffered and inhibited in Canada by the existence of a national health insurance plan, coupled with the trend we have termed deprivatization. Since Canadian patients had already retained the freedom to choose their own physicians, Canada has faced the pressures for "private medicine" now affecting the national health plans in the United Kingdom and Sweden as their health consumers become more affluent and more demanding. However, provincial government control of the way physicians obtain their income and, in some cases, the location of their practices, is increasing. Services previously not available or provided privately are increasingly coming under the umbrella of provincial plans, and thus subject to greater government control and regulation. This trend is encouraged by the acceptance in Canada of the beliefs that health care is a public good, and that government involvement in the financing and regulating of health services is appropriate. On the provincial level, from which many challenges would originate, there is little incentive for structural changes in the health care system. Instead, the system's strong public support places constraints even on experimentation with alternative modes of health service financing, organization, and delivery.

Does this imply inefficiency in the future organization and delivery of health care, and the bankrupting of the nation? We think not. The major sources of cost increase relate to changes in servicing patterns, particularly for the elderly (63), and expansions in the number of health services to be covered. Except for providing a temporary buffer against demands for care, private sector involvement is unlikely to address these factors. As current pressure on government to ensure high quality of care in private nursing homes indicates, private sector involvement complicates government accountability and control over spending, but does not eliminate pressures and demands.

There is considerable scope for savings through more systematic peer evaluation of medical practice and scrutiny of test ordering; prospective global budgets can provide incentives for institutions to find such internal economies. The major problem is political will in enforcing existing policies; mechanisms must be found that can, even when elections are impending, avoid rewarding those violating controls (16, 42).

The Canadian system is dynamic and changing enough to accommodate new demands. The advantage of public control is that government retains the ability to dictate the sorts of things for which any savings realized from new organizational forms will be used. To the extent that the Canadian system has chosen to allocate services on the basis of need, it has recognized that government is the payer of last resort. Canadian pragmatism thus far has led to a rejection of ideological blinkers that would offer a blank cheque to private companies or, in reaction to the inevitable cost increases, permit the abandonment of classes of society unable to meet the increased costs. The problem Canada must confront in the future is somewhat different: In an era of diminishing economic carrying capacity, but undiminished public pressure to expand the scope of services, how long can we hold on to a good thing?

REFERENCES

1. Ewell, C. M. Organizing along corporate lines. *Hospitals* 46: 58–62, June 1, 1972.
2. Leatt, P., and Fried, B. Organizational designs and CEOs. *Health Man. Forum*, Summer 1985, pp. 65–79.
3. McLachlan, G., and Maynard, A. (eds.). *The Public/Private Mix for Health*. Nuffield Provincial Hospitals Trust, London, 1982.
4. Weller, G. R., and Manga, P. The push for reprivatization of health care services in Canada, Britain, and the United States. *J. Health Pol., Policy and Law* 8(13): 495–518, 1983.
5. Evans, R. G. *Strained Mercy: The Economics of Canadian Health Care*. Butterworths, Toronto, 1984.
6. Brown, L. D. *New Policies, New Politics: Government's Response to Government's Growth*. The Brookings Institution, Washington, D.C., 1983.
7. Health and Welfare Canada. *Preserving Universal Medicare: A Government of Canada Position Paper*, Supply and Services Canada, Ottawa, 1983.
8. World Health Organization. *Constitution of the World Health Organization*. Official Records of the World Health Organization, no. 2, Summary Report on Proceedings, Minutes and Final Acts of the International Health Conference held in New York, June 19–July 22, 1946.
9. Lalonde, M. *A New Perspective on the Health of Canadians*. Minister of Supply and Services, Ottawa, 1974.

10. Epp, J. *Achieving Health for All: A Framework for Health Promotion*. Minister of Supply and Services Canada, Ottawa, 1986.
11. Andreopoulos, S. *National Health Insurance, Can We Learn From Canada?* Wiley, Toronto, 1975.
12. Glaser, W. A. Canadian health care problems and foreign solutions. Presentation to the Economic Council of Canada Colloquium on Aging with Limited Health Resources, Winnipeg, May 5–6, 1986.
13. Kane, R. L. An American's view of the Canadian health care system: The not so innocents abroad. Presentation to the Economic Council of Canada Colloquium on Aging with Limited Health Resources, Winnipeg, May 5–6, 1986.
14. Freedman, S. A. Megacorporate health care: A choice for the future. *New Engl. J. Med.* 312(9): 579–582, 1985.
15. Taylor, M. *Health Insurance and Canadian Public Policy*. McGill-Queen's University Press, Montreal, 1978.
16. Deber, R. B., and Vayda, E. The environment of health policy implementation: The Ontario, Canada example. Chapter 29 in *Investigative Methods in Public Health*. Edited by G. Knox. Oxford University Press, Oxford, 1985.
17. Vayda, E., and Deber, R. B. The Canadian health care system: An overview. *Soc. Sci. Med.* 18: 191–197, 1984.
18. Hastings, J. Canada's health care system. In *Introduction to Nursing Management: A Canadian Perspective*. Canadian Hospital Association, Ottawa, 1985, pp. 1–38.
19. Torrance, G. M. Socio-historical overview: The development of the Canadian health system. Chapter 1 in *Health and Canadian Society: Sociological Perspectives*, Second Edition. Edited by D. Coburn, C. D'Arcy, G. M. Torrance, and P. New. Fitzhenry and Whiteside, Markham, Ontario, 1987.
20. Van Loon, R. J., and Whittington, M. S. *The Canadian Political System: Environment, Structure and Process*. McGraw-Hill Ryerson, Toronto, 1981.
21. Macdonald, D. C. (ed.). *The Government and Politics of Ontario* (third edition). Nelson, Toronto, 1985.
22. Deber, R. B. Winning points and influencing policy. *Health Man. Forum* Spring: 39–45, 1986.
23. Soderstrom, L. *The Canadian Health System*. Croom Helm, London, 1978.
24. Van Loon, R. J. From shared cost to block funding and beyond: The politics of health insurance in Canada. *J. Health Pol., Policy and Law* 2: 454–478, 1978.
25. Ginzberg, E. The destabilization of health care. *New Engl. J. Med.* 315(12): 757–761, 1986.
26. Nutter, D. O. Access to care and the evolution of corporate, for-profit medicine. *New Engl. J. Med.* 311: 917–919, 1984.
27. Iglehart, J. K. Medical care of the poor—a growing problem. *New Engl. J. Med.* 313: 59–63, 1985.
28. Schiff, R. L., Ansell, D. A., Schlosser, J. E., Idris, A. H., Morrison, A., and Whitman, S. Transfers to a public hospital: A prospective study of 467 patients. *New Engl. J. Med.* 314: 552–557, 1986.
29. Relman, A. S. The new medical-industrial complex. *New Engl. J. Med.* 303: 963–970, 1980.
30. Relman, A. S. Texas eliminates dumping: A start toward equity in hospital care. *New Engl. J. Med.* 311(9): 578–579, 1986.
31. Salmon, J. W. Profit and health care: Trends in corporatization and proprietarization. *Int. J. Health Serv.* 15(3): 395–418, 1985.
32. Heiber, S., and Deber, R. Banning extra-billing in Canada: Just what the doctor didn't order. *Can. Pub. Policy* 13(1): 62–74, 1987.
33. Detsky, A. S., Stacey, S. R., and Bombardier, C. The effectiveness of a regulatory strategy in containing hospital costs: The Ontario experience, 1967–1981. *New Engl. J. Med.* 309: 151–159, 1983.
34. Bergthold, L. A. Business and the pushcart vendors in an age of supermarkets. *Int. J. Health Serv.* 17(1): 7–26, 1987.

35. Barer, M. L. Regulating physicial supply: The evolution of British Columbia's Bill 41. *J. Health Polit., Policy and Law* 13(1): 1-25, 1988.
36. Deber, R., and Heiber, S. Freedom, equality, and the charter of rights: Policy and legal aspects of regulating physician reimbursement. *Can. Pub. Admin.* 31(4): 566-589, 1988.
37. Starr, P. *The Social Transformation of American Medicine.* Basic Books, New York, 1982.
38. Tuohy, C. Post-Medicare politics in Ontario. *Can. Pub. Policy* 2(2): 192-210, 1976.
39. Stevenson, H. M., and Williams, A. P. Physicians and Medicare: Professional ideology and Canadian health care policy. *Can. Pub. Policy* 11(3): 504-521, 1985.
40. Stoddart, G. L. Economic evaluation methods and health policy. In *Choices in Health Care.* Edited by R. B. Deber and G. Thompson. Department of Health Administration, University of Toronto, 1982.
41. Deber R. B. Your money and your life. *Health Man. Forum* 6(3): 25-31, 1986.
42. Deber, R. B., Thompson, G. G., and Leatt, P. Technology acquisition in Canada: Control in a regulated market. *Int. J. Tech. Assess. Health Care* 4(2): 185-206, 1988.
43. Naylor, C. D. *Private Practice, Public Payment: Canadian Medicine and the Politics of Health Insurance 1911-1966.* McGill-Queen's University Press, Kingston and Montreal, 1986.
44. National Council of Welfare. *Medicare: The Public Good and Private Practice.* Supply and Services, Ottawa, 1982.
45. Ermann, D., and Gabel, J. Multihospital systems: Issues and empirical findings. *Health Aff.* 3(1): 50-64, 1984.
46. Starkweather, D. B. *Hospital Mergers in the Making.* Health Administration Press, Ann Arbor, Michigan, 1981.
47. Gelmon, S. B., and Fried, B. J. *Multi-Institutional Arrangements and the Canadian Health System.* Canadian Hospital Association, Ottawa, 1987.
48. Salmon, J. W. Introduction: Special section on the corporatization of medicine. *Int. J. Health Serv.* 17(1): 1-6, 1987.
49. Shortell, S. M., Morrison, E. M., Hughes, S. L., Friedman, B., Coverdill, J., and Berg, L. The effects of hospital ownership on nontraditional services. *Health Aff.* 5(4): 97-111, 1986.
50. Pattison, R. V., and Katz, H. M. Investor-owned and not-for-profit hospitals: A comparison based on California data. *New Engl. J. Med.* 309: 347-353, 1983.
51. Leatt, P. Multi-institutional arrangements among hospitals in Ontario. Presented at the 8th Jean-Yves-Rivard Conference, The Ontario Health Care System: Lessons for Quebec, October 2 and 3, 1986, Montreal, Quebec.
52. Lacroix, R. The Hawkesbury experiment: A major step forward. *Dimen. Health Serv.* 61(1), 1984.
53. Canadian Medical Association (CMA). *Submission to the Parliamentary Task Force on Federal-Provincial Fiscal Arrangements.* CMA, Ottawa, 1981.
54. Canadian Hospital Association (CHA). *Brief to the Parliamentary Task Force on Federal-Provincial Fiscal Arrangements.* CHA, Ottawa, 1981.
55. Hall, Hon. E. M. *Canada's National-Provincial Health Program for the 1980s.* Health Services Review, Craft Litho, Saskatoon, 1980.
56. Evans, R. G. Health care in Canada: Patterns of funding and regulation. In *The Public/ Private Mix for Health.* Edited by G. McLachlan and A. Maynard. Nuffield Provincial Hospitals Trust, London, 1982.
57. Manga, P. The underfunding of Canada's health care system: Myth or reality? In *Medicare: The Decisive Years,* Proceedings of the CCPA Conference on Medicare, Montreal, November 12-13, 1982, Ottawa: Canadian Centre for Policy Alternatives.
58. Stoddart, G. L., and Labelle, R. J. *Privatization in the Canadian Health Care System: Assertions, Evidence, Ideology and Options.* Health and Welfare Canada, Ottawa, October 1985.
59. Thompson, C., Youmans, J., and LeTouzé, D. Hospital capital shows signs of old age, Part 1. *Dimen. Health Serv.* 61(1): 34-36, 1984.
60. Thompson, C., and LeTouze, D. Hospital capital shows signs of old age, Part 2. *Dimen. Health Serv.* 61(2): 19-22, 1984.

61. Wilson, C. Fundraising: The search for discretionary income. *Dimen. Health Serv.* 60(7): 11–12, 1983.
62. Ruth, S., and Miller, L. S. The volunteer/government/provider relationship. *Health Man. Forum* 6(3): 18–24, 1985.
63. Barer, M. L., Evans, R. G., Hertzman, C., and Lomas, J. Toward Efficient Aging: Rhetoric and Evidence. Paper presented at the Third Canadian Conference on Health Economics, Winnipeg, Manitoba, May 29–30, 1986.

CHAPTER 10

Lessons from America:
The Commercialization and Growth
of Private Health Care in Britain

Geof Rayner

In real terms, the private sector in Britain has doubled in size over the last decade (1), and in comparative terms, the average Briton is five times more likely to purchase private treatment than he or she was at the inception of the National Health Service (NHS) in 1948 (2). Today, slightly more than one in 10 of the British population is covered by private medical insurance. Private medicine, which for most of the period of the war was written off by the Left as an irksome irrelevance, is now portrayed as a spectre haunting the NHS. Nevertheless, the private sector has not encountered the spectacular growth many expected following the Conservative Party election victory in 1979, and although the private sector is in many ways a different creature from what it was a decade ago, it is still a little wheel in comparison to the far bigger wheel of the NHS. This may now be also set to change. In early 1988 the Thatcher Government launched a review of the workings of the National Health Service, to be conducted behind closed doors. The findings of this review were published in January 1989. This chapter focuses upon recent changes in the private sector and its links to the NHS. The future over the next decade will see an intensification of some of the trends defined here.

HOW BIG IS PRIVATE MEDICINE?

British private medicine is tiny in proportion to the NHS, and the image of private sector growth and public sector decline is misleading. The yearly revenues of the private sector are about £1 billion per year ($1.5 billion) (3) compared with about £19 billion ($29 billion) for the NHS. The private sector is

187

composed of approximately 200 hospitals, mostly very small, with an average size of 50 beds. Construction of private hospitals represents approximately 1 percent of the total U.K. building market, compared with 10 percent for the NHS (4). The private sector possesses no full-service general hospitals and is neither equipped nor staffed to offer comprehensive care. There are less than 100 resident staff physicians in private hospitals, and the sector provides no contribution to the training of physicians and offers only a paltry number of courses to nurses. Centers of excellence in British medicine remain inside the public sector.

British private medicine should not, however, be dismissed too lightly. It should not be judged merely by the number of hospitals, one reason being that it is only recently that private work has been of more significance outside the public sector than within it. The private sector possesses a growing political significance that represents a dilemma for each of the major political parties. As its right-wing advocates have argued, the private sector's rapid growth reveals unfulfilled consumer demand for medical services. This is not merely consumer "commodity fetishism:" the most recent figure for NHS waiting lists, the register of elective operations waiting to be carried out, reveals that in September 1985, 661,000 people were having to wait for some degree of time to obtain in-hospital treatment (5). However, the "waiting list" is not a good indicator of unmet demand, and lists vary considerably in different parts of Britain (6). The private sector undertakes about 300 thousand elective operations per year,[1] compared with 6,178 thousand in-hospital treatments in the NHS (1975 figures) (7). While waiting lists are not the sole explanatory factor, they do explain in part why almost 5 million people are currently covered by private medical insurance (this figure includes dependents). Although most "subscribers" to private insurance schemes are drawn from among the better off (8), the size of the subscriber base—one in 10 of the population—does indicate a weakening of the socially comprehensive character of the Health Service. The growth of the private sector also acts as a beacon to those of the anti-welfare state Right. If so many people are prepared to pay twice (since they have already paid for the NHS), does this not mean that the public might prefer a private replacement for the NHS which promises quicker responses to consumer demand?

This suggestion, which Conservative intellectuals have seen as the Achilles' heel of the NHS, has been pushed to the perimeter of progressive thinking: although opposition to private treatment and "queue jumping" has declined, high public support for the philosophy of the NHS continues undiminished (9). There are reasons why this support continues. One must remember that for most of the period since the end of the Second World War, private medicine only

---

[1] This is an estimate based on the sole available figures and updated to take account of increases in the numbers of medically insured persons. The figures are found in reference (7).

meant first access to the NHS through pay-beds. Only a handful of doctors work full time in the private sector, and all "life and death" services are provided, very efficiently, by the NHS. Until the private sector really does offer a comprehensive alternative, the NHS, with all its failings, provides the sense of security many British people seem to desire. Unlike in the United States, the public sector in Britain represents the mainstream; it is not an add-on to or a safety net for private services. Indeed, the reverse is true.

BEFORE THE BOOM

The public image of the private medical sector today is one of unbounded confidence in its own abilities. Claims are made that private hospitals are at the leading edge of technological development or that they are able to offer personalized service. All this is quite new. In 1972, when the British United Provident Association (BUPA), the largest British insurance company wholly committed to this market, played host to an assembly of international insurance schemes, such expansive thoughts were hardly in evidence.

Representatives of the international insurance funds met again in early 1986 in Ireland (10). The tone of this conference was certainly less self effacing; since Thatcher's Britain, the mood surrounding the NHS in the mid-1980s could hardly have been in sharper contrast. The NHS is pervaded by a crisis imagery, and as a result of propaganda efforts, is portrayed as inefficient, ineffective, and lacking innovation. The private sector, with its U.S. management styles, is presented as the effective counterpoint (11-13).

THE CONSERVATIVES AND PRIVATE MEDICINE

The appearance of the newly fashioned image of private medicine coincided with the election of the Conservative Government in 1979. Mrs. Thatcher's government not only brought to an end the policies of outright hostility to NHS private medicine pursued by the former Labour administration, but also instituted radical new departures in Tory policy. Mrs. Thatcher's *nouveau riche* conservatism represented a sharp break with the consensual policies formerly pursued by the Conservative Party, policies that Sir Keith Joseph, one of the founders of "Thatcherism," has termed the "semi-socialist" policies of the past. Adopting themes developed by the Institute of Economic Affairs and the newer Adam Smith Institute (14-20)—the British equivalent of the U.S. American Enterprise Institute and Heritage Foundation—Conservative ministers welcomed rising demand for private medical insurance and the private hospital sector's ambitious plans to satisfy it. The Institute of Economic Affairs had long argued that public opinion toward the NHS had shifted, and that people were now ready for radical alternatives that provided them with "freedom of choice," although the precise route to be taken still needed to be charted. Rejecting the argument of a Royal Commission into the workings of the National Health Service, which reported soon after the Conservatives arrived in office (21), civil servants were sent to the European states and the United States to study alternative health finance arrangements. The Government's aspirations were to receive their first, technical rebuff: to Ministers' dismay, civil servants reported that foreign schemes were costly and cumbersome to administer. However, neither the Treasury nor the radical members of the Cabinet were satisfied, and over the next half decade, separate enquiries were conducted in secret by government advisers (22).

By raising the spectre of an NHS replaced by services based on the ability to pay, these plans had touched a public nerve, and the government hastily denied that these suggestions were anything more than a review of the options. However, in the period up to the 1983 election, with the deterioration of the NHS being made a major electoral theme by the Government's opponents, support for private medicine, if undiminished, became more carefully worded. Thus the Government was saddled with an electoral commitment to retain the Health Service in its present form. In public, therefore, Ministers avoid being seen extending privileges to the private sector, at a time when there are widespread public expressions of concern for the safety of the NHS, which is viewed as severely underfunded. However, the main current of radical opinion within the Conservative Party, represented by the current leadership, is that such commitments present a serious handicap. The Government is criticized for failing to support the Health Service even though spending has increased substantially (though not enough to cover demographic and technological changes and wage increases), and because its efforts to privatize have not been substantial enough, the Government has not been able to set in place an alternative system or to allow those who now use the private sector to be wholly reliant upon it. It is for reasons that the Government decided to launch a wide-ranging review of the working of the NHS in early 1988.

The Government's failure to resolve this dilemma has been at some cost to the private sector. The expectations generated during the first two years of the Conservative Government launched a speculative building boom. In 1981 (the first full year in which hospital developers were required to notify their intentions to construct hospitals), 37 new building schemes, including almost 2000 beds, were announced, followed by 20 in 1982 and 26 in 1983 (23). These expectations were in line with growth rates for the main private insurance companies of about 25 to 30 percent in 1980. But in subsequent years, growth declined, partly due to the industrial recession, and partly due to the rising costs of private medical insurance. The Government failed to intervene to provide additional incentives, as the developers had expected it to, producing over capacity in some parts of the country. This is not to say that specific policies to advance the cause of private medicine were not pursued. Certainly, the decision to liberalize senior physicians' obligations to the Health Service was a major pro-private measure. However, the benefits that this bestowed were intermingled with factors that brought the Government embarrassment and setback.

PRIVATE PRACTICE

Consultants are the elite grade of the British medical profession, in what is traditionally a very hierarchical medical care system. Even before the NHS, medical prestige was developed through the association of private practitioners with a teaching hospital, and at the very minimum it is essential for the more highly ranked private physicians to obtain honorary (i.e., unpaid) consultancies with an NHS hospital. The number of wholly private general practitioners, on the other hand, is very small—estimated around 300—and since most of the clinical activity of the private acute care sector is elective surgery, it is essential that a major part of the work of the private hospitals is undertaken by physicians who normally spend the majority of their time in salaried NHS employment.

Before 1979, NHS consultants came in four types: those with full-time contracts; those with maximum part-time contracts, obligated to give a full commitment to the Health Service but able to practice privately and paid 9/11 of the full-time salary; other "part-time" consultants, paid according to the number of sessions worked; and "honorary consultants," not paid at all. The Government's change of rule meant that full-time consultants were given the right to earn up to 10 percent of their NHS salary from private practice without any deduction from their salary and "maximum part-timers" were now paid 10/11 of the full-time salary (24). As a result, many consultants switched contracts. The number of maximum part-timers rose by 28 percent in 1979–1980, and the number choosing whole-term work rose by 7 percent that year and by 5 percent in 1980–1981. More private work could thus be undertaken, although the exact amount (and the resultant enhancement to income) was knowledge only to be shared between the physician and his or her accountant.

Consultant contracts favor private practice, and also help place physicians outside public accountability. Most consultant contracts are held by Regional Health Authorities and not by local health districts, which administer services and employ almost all of the other workers. This feature, together with the practice of "merit awards" whereby acclaimed consultants, usually in the glamour specialities, are given extra income of up to half their salary, provides a material basis for the stark elitism that infects the NHS. Since 1980, a series of frauds has been uncovered indicating that a significant minority of consultants have taken advantage of existing lax administrative practices by failing to pass on the element of their fees that is due to the NHS (25). In some cases, private patients fail to pay their bills. In Bloomsbury Health Authority of central London, these amounted to £1.39 million by March 1986. The previous

December, the major district teaching hospital closed its doors to non-urgent cases for four weeks to save £450 thousand (26). Guidelines on private practice have now been considerably revised (27). Although the evidence is anecdotal, concern has been expressed, even by a Conservative Health Minister, that the size of the NHS waiting lists was linked to consultants' desire to filter patients into the private sector. There has also been some indication, following a highly publicized case involving a child death in an American Medical International-managed hospital in Scotland, that the new commercial links between investor-owned hospitals and some consultants have resulted in some cases in inappropriate admissions and surgery. Fear of the proliferation of these practices led to a ruling by the Charity Commissioner in May 1984 that consultants who were directors of private hospitals with charitable status must not treat patients in these hospitals privately, and the General Medical Council was asked to declare that the same prohibition should apply to noncharitable private hospitals.

The British Left has long been highly critical of consultants in the Health Service, and the Right has been more defensive. However, critical voices are being heard on the intellectual Right, reminiscent of free market thought in the United States, and one emergent "libertarian" critique is that the medical profession and its protection by the state form an obstacle to the development of "competitive" health care organization (28).

Collaboration Between the National Health Service and Private Medicine

The Government's initial approach to privatization in response to adverse publicity has been for its policies to be determined in a more piecemeal manner. Individual Health Authorities have been encouraged to develop cooperative arrangements between the NHS and the private sector, and the NHS has been obliged to take private hospitals into account during the formulation of NHS service planning (which runs along a strict cycle). Prior to 1981, Health Authorities were not being allowed to contract with profit-making organizations, but in 1981, an informal Department of Health and Social Security (DHSS) circular was sent to Chairpersons of Regional Health Authorities (the upper tier administration between the Department of Health and local health districts) claiming (29):

> Although the private sector of health care is comparatively small, the benefits of partnership with it are disproportionate to its size. . . . Independent sector capital might be used to provide expensive equipment for, say, a district general hospital on the basis of a leasing/rental agreement (or for joint use by an NHS or independent hospital).

Pay-beds could be "managed for a fee by the independent sector;" wards could be "sold to the independent sector, which would then run [them] outside the NHS but would have guaranteed access to the main hospital facilities" (29).

It was expected that these proposals would be followed by Government directives; none has so far emerged.

Cooperative links between the NHS and private sector have therefore been of limited significance, despite their encouragement by pro-private sector academics (30), the business press (31), and Conservative Ministers. The first links occurred not so much as outright business ventures in their own right, but rather as marketing tactics by hospital management companies and insurers (such as American Medical International and BUPA) anxious not to appear as predators on the Health Service (32). More recently, with the squeeze on NHS finances, Health Authorities have begun to look to hospital management companies to take over the running of their private wings whose refurbishment the Authorities were unable to finance (33). Researchers who have studied contract arrangements have indicated that such emerging public private links can distort NHS planning (34).

However, with certain exceptions, most acts of collaboration have been undertaken voluntarily by Health Authorities (35). The Prime Minister's own statement in Parliament in May 1985 revealed that many discussions had occurred between Ministers and the private hospitals over how cooperative links could be forged, but that there were no plans for a centrally promoted scheme, though any schemes suggested by local health districts would be looked at "sympathetically" (36).

The Government has pursued a different strategy with regard to lower grade NHS staff, instructing District Health Authorities to tender domestic, catering and laundry services on the market. Ancillary workers in the Health Service, a large proportion of whom are from ethnic minorities, are among the lowest paid workers in Britain. However, at least in comparison with the equivalent jobs in private industry, ancillary workers in the Health Service have enjoyed more security of employment, holiday entitlements, union representation, and so on. The Government's decision to place domestic, catering, and laundry services out to contract was based on the belief that rates of pay could be further reduced, that workforce representation could be weakened by casualization, and that the number of employees could be reduced by intensification and the introduction of new technology (e.g., the introduction of "cook-chill" methods in catering, and capital investment in new plant to enhance economies of scale). This process has been accompanied by a rhetoric whose main theme is that the resulting "savings" could be released for patient care. In a direct sense, therefore, pay reductions are to be used to compensate for the failure to adequately finance the Health Service.

Tendering of services began in 1983-1984, and the total "savings" claimed by the Government by March 31, 1986, were £52 million ($77 million). Of these, 148 contracts have been let to private contractors with estimated "savings" of £21.5 million ($33 million); 522 tenders were secured in-house with estimated "savings" of £30.5 million ($46 million) (37). The financial benefits to the NHS are overstated in these figures: there is no account made of redundancy payments, the administrative costs of putting services out to tender, and the cost of supervising the contracts. Estimates of the "savings" were made on the basis of the previous year's cost of the service and not by comparison with the in-house tender price. With regard to "efficiency gains," these apparently occurred through staff reductions and reductions in conditions of service. A second nondiscretional policy concerns NHS land sales. Health Authorities are now forced to sell off redundant land to the highest bidder, whereas previously, Health Authorities, local authorities, and the voluntary sector had first choice at preferential rates.

In its eagerness to reverse Labour's policies on the private sector, the Government "rescued" NHS pay-beds and abolished Labour's Health Services Board. Although these measures suited consultants, they did not find favor with the private sector, some of whose spokespersons had argued that pay-beds should be phased out since they represented "unfair competition." Under pressure to show that the private sector gained no financial advantages from the Health Service, the Government increased pay-bed charges and brought in administrative charges for the supply of blood collected by the National Blood Transfusion Service. These measures contributed to the private sector's rising costs. Furthermore, the Government has resisted the private sector's long-standing pleas for additional tax advantages for private patients and access to subsidized NHS drug prescriptions.

Compared to the policies proposed by its right-wing advisors, these steps are relatively minor and hardly compare with the Thatcher Government's policies on industrial privatization. Conservative university economist Patrick Minford has suggested that public hospitals should simply be sold off (38). Right-wing Conservative Members of Parliament and their advisers have suggested the introduction of tax incentives for private insurance and the privatization of management (39–42).

Not only those on the right of the Conservative Party are in favor of privatization. Some notable British and U.S. economists, occupying perhaps the middle ground of politics, have suggested that certain new market-based management approaches from the United States might find applicability in Britain. The Health Economics Research Centre at York University, and Stanford Professor Alain Enthoven have been promoting the adoption of U.S.-style financial incentives. Enthoven's views, which have been promoted by Nuffield Provincial Hospital's Trust (43) (not associated with the Hospitals Group) and the *Economist* (44), are an adaptation of his "pro-competition" policies in the United States (45). While his first preference is the abandonment of the NHS in favor of competitive health maintenance organizations, his immediate suggestion is for the phased introduction of competition between existing District Health Authorities. The crux of his argument is that efficiency-inducing incentives should be introduced through which Health Districts would "import" from and "export" to other Districts using negotiated prices, the implication being that the more efficient (including private groups) would take over the work of the less efficient by underbidding. In a sense this approach compares with the Government's existing policy of enforced contracting for ancillary services.

The Government wholly welcomes market perspectives and the introduction of business methods into the management of the NHS. Former Labour Party economist Nick Bosanquet, who has criticized the Government for its mishandling of NHS finance, has applied Enthoven's ideas to primary care, suggesting that general practitioners should be encouraged to be "active economic agents in the provision of primary care," and acting as local firms, they might offer services for children "which would mean that the school health service would be redundant" (46). His York University colleague Professor Alan Maynard has actively canvassed the application of HMOs to Britain (47,48). HMOs have caught the attention, though perhaps not the support, of the British Medical Association (49,50), and have attracted the Government's interest in the shape of the idea of multidisciplinary "health shops," which could be run under contract management by the private sector (51). Without the support of the professions, which have recently witnessed the introduction of competitive arrangement within the retail optical business, these suggestions at present appear stuck at the ideas stage.

The most visible sign of Government action to introduce the processes of the business system into the Health Service has been the installation of "general management" into the running of District and Regional Health Authorities, thereby displacing the older approach of "consensus management" introduced in the Health Service reorganization of the mid-1970s. This management system, along the lines suggested by supermarket boss Roy Griffiths of the successful Sainsbury's chain [whose owners, once Labour Party supporters, are now linked with the Social Democratic Party (SDP)], suggested that the Health Service would run more efficiently by having a command structure with a manager who took final responsibility for getting things done. As former colonels and business people began to occupy general management posts, many on the Left saw the Griffiths approach as merely a way of preparing the NHS for privatization. This intention cannot be ruled out, though in practice, managers are still politically constrained, both by local Health Authority members—a mix of appointees, physicians and local government councillors—and ironically, the Government itself. In June 1986, the senior officer of the new NHS Management Board resigned because neither the Minister nor the DHSS had been willing to cede the Board sufficient authority (52).

Although academics and business people may have some influence at the fringes of policy formation, the future of the public-private mix in Britain is tied to political events. Private medicine survived the formation of the Health Service by an act of toleration and pragmatism by a Labour minister, and it has grown since as a result of the twin processes of action and inaction by successive

Labour and Conservative administrations. Public acceptance of the NHS is perhaps ingrained too deeply to be easily dislodged, and private medicine is only tolerated (even by many of its medical advocates), marginalizing it to a fringe role beside a much larger NHS.

One York health economist, Anthony Culyer, a former author with the Institute of Economic Affairs, has noted that a genuine free market in health is mere fantasy (53). However, it is a fantasy that still continues to fascinate many in the Conservative Party, though it is perhaps more a danger to the Party itself than, as yet, to the NHS.

Although the Government has tried to promote private medicine as a measure that facilitates individual choice, and has attempted to uncouple the putative advantages of "going private" from the financial problems of the Health Service, the private sector and the Government's policies toward it remain vulnerable to attack. The highly publicized problems of the NHS are not seen, as the Government would have wished, to be intrinsically linked to its statist nature, but to the Government's failure to make proper financial allowance for it (54). In any case, the time has passed when private medicine could be presented solely as a matter of individual choice, since most policies are paid for collectively by employers.

OPPOSITION VIEWS ON PRIVATE MEDICINE

The British centre parties have sympathized with the consumerist notions found within the private sector. Despite Labour's fierce broadsides against private medicine, and the Party's 1983 manifesto commitment to remove private practice from the NHS and nationalize the commercial hospitals, the party has generally recognized that the private sector represented something that they had to live with rather than abolish. At a conference organized for the private sector by the Financial Times in 1985, the former opposition Health Secretary Michael Meacher (55) outlined a series of seven initiatives the Labour Party would want to make toward the private sector, including: 1) introducing new incentives to encourage consultants to work full time for the NHS and in the understaffed specialities, 2) removing tax concessions, 3) reviewing pay-bed fees, 4) increasing NHS amenity beds, 5) stricter auditing of consultants, 6) the introduction of an inspectorate, and 7) the reinstatement of the Health Services Board. While these proposals hardly constitute a full blooded assault on the private sector, the overall aim being to promote "fair competition between both sides," they would nevertheless produce a substantial impact. Certainly, one apparent result would be the weakening of the position of ostensibly "charitable" hospitals. Given the present size of the private insurance market, there may be some gulf between what Labour policy makers are likely to want to do and what they are able to do. Policy change is therefore likely to occur at the fringes. The Labour Party has offered a commitment to end the contracting of ancillary services (56), and, in the face of internal disputes on a future Labour Government's spending commitments, had pledged 3 percent real growth in NHS financing.

PRIVATE HEALTH INSURANCE

Policies toward the private sector have to take account of how the private sector operates and what support it has among the public. The starting place for the investigation of the first aspect is private health insurance. Private health insurance in Britain is an optional extra, and does not, in a strict sense, offer an alternative way of financing comprehensive services for all groups. The key to understanding private medical insurance in Britain is that it is mainly a way of paying for hospital expenses and surgeon's fees.

Although the origin of medical insurance in Britain, like that of the U.S. Blue Cross system, lay in the voluntary hospitals, its development in Britain was far more fragmented and low key. This is not to underestimate the significance of the medical insurance companies. Before the mid-1940s, private insurance was composed of literally hundreds of little hospital-based or geographically-based "provident associations." Their amalgamation, under the paternal eye of Lord Nuffield, the motor magnate and patron saint of private medicine, allowed them to survive the crisis of 1948 (i.e., the formation of a "free" NHS). The handful of schemes that survived in turn ensured the survival of private medicine throughout the wilderness years of the early 1950s.

Medical insurance was originally devised to provide a form of a prepayment for the costs of a private bed in a pre-NHS voluntary hospital. It was intended especially for the lower middle class—the rich paid for themselves. Today, insurance companies are well organized marketing organizations that skillfully exploit fear of the NHS "waiting list" to recruit new subscribers. As the attraction of private medicine has grown, the traditional clientele has been joined by a substantial number of the upper-salary grade and a sprinkling of the workers (and the rich). Health insurance has joined company cars and expense accounts as a key "perk" (fringe benefit). Information collected by market analysts suggests that there is considerable inequality between quality of cover offered to diffent grades of employees and the burden of costs assumed by employers. Broadly speaking, the higher up the employment ladder, the better the insurance cover (57).

In 1977, individual subscribers formed about 45 percent of the total, though today this figure has fallen to around 20 percent. In part, the growth of company benefits such as private health insurance has been due to a mixture of things, including perceived high taxation rates among executive grades, wage freezes, and perceptions of status. Despite their name, "provident associations" are ordinary insurance companies (though they have no shareholders). While they still retain the majority share of the private insurance market, this has been recently challenged by investor-owned companies.

A breakdown of the insurance market shows that the top three insurers—led by the British United Provident Association—control around 85 percent of the market; the remainder is divided between another five nonprofit groups and seven for-profit groups. The chief characteristics of the change in market share over the last five years have been the relative decline in BUPA's hold on the market (though against a background of considerable absolute growth) and the emergence of the for-profit sector. Alongside these traditional insurance schemes are a number of new self-insurance companies.

If Labour's opposition to private medicine has been a continual threat, it does not seem to have affected the growth prospects of the industry. The two main problems facing the industry are of their own making. The first is that of climbing premium costs (58), which are related to the increasing charges levied by hospitals, surgeons, and the NHS (pay-bed charges). Medical insurance, while highly favored by personnel managers in British industry, is liable to fall out of favor if it is seen to be as burdensome as insurance costs are to employers in the United States—a topic that has received attention in the British business press (59). After all, private medicine is only a standby to public treatment, and lack of access to private services only means a wait for treatment, not absolute denial. The recent rapid cost increases levied by insurers has led to companies holding experience-rated cover switching to rivals to moderate the impact of sharp yearly price increases. For the insurers this has resulted in highly variable yearly growth rates. There are substantial differences between rates for young and old, city dwellers and country dwellers. Cover is not comprehensive and the list of exclusions is very broad. For example, BUPA runs nursing homes for the elderly, but does not provide an insurance plan to cover the cost.

The second problem facing private medical insurance is the demand for a wider mix of services, some of which are extremely costly. Because of resource difficulties, the NHS has only one center for in vitro fertilization that it runs completely free of charge; the rest are either wholly private or supported by private patients (60). In 1985, in response to moves by commercial hospital chains to expand psychiatric and drug addiction treatment, the provident associations removed these treatments from their benefit plans (61). In the case of transplant surgery, kidneys were being imported on a commercial basis from the United States, and the Government acted to dampen the trade (62). What has emerged over the last half-decade is a deep conflict of interest between companies that are the main providers of medical care, and others that offer third-party insurance. Providers wish to expand the market (63) and to charge fees that amply cover their overheads and give a return to their investors; payers wish to restrain their costs to maintain their market share. The issue of restricted resources, which bedevils the NHS, also affects the private sector.

The private insurance market is now undergoing rapid change, particularly with the entry of U.S. companies such as Mutual of Omaha, which is investing heavily to obtain market share. However, the long established companies continue to use their considerable market advantage to shape the market and place restrictions on care providers.

NATIONAL HEALTH SERVICE PAY-BEDS

Until the early 1970s, private medicine in Britain was more simple to grasp and its impact was disputed (but largely inconsequential) (64). Over 2/3 of private hospital treatment occurred in NHS private beds, known as pay-beds; treatment outside the NHS was either of the simplest variety or entailed considerable risk. Because of the expansion of facilities outside the NHS, pay-beds constitute only about 1/4 of private acute care.

Pay-beds, which existed in voluntary hospitals before nationalization, formed part of a political bargain between the medical establishment and the postWar Labour Government committed to socialized medicine (as it is called everywhere but in Britain). Pay-beds were therefore viewed as an unpleasant anachronism that would fade away over time. The opposite was true: the more the NHS was patently unable to deal with every ache and pain, and the more the demand for elective surgery exceeded supply (and the more the public attention was drawn to this), the greater was the attention placed on pay-beds as a source of continuing inequality.

The main critique of pay-beds and their effect on the Health Service was made in a House of Commons Select Committee in 1971 (65): pay-beds encouraged queue jumping, resulted in neglect of NHS patients and lengthened waiting lists, and provided the opportunity for consultants to abuse NHS facilities for their private practice. Following pressure from Health Service Unions, the 1974–1979 Labour Government proceeded to phase them out. In practice, Labour's policies on NHS pay-beds were little short of disastrous. The number of beds declined only 40 percent and the number of patients treated declined hardly at all. In 1974 there were 4,302 pay-beds in England with an average occupancy of 48.3 percent. Today the figure stands at 3,000 beds with average occupancy below 40 percent. About 83,000 patients were treated in pay-beds in England in 1984, a fall of more than 8,000 patients over 1979 (66). The true picture of pay-bed occupancy is unclear because these beds can be used by patients who do not pay (67).

Labour's attack on private medicine also produced its opposite effect, the encouragement of the "independent" sector. One part of this was the result of Labour policy. It was agreed with the private medicine lobby that the phased withdrawal of pay-beds would be accompanied by the gradual growth of facilities outside the NHS, and the government-backed Health Services Board was formed to oversee this process.

Although Labour policy had the expressed intention of separating private practice from the Health Service, no impediments were placed on NHS consultants working privately. Therefore, what some had anticipated to be the death-knell for private practice became its saving grace. David Bolt, then Chairperson of the British Medical Association's Central Committee for Hospital Medical Services, which negotiates for Britain's 16,000 consultants, eagerly responded by suggesting to consultants that they should merely direct their patients out of NHS pay-beds into independent clinics (68):

> [W]e put a fair amount of pressure on consultants to move towards facilities outside the NHS. Even after the change of government in 1979 we used to impress on consultants that they now had a five year "breathing space" which they should use since, if at the end of that time the opposition were to come to power, there would be very little notice before all NHS facilities were closed to private patients. As a result there has been a very striking development in terms of provision of private facilities over the period.

The reduced reliance on the NHS provided new opportunities for private hospital developers. However, when the Thatcher Government entered office in 1979, it pursued its electoral commitment to halt the removal of pay-beds: "We shall . . . allow pay-beds to be provided where there is a demand for them." Ironically then, while the private hospital associations now support the removal of pay-beds from the NHS, it is the Conservative Government that is responsible for maintaining them.

PRIVATE HOSPITALS

Although NHS pay-bed prices undercut those of private hospitals, consultants' commitments to divert private patients to external facilities, combined with the unmet demand for private treatment, provided a vision of a lucrative future to both foreign and domestic hospital management companies.

Historically, most private hospital care has been provided by charitable and religious organizations financed by loans, legacies, contributions, covenants, etc. As in the United States, private hospitals, clinics, and nursing homes come in three main types: secular "non-profit," religious "non-profit," and investor-owned "for-profit." Also as in the United States, differences in emphasis and strategy exist between—and indeed within—these groups.

The charitable sector is, on the whole, composed of small and financially vulnerable hospitals, many of which resent the commercialism represented by the big groups, which is partly why there are two private hospital associations. While some hospitals, and most hospices, are entirely charitable (indeed, do not charge fees), for others there is often a fine line between "nonprofit" and profit-making. For the most part, charitable hospitals, like their counterparts in the United States, retain their charity status primarily for tax advantage.

For many years however, the largest hospital chain in Britain, the Nuffield Nursing Homes Trust (which changed its name to Nuffield Hospitals in 1984) was the largest multihospital system in Britain. There are special reasons that explain Nuffield's growth and set it apart from the other charities. Nuffield was formed by BUPA in 1957 as a supplement to NHS pay-bed provision in order to ensure that independent surgical nursing homes would not suffer extinction. Nuffield's original marketing strategy was determined by its relationship to the BUPA and pay-bed pricing policy (often below cost). Although, with 32 hospitals, Nuffield is the largest hospital chain in Britain (though it would obtain a rank of somewhere between 60th and 70th in size in the United States), it has been handicapped by its policy of maintaining moderate fee structures, and its policy of maintaining pay structures similar to those in the NHS so as not to appear to be acting to "poach" staff. The company was therefore not able to respond as quickly as its well-financed investor-owned competitors to meet the challenge of market growth in the late 1970s. This it now regrets.

One result has been that the commercial hospital chains [in rank order, U.S., British, and Arab (financed) companies] have led the field. The U.S. for-profit chains view their foreign operations as medium investments, strictly subsidiary to their domestic assets. Although their growing commitment to the British market might indicate strong returns, profits have so far been limited. The best known companies, including American Medical International (AMI), Hospital Corporation of America (HCA), and the Humana Corporation, have had offices or facilities in Britain for well over a decade. London was a useful stage post for medical staff recruitment for their managed hospitals in the Middle East. The U.S. companies typically recruited British physicians, who are used to much lower salaries and do not, unlike their U.S. counterparts, have to declare foreign earning for taxation. Private medicine in London also offered a comparative advantage over Continental European and U.S. hospitals, and therefore attracted many overseas patients, who could combine their routine surgery with sight-seeing and shopping at Harrods.

By 1986, there were nine U.S. hospital management companies operating in Britain. Besides those mentioned, these include National Medical Enterprises (NME), Community Psychiatric Centres, Charter Medical, Universal Health Services, Nu-Med Inc., and Family Health Plan, the sole HMO.

Despite the present difficulties of its parent company (69), AMI maintains a clear lead, (and in 1988 obtained listing on the London stock exchange) with a presence that compares to BUPA (which runs some hospitals, besides its main insurance business). It is also the most publicity-conscious of the hospital groups, and while not exactly hiding its U.S. ownership, never advertises the fact. Indeed, AMI claims to have only one American employee (though he is the Managing Director). HCA has been rather less than successful. Late into the market, its sole, medium-sized unit in Southampton has faced continual occupancy problems, and thus most of the company's effort has been devoted to smaller and less profitable units outside the cities. Humana has restricted itself to one major central London facility, and remained keyed into the foreign market. Community Psychiatric Centres and Charter Medical have stuck to what they know best, and thus dominate the elite market for drug, alcohol, and stress therapy. The other groups, NME, Universal, and Nu-Med have gained a foothold in the market.

U.S. investment in Britain has been supplemented by Arab capital. Devonshire Hospitals, for example, a highly financed facility in central London (one of the two hospitals in Britain with a Dornier lithotripter for kidney stone crushing) is owned by the Kuwait Investment office. The expensive Cromwell Hospital in West London is also Arab-financed.

A number of British commercial chains have been formed. The largest of them, Community Hospitals, projects a style reminiscent of its U.S. rivals. British finance houses, with the exception of one or two merchant banks, have viewed the private sector as a risky investment, hence these companies have looked to local consortia, including consultants, the Government's Business Expansion Scheme and in some cases the Unlisted Securities Market (a City funding mechanism cheaper than full stock exchange listing), to launch hospital schemes (70).

British groups do not possess the confidence of the large financial institutions. As a result, buy-outs and liquidations, common among proprietary hospitals in the United States, are occurring with increasing rapidity. A sign of the times was the sell-out of the domestic hospital holding of United Medical Enterprises, formerly owned by the British Government (through the National Enterprise Board), to U.S. competitors (71).

The Provident Associations possess an intense dislike of the commercial hospitals ostensibly because they overcharge, but also because they have disrupted the cosy oligopolistic marketplace that formerly existed. Their response has taken a variety of forms, from scaling back the level of charges that they are willing to meet, to eliminating benefits (such as private psychiatric care) from their insurance policies when the companies began to market new services. AMI's response to this threat is the introduction of its own payment by credit system and by the announcement of its own HMO. As with AMI's parent company, there is some ambivalence as to whether it should take this route.

A further response by the main insurer, BUPA, has been to develop its own chain of commercial hospitals, building on its experience as sponsor to the Nuffield chain. BUPA has a very strong brand image, and has attempted to present its activities as the "BUPA Health Service:" "BUPA's involvement in health insurance and its own centres of excellence—hospitals, screening centres and clinics, make it the largest independent [sic] health care service in Britain" (72).

PRIVATE HOSPITAL DEVELOPMENT

The number of beds in the acute private sector has risen from about 4,000 in 1978 to over 10,000 today. One reason for the rapid growth since 1979, apart from the change in government, is that the private sector has been freed of all the restrictions placed upon it by the previous Labour Administration. Although private hospitals are required to be licensed, no hospital has ever been refused, even when the plans have to be referred explicitly nearby NHS hospitals as a source of staff and patient recruitment and as a location for back-up services. Although, as noted earlier, private hospital developers are required to notify the Secretary of State of their intention to build, some have even gone ahead without such notification.

In 1980, a Government circular to local planning authorities aimed: "to ensure that development is only prevented or restricted when this serves a clear planning purpose and the economic effects have been taken into account" (73). The following year, another circular included a memorandum insisting that (74):

> [Authorities] decisions in respect of each application will continue to be based solely on planning considerations, regardless of whether, in their view, the proposal to develop a private nursing home or hospital would be prejudicial to the interests of the National Health Service. Nor should their decision be influenced by the fact that the proposed development is in the private sector rather than the public sector.

Given that private hospitals can locate wherever they like, they are heavily concentrated in the better-off south-east of Britain, and especially in central London. Of the 14 Health Regions in Britain, North-West Thames has the highest percentage of beds—over 40 per 100,000 inhabitants—contrasted with the very low density of beds in the north of the country—Northern Regional Health Authority has 2.1 beds per 100,000. Over half of existing beds are located in the four Thames Regional Health Authorities.

The Harley Street area in London is the focus for private medical practice, with individual practitioners renting or sharing consulting rooms. Just as the location of central London teaching hospitals is explained by their proximity to Harley Street, so this also explains the high density of private hospitals in the Westminster and Bloomsbury areas of London. Outside London, hospital locations were selected for a variety of reasons. In the case of the Nuffield chain, clinics were developed because of local initiative and to supplement pay-beds. In the case of the U.S. companies, hospitals (outside London) are developed where local consultants are willing to support new schemes and where there is evidence of a growing subscriber base. Additionally, a new hospital may need to be near to existing NHS hospitals, not simply for ease of access by consultants, but also because private hospitals are usually poorly equipped and unlikely to be properly staffed for emergencies. Less than one in two has a radiology department. Only 53 hospitals with operating rooms contained resident doctors (75).

Unrestricted growth has brought in its train one key difficulty: maintaining occupancy. While few of the companies publish occupancy figures and it remains very difficult to obtain a reliable picture of company accounts (because of recent heavy investment that dampens profits or their disguising of accounts), from those figures that are published it is possible to assemble a picture of falling occupancy and, because of cost-cutting measures pursued by insurers, narrowing margins. Nuffield Hospitals, for example, has always published a reasonable amount of data about itself, and recent reports indicate a considerable reduced surplus and falling occupancy, down to about 70 percent. In some of the smaller independent hospitals, occupancy has fallen to below 50 percent.

CONCLUSIONS

Private health care in Britain was, for a relatively brief period, a boom industry. It is hardly in a slump today, but neither has experienced an unparalled boom. Many on the Left have drawn a straight parallel between the Conservatives' attack on the NHS, and the growth of the private sector. Certainly, this seemed to be borne out, but the private sector has many problems of its own. Like their counterparts in the United States (in some cases parent companies), the new commercial chains welcomed competition and the chance to exhibit their efficiency in comparison with what they perceived to be a dowdy, bureaucratic NHS. But also as in the United States, profits now seem more difficult to find. The marketplace for private medical care is now highly competitive, and overbedding (and outpatient surgery) has cut into hospital occupancy rates. Providing the U.S. companies keep their nerve and continue to receive financial backing, they do have the opportunity of obtaining market dominance. Assuming that the radical reforms proposed by the Government in early 1989 come into effect, their role may even be considerably enlarged.

Caution should be exercised in making direct comparison between British private medicine and the U.S. proprietary (or voluntary) sectors. Corporate names are in some cases the same, but the political context, the role of physicians, the relationship to the public sector, and indeed the overall nature of private medicine are markedly different.

Commercialization is occurring in several different ways, each of which has a clear resonance with events in the United States: (a) the commitment of the Government to privatization and private sector solutions; (b) the application of more marketing-led activities by medical insurance companies, the market entry of proprietary groups, and the investigation of vertical markets; and (c) the development of investor-owned multihospital systems, and the displacement, or transformation, of charity-based hospital care. A final trait emerging from this thesis is changes in medical practice. Aaron and Schwartz (76) have observed that British physicians undertake a more cautious, economic, and reflective approach to the application of their skills. Should the fee-for-service system, as applied through the British private sector, displace the now traditional salaried mode of compensation as a significant element of a physician's income, then this aspect may pull Britain into line with the United States, with as yet unknown results.

REFERENCES

1. Association of Independent Hospitals. *Nursing Home Beds*. London, November 1985.
2. McPherson, K., Coulter, A., and Stratton, I. Increasing use of private practice by patients in Oxford requiring common elective surgical operations. *Br. Med. J.* 291: 797–799, 1985.
3. Grant, C. *Private Health Care in the UK: A Review*. Economist Intelligence Unit, London, 1985.
4. Anderson, J. R. Business opportunities for construction companies. Speech at the Financial Times Conference on Private Health Care, March 1985.
5. Hildrew, P. Fowler orders check on hospital queues. *The Guardian*, July 22, 1986.
6. College of Health. *Guide to Hospital Waiting Lists, 1985*. London, November 1985.
7. Nicoll, J. P., et al. Contribution of the private sector to elective surgery in England and Wales. *Lancet*, July 14, 1984, pp. 89–92.
8. Office of Population, Census and Surveys. *General Household Survey 1982*. London, June 1984.
9. Public versus private provision: What people think. *Public Money*, December 1984, pp. 63–66.
10. Pitcher, G. A matter of life and luxury. *Observer*, April 27, 1986, p. 39.
11. Larson, J. G. The role of private enterprise in providing health care: Lessons of the American experience. *National Westminster Bank Rev.*, November 1980, pp. 58–65.
12. Goodman, J. C. *National Health Care in Great Britain: Lessons for the U.S.A.* Fisher Institute, Dallas, Texas, 1980.
13. Lindsay, C. M. *National Health Issues: The British Experience*. Hoffman La Roche Inc., 1980.
14. Seldon, A. (ed.). *The Litmus Papers: A National Health Disservice*. Centre for Policy Studies, London, 1980.
15. Adam Smith Institute. *Health and the Public Sector: A Report to the Minister of Health*. London, 1981.
16. Buchanan, J. M. *The Inconsistencies of the NHS*. Institute of Economic Affairs, London, 1964.
17. Jewkes, J., and Jewkes, S. *The Genesis of the British National Health Service*. Basil Blackwell, Oxford, 1962.
18. Lees, D. S. *Health Through Choice*. Institute of Economic Affairs, London, 1961.
19. Seldon, A. *After the NHS*. Institute of Economic Affairs, London, 1968.
20. Adam Smith Institute. *Privatization Worldwide*. London, 1986.
21. Royal Commission on the National Health Service. Report (Cmnd 7615). Her Majesty's Stationery Office, London, July 1977.
22. Thatcher's think tank takes aim at the Welfare State. *Economist*, September 18, 1982, pp. 25–26.
23. Hansard, March 21, 1984.
24. Department of Health and Social Security. *Health Service Development, Health Service Act 1980: Private Medical Practice in Health Service Hospitals and Control of Private Hospital Beds*, DHSS HC (80)10. London, 1980.
25. Report of the Controller and Auditor General on the Accounts. National Health Service Accounts. London, 1986.
26. Press release from Frank Dobson, MP, July 24, 1986.
27. Department of Health and Social Security. *Management of Private Practice in Health Service Hospitals*. London, 1986.
28. Green, D. *Which Doctor?: A Critical Analysis of the Professional Barriers to Competition in Health Care*. Institute of Economic Affairs, London, 1985.
29. Cooperation between the NHS and the private sector at district level. *The Health Services*, June 3, 1983, p. 5.
30. Williams, B. T. Will the NHS and private sector collaborate? *Br. Med. J.*, July 5, 1982.
31. Loshak, D. Healing partnership with the NHS. *Financial Times*, June 7, 1985, p. 16.

32. West, P. A. Sharing the costs of high technology: The economics of public and private cooperation. *Hosp. Health Serv. Rev.,* January 1986, pp. 15–17.
33. Anderson, F. Private management for St. Mary's. *Health Soc. Serv. J.,* January 23, 1986, p. 95.
34. Birch, S. Policy implications of contracting out care: The case of total hip replacements. *Hosp. Health Serv. Rev.* 81(1): 281–284, 1985.
35. Rathwell, T., Sics, A., and Williams, S. *Towards a New Understanding.* Nuffield Centre for Health Services Research, Leeds, 1985.
36. Hansard, June 10, 1985.
37. Hansard, June 23, 1986.
38. Minford, P. State expenditure: A study in waste. *Econ. Aff. Suppl.* 4(3): i–xix, 1984.
39. Davis, D. *Public Hospitals: Private Management.* Adam Smith Institute, London, 1985.
40. No Turning Back: A Radical Political Agenda from a Group of Conservative MPs. Conservative Political Centre, London, 1985.
41. Elwell, H. NHS lessons Norman Fowler has yet to hammer home. *Daily Telegraph,* October 26, 1983.
42. Burton, J. *Why No Cuts? An Inquiry into the Fiscal Anarchy of Uncontrolled Government Expenditure,* Hobart Paper No. 104. Institute of Economic Affairs, London, 1985.
43. Enthoven, A. *Reflections on the Management of the National Health Service.* Nuffield Provincial Hospital's Trust, Oxford, 1985.
44. Enthoven, A. National Health Service: Some reforms that might be politically feasible. *Economist,* June 22, 1985, pp. 19–22.
45. Enthoven, A. *Health Plan: The Only Practical Solution to the Soaring Cost of Medical Care.* Addison Wesley Publishing, Reading, Mass., 1983.
46. Bosanquet, N. GP's as firms: Creating an internal market for primary care. In: *Health Care UK 1986,* edited by A. Harrison and J. Gretton, pp. 65–68. Hermitage, Berks, 1986.
47. Maynard, A. Reassessing the NHS: Evaluation could be a blooming success. *Health Soc. Serv. J.,* December 13, 1984, pp. 1467–1468.
48. For a full discussion on the attempt to apply HMOs to Britain, see: Rayner, G., HMOs in the USA and Britain: A New Prospect for Health Care?, *Soc. Sci. Med.* 27(4): 305–320, 1988.
49. Richards, T. Medicine American style and the growth of HMOs. *Br. Med. J.* 292: 392–394, 1986.
50. Richards, T. HMOs: American today, Britain tomorrow. *Br. Med. J.* 292: 392–394, 1986.
51. Department of Health and Social Security. *Primary Health Care: An Agenda for Discussion.* Her Majesty's Stationery Office, 1986.
52. Johnson, P. Early exit for NHS's "Managing Director." *Br. Med. J.* 292: 1609, 1986.
53. Culyer, A. J. The NHS and the market: Images and realities. In: *The Public/Private Mix for Health,* edited by A. Maynard and G. McLachlan. London Provincial Hospitals Trust, London, 1982.
54. Johnson, P. Government condemned by its own statistics. *Br. Med. J.* 293: 86, 1986.
55. Meacher, M. Speech at the Financial Times Conference on Private Health Care, March 1985.
56. Hencke, D. Labour vows to axe Health Service deals. *The Guardian,* April 18, 1986.
57. Income Data Services. *Private Health Insurance.* London, June 1985.
58. Wood, L. Containment of costs is the main problem. *Financial Times,* January 22, 1986.
59. Kleber, L. Corporate health care: Why a time bomb is fizzing in the U.S. *Financial Times,* June 2, 1986.
60. Veitch, A. Test tube babies "only for the rich." *The Guardian,* April 24, 1986.
61. Timmins, N. Private health insurer to ban drug abuse and alcoholism patients. *The Times* (London), December 5, 1985.
62. Veitch, A. Hospitals told to stop kidney deals or close. *The Guardian,* June 11, 1986.

63. Pauley, R. Plea for a wider market. *Financial Times,* January 22, 1986, p. 17.
64. Mencher, S. *Private Practice in Britain: The Relationship of Private Medical Care to the National Health Service, Occasional Papers in Social Administration.* G. Bell and Sons, London, 1967.
65. House of Commons Employment and Social Services Sub-Committee of the Expenditure Committee. *National Health Facilities for Private Patients.* London, 1972.
66. Rayner, G. *Public Money*, December 1984.
67. Parliamentary Questions, February 4, 1985.
68. Independent Medical Care, February/March 1984.
69. Dodsworth, T. For-profit hospitals feel the pinch. *Financial Times,* January 22, 1986.
70. Sandison, C. R. Using the stock market to fund private hospital projects. *Br. J. Hosp. Med.* 23(4): 400, 1980.
71. Hall, W. AMI sees loss after $175 million write-off. *Financial Times,* March 15, 1986.
72. British United Provident Association. *Private Medicine: The Facts.* London, October 1983.
73. Department of Environment. Circular 22/80. London, 1980.
74. Department of Environment. Circular 2/81. London, 1981.
75. Hansard, April 4, 1985.
76. Schwartz, W. B., and Aaron, H. J. Rationing health care: Lessons from Britain. *N. Engl. J. Med.* 310: 52–56, 1984.

PART 4

Critique of Influences on Popular Thinking

Reaching the public to raise consciousness about the changing control of the health sector, and to promote a popular movement for different terms for health services delivery, is indeed difficult. Academic writings rarely penetrate a broad audience, though there are a few exceptions. Beyond individual and family member experiences in health care institutions, information and critique are limited mainly to the popular media's portrayals of health care, which have not been generally that favorable, but also are not that very incisive. Mobilizing information is often absent from media descriptions so social struggles are not supported. While critical, though usually incomplete, perceptions get created among the public, much needs to be done to move from sentiments to actions.

Over time opinion polls have indicated a majority of Americans growing more disenchanted with the health care system, feeling that major changes are in order (1, 2). They also express dissatisfaction with the major political, social and economic institutions of this nation, thus they are not so likely to favorably witness a corporate transformation of health care.

The four books under review in this section directly relate to the theme of this volume. Each in its own right has gained a wide, but varied, readership, though there are obvious differences in their scope and size. Two are popularized renditions of the history, development, and current dynamics of health care organizations that found audiences beyond the usual distribution for such accounts. The two works of fiction under review are most interesting in that each, in a not so subtle manner, attacks corporate medicine. For these reasons, they are important to analyze in the context of the previous selections of our volume here.

In "Medical History as Justification Rather than Explanation," Navarro critiques the Pulitzer Prize winner, *The Social Transformation of American Medicine* (3). He analyzes the major ideological and political assumptions that sustain Starr's explanation of the evolution of the institutions of medicine in the United States. These assumptions include: 1) that its evolution is an outcome of conflicts among different interest groups that exist within medicine, interacting within parameters defined by the majority of Americans whose beliefs and wants eventually determine what occurs in medicine; and 2) that the hegemonic positions in the ideology, practice and institutions of medicine are dominant because of their powers of persuasion. Navarro's chapter presents an alternative explanation of the evolution of medicine, including its recent corporatization (which Starr treats so lightly), to view it as an outcome of power relations defined not by the majority of Americans but by a series of conflicts between classes, races, genders, and other power groupings within a matrix of dominant-dominated relations. He finds that the dominance is reproduced by coercion and repression, and not merely by persuasion.

In "Physicians as Employees" Feinglass delineates both theoretical and empirical shortcomings of *The Medical Industrial Complex* (4). Neurosurgeon and author Wohl wrote this populist-styled indictment of corporate medicine in

1984; it goes beyond being merely a doctor's lament. Feinglass, however, enlarges Wohl's perspective as he analyzes how the for-profit forces in health care delivery may more specifically affect physicians. He sees the profession at a crossroads, with a segment of physicians ready to succumb to their eventual "proletarianization."

The third chapter turns attention to contemporary fiction. In "Mystery as a Means of Raising Doubts About Health Care for Profit," Gallo reviews the Paretsky novel, *Bitter Medicine* (5). She sees a plausible situation in the plot by a for-profit hospital executive and physician to carry out murder and cover-ups for the sake of corporate greed. Gallo notes how this author's progressive values led to the decision to explore profit maximization effects on health care and people's lives, and thus shaped her fictional characters and their actions.

The last chapter, "Mindbend Against Corporate Intrusion into Health Care," examines best-seller author Robin Cook's *Mindbend* (6). This was the first indictment of corporate medicine in a mass paperback novel. Strobeck places his review of it in a context of the recent and relevant medical care literature. He points out that Cook, himself a physician, wrote the book as an anti-big business polemic, but Strobeck raises specific criticisms about the projected story. He links Cook with Starr, Wohl and others in failing to understand the nature and consequences of large-scale corporate involvement in health care.

REFERENCES

1. Navarro, V. Where is the popular mandate? *New Engl. J. Med.* 13(1), 1983.
2. Smith, K. M., and Spinard, W. The popular political mood. *Soc. Policy*, March-April, 1981.
3. Starr, P. *The Social Transformation of American Medicine.* Basic Books, New York, 1982.
4. Wohl, S. *The Medical Industrial Complex.* Harmony Books, New York, 1984.
5. Paretsky, S. *Bitter Medicine: A V.I. Warshawski Mystery.* William Morrow and Co., New York, 1987.
6. Cook, R. *Mindbend.* New American Library, New York, 1986.

CHAPTER 11

Medical History as Justification Rather than Explanation: A Critique of Starr's *The Social Transformation of American Medicine*

Vicente Navarro

STARR'S MAJOR POSITION: AMERICANS' BELIEFS AS THE MOTOR OF HISTORY

Very few books on medical history have received so much acclaim as Paul Starr's *The Social Transformation of American Medicine* (1). Not only professional journals, but also the lay press have defined this publication—which received the Pulitzer Prize—as an indispensable reference to understanding the evolution of the institutions of medicine in the United States, referred to as the institutions of "American medicine." Starr, in no less than 154 pages, explains why American medicine has evolved the way that it has. His explanation covers many subjects, including why American medicine was born at the time that it was, why there is no national health insurance in this country, why there is a large involvement of corporate interests in the field of medicine, why we are witnessing a retrenchment of the expansion of government intervention in American medicine, and many other important questions. We all should agree that the answers to these questions have enormous importance for the resolution of many health policy issues that the United States faces today. History is, after all, a much needed element in the explanation of today's realities.

Before answering these questions, Starr criticizes and dismisses previous explanations which have emerged from different ideological poles. One, defined by him (1, p. 16) as the "most influential explanation of the structure of American medicine," traces the evolution of medicine to forces within medicine, and very much in particular to the scientific and technological advances that have acted as the primary motors in the evolution of medicine. While Starr agrees that these forces are important, he maintains that they cannot by themselves explain the evolution of American medicine. Scientists need to be reminded of the need for humility, after all.

The other explanation of American medicine is the instrumentalist interpretation that Starr attributes to Marxist authors. According to him (1, p. 17), Marxists view the development of American medicine as an "outcome of the objective interests of the capitalist class or the capitalist system." In this theoretical scenario, American medicine is what the capitalist class wants it to be. That class uses and shapes medicine in the way that best serves its class interests. Starr dismisses this interpretation, which he defines as *the* Marxist interpretation, as erroneous, i.e., it does not actually explain the evolution of American medicine. A proof that Marxists are wrong is that the capitalist class has attempted to rationalize medicine many times and has failed miserably. For example, Starr observes (1, p. 17), "The [capitalist] foundations have made repeated efforts to rationalize medical care [and] it is impressive how little these efforts have succeeded." Marxists and the Marxist historical method are thus plain wrong.

Starr's book represents in large degree an intent of offering an alternative explanation of American medicine to the ones recently presented by radicals and Marxist scholars. Thus, after dismissing these types of explanations of American medicine, he provides his own answer to the key question of why American medicine has evolved in the way it has. His explanation is remarkably simple: *American medicine has evolved as it has because Americans have wanted it that way.* American beliefs, concerns and wants have been the determinants of what has taken place in America's medicine, from its birth to the present. Needless to say, an interaction exists between forces within medicine (such as the power of physicians and other interest groups) and forces outside of medicine (such as Americans' beliefs). But of these forces, Starr maintains, the ones that determine the parameters of what happens or does not happen within medicine are the forces outside of medicine, of which the most important ones are the values and beliefs of Americans, by which it must be assumed Starr means the values and beliefs of the majority of Americans.

For example, the birth of what became known as scientific medicine is presented as an outcome of the power of persuasion of the physicians who convinced a responsive American public of the value of their tools and skills. Starr writes (1, p. 142) that "professional medicine drew its authority in part from the changing beliefs people held about their own abilities and understanding." At the time when medicine started, "there were profound changes in Americans' way of life and forms of consciousness that made them more dependent upon professional authority and more willing to accept it as legitimate" (1, p. 18). Also, "towards the end of the nineteenth century . . . Americans became more accustomed to relying on the specialized skills of strangers . . . Bolstered by genuine advances in science and technology, the claims of the professions to competent authority became more plausible, even when they were not yet objectively true; for science worked even greater changes on the imagination than it worked on the processes of disease" (1, p. 15). Consequently, Americans were convinced and persuaded that they needed the medical profession to solve their health problems: "Rather than trusting one's own skills and knowledge or those of competing sects or groups, Americans were persuaded to rely on the skills of the nascent medical profession; the less one could believe 'one's own eyes' . . . the more receptive one became to seeing the world through the eyes of those who claimed specialized, technical knowledge validated by a community of their peers" (1, p. 19).

In summary, Starr sees the rise of the medical profession as an outcome of Americans' beliefs, a result of their being persuaded by the medical profession's claims of the value of their skills. Once again, he castigates Marxists for believing that the monopolization of medical practice by regular physicians was accompanied by the repression of competing systems of medicine. He indicates (1, p. 229) that "to see the rise of the [medical] profession as coercive is to underestimate how deeply its authority penetrated the beliefs of ordinary people and how firmly it had seized the imagination even of its rivals."

Thus, Starr sees persuasion of the majority of Americans by a minority as the primary intellectual force behind social change in America. Several pages after having explained the birth of medicine as the result of the medical profession's powers of persuasion, Starr goes on to interpret the failure to establish a national health insurance, on the eve of World War I, as a result of the failure of social reformers to persuade Americans of the merits of that program. To the same degree that Americans have been "persuaded to adopt compulsory insurance against industrial accident, Americans could have been persuaded to adopt compulsory insurance against sickness" (1, p. 236). Social reformers, however, failed to do so. In conclusion, American did not get national health insurance at that time because Americans did not want it.

American beliefs, wants and values appear again as the primary explanation of the events that took place in American medicine after World War II. This period is presented by Starr as characterized by the efforts of different interest groups to win the hearts and minds of the American people. Thus, one of the most conflictive periods in the history of the United States—which included the nightmare of McCarthyism, with brutal repression against radical and Marxist forces—is presented by Starr (in a chapter meaningfully entitled the "Triumph of Accommodation") as merely an outcome of U.S. labor's decision to change its image, style and strategy. Labor decided to change from radical to moderate in order to accommodate its interests to business interests and, in doing so, avoid antagonizing the majority of Americans, now redefined as the middle class public (1, p. 312). Indeed, Starr writes (1, p. 313), "The unions' struggle for influence in welfare programs was one of their few political successes during the post war period. Strikes during and immediately after the war antagonized much of the middle class public, and in the backlash against the unions, employers took the opportunity to get back some of the control they had lost." According to Starr, moderation as a tactic for persuasion was successful. Americans, via Senator Taft and the Supreme Court, included the right to bargain health care benefits in the Taft-Hartley Act. In this way, "unions have won the right to a say in health care" (1, p. 313).

American beliefs, values and wants are also perceived to be responsible for what happened in American medicine in the 1960s, with the establishment of new programs such as Medicare and Medicaid that were not allowed to interfere with the power relationships in existence in the institutions of medicine. According to Starr (1, p. 364), Americans "in the early 60s wanted to change, but did not want *to be changed*. This was very much the case with regard to medical care. Americans wanted medicine to bring them change (new advances, more services), but they were not yet prepared for the sake of health to make changes in their way of life or their institutions." Needless to say, the final shape of those government programs also depended on the interplay of the different interest groups that operated within the institutions of medicine. Starr (1, p. 367) quickly adds, however, that American beliefs and public concern were the main forces responsible for the establishment and development of these programs.

Rolling along with time and moving on to the next historical period, American beliefs appear once again as the main force behind changes in American medicine in the 1970s and 80s. Thus, the expansion of government health interventions (expenditures and regulations) at the beginning and middle of the 70s and their reduction in the early 80s is explained as an outcome of a particular change in American beliefs. At the beginning of this period, Americans believed in government; at the end of the period, they did not. Starr summarizes this development as follows (1, p. 380); "Like American politics more generally, the politics of health care passed through three phases in the 1970's: (1) a period of agitation and reform in the first half of the decade when broader entitlements in social welfare and stricter regulation of industry gained ground in public opinion and law, (2) a prolonged stalemate, beginning around 1975 . . . and (3) a growing reaction against liberalism and government, culminating in the election of President Reagan in 1980 and the reversal of many earlier regulatory programs." While at the beginning of the 70s the majority of Americans favored government expansion, by 1980 "the majority of Americans clearly shared a general antipathy to government" (1, p. 418). According to Starr (1, p. 416), when the decade began, reformers were criticizing the inefficiency of the health care industry and they were able to persuade Americans of the need for government intervention; when the decade ended, the industry was criticizing the inefficiency of reform and was able to persuade Americans of the need to curtail government intervention. As a result of this situation and effective persuasion, "the public seems to be expressing a desire to return to older and simpler ways"

(1, p. 419). Thus, Reagan's current drastic policies of cutting health expenditures for the elderly, poor, disabled and children, and of weakening government interventions, are perceived as responding to a popular mandate; these policies are the ones that Americans want.

Starr's interpretation of current events is a logical extension of his historical interpretation of American medicine. In his history, the social transformation of medicine is reduced to the ideological transformation of American beliefs and wants expressed either through the market or through their representative public institutions. In this theoretical scenario, the history of American medicine becomes the history of how interest groups have or have not been successful in persuading Americans of the merits of their proposals and ideas and how these groups have interacted among themselves to define the probable within the parameters of what Americans have already defined as possible. It is therefore not surprising that Starr concludes his explanations of the past and present of American medicine by predicting that the future of American medicine will depend primarily on what Americans want to happen. The last sentence of the book (1, p. 449) summarizes it well: The future of American medicine depends on "choices that Americans have still to make." History is, after all, a way of reading our own future.

STARR'S IDEOLOGICAL AND POLITICAL ASSUMPTIONS

I have gone to great lengths to summarize Starr's explanation of American medicine and to quote extensively from his acclaimed work because his views are highly representative of the view toward the workings of health policy upheld by large sectors of U.S. academia, government and media. His view sustains the ideological position that whatever has happened and will happen in America and its institutions is very much the result of what Americans want and believe.

Starr's interpretation of America sees the past and present structure of power in the United States as reflecting the wishes of the majority of Americans. To see the structure of power in America as the outcome of what Americans want, however, is to beg the question of which Americans. If by Americans it is meant the majority of Americans, then two assumptions are being made. One is that the majority of Americans share a set of beliefs, values and wants that provide an ideological cohesiveness to the totality of the unit called America. The other assumption is that the majority of Americans have had and continue to have the power to determine what happens both in the private sector of America (through the market forces) and in the public sector (through the representative public institutions). To these two assumptions Starr adds a third one: the dominant ideologies and positions become dominant through their powers of persuasion rather than through coercion and repression of alternative ideologies and positions.

These are the assumptions that sustain Starr's theoretical position and discourse. Needless to say, this interpretation of America is the one favored by those who benefit from current power relations in the U.S. It rationalizes the power of the establishment. They are there, on the top, because people want them there. Moreover, theirs is the power of persuasion rather than the power of coercion and repression. This legitimization function, incidentally, is what explains the "popularity" of Starr's book in the establishment's media and academia. Indeed, that acclaim cannot be attributed to the book's explanatory value of our realities (which is limited) but rather to its propagandizing function within that reality (which is large).

AN ALTERNATIVE EXPLANATION OF OUR REALITIES

A historical analysis of U.S. realities in general and of American medicine in particular shows that none of Starr's assumptions is correct. The historical analysis of the United States shows that Americans have been and continue to be divided into classes, races, genders and other power groupings, each with its own interests, set of beliefs and wants that are in continuous conflict and struggle. And these conflicts appear because, given the economic, social and political structure of the United States, certain classes, races, gender, and other groups have more power than others. Moreover, these power differentials are structural rather than conjunctural; they are built into the fabric of American society. In terms of classes, corporate America, for example, has far more power than working class America. This power differential results from the dominant position that the capitalist class—Corporate America—has over the means of production, consumption and exchange. And the hegemony of that class in the ideological and cultural sphere is due to its overwhelming influence over the means of value formation and legitimation. Needless to say, dominance and hegemony do not mean absolute control. The working class can also win victories. Power competition does exist after all. However, this competition is consistently and unavoidably unequal, skewed, and biased in favor of the document classes (and races and gender). As Miliband (2, p. 278) has indicated:

> There is competition, and defeat for powerful capitalist interests as well as victories. After all, David did overcome Goliath. But the point of the story is that David was smaller than Goliath and that the odds were heavily against him.

To believe that some classes, races and a gender are dominant does not mean that they alone determine the nature of what happens in the United States and its institutions, including the institutions of medicine. Indeed, to have a dominant class, race and gender means that there are dominated classes, races and a gender who do not necessarily accept the formers' domination in a passive way.

Conflict and struggle continuously take place; and it is this struggle and conflict (rather than merely what one class wants) that determines changes in U.S. society and in American medicine. Starr is unaware of this reality. He indulges in facile stereotyping of Marxist positions by defining them as instrumentalist, i.e., they see the evolution of government and medicine as the outcome of the wishes of the capitalist class, which in a rather omnipotent fashion, shapes government and medicine to optimize its own interests. Starr's acquaintance with Marxist scholarship is characteristically limited. He would have benefited from a more rigorous reading and familiarity with that branch of scholarship before dismissing it so quickly. To reduce the large body of historical scholarship rooted in Marx to instrumentalism is abusive to an extreme. (For a critique of instrumentalism, see reference 3.) Actually, it was neither Marx nor any of his followers, but rather President Woodrow Wilson, who said that "the masters of the government of the United States are the combined capitalists and manufacturers of the United States" (quoted in 4). Although I find this instrumentalist vision of government too simplistic, I consider it equally simplistic to believe, as Starr does, that it is not the capitalist class but rather the will of the American people which defines government policies.

American institutions, including the institutions of government and medicine, are the results of conflicts and struggles, of which class conflict is a key one. And by key I do not mean that class conflict is the only one. Other types of conflict do exist, of course, but class conflict is the one that explains the parameters within which all other conflicts unfold. And that conflict appears and has consequences in all societal institutions, including medicine. Moreover, that conflict emerges within a set of class (as well as race, gender, and other) forms of dominant/dominated power relations which *are reproduced not only by persuasion* (as Starr believes) *but, more importantly, by coercion and repression.*

In summary, and as I have shown elsewhere (6), to understand the evolution of the United States and of American medicine, one has to understand the economic, social, and political structure of the U.S. and how it is reproduced through conflicts and tension among different groups and classes, conflicts that appear in all realms of society, including medicine. What happens in medicine is not the outcome of the conflicts between the different interest groups that exist within medicine, interacting within the parameters defined by the majority of Americans whose beliefs and wants eventually define what does or does not occur in medicine. These interest groups are, in reality, segments of classes (and other power categories) which, when considered in a systemic and not just sectoral fashion, are found to possess a degree of cohesion far transcending their specific differences and tactical disagreements. Thus, to understand the behavior and dynamics of the visible, and equally important, nonvisible actors in the medical sector, we have to understand their position within the overall economic and political scheme of the United States, i.e., their class and power position. Their position within a matrix of class, as well as sex, race and other types of power relations, explains why certain possibilities are being reproduced and others are being inhibited and repressed.

REPRESSION, BESIDES PERSUASION: THE ESTABLISHMENT OF DOMINANCE

From its inception, the occupational branch of medicine was very close to management. As indicated in 1919 by one of the founders of occupational medicine, Dr. C. D. Relby (quoted in 7, p. 26), "industrial medicine is a specialty in the service of management." Forty-two years later, the head of the Council for Occupational Medicine of the American Medical Association, Dr. W. Shepard, put it equally well (7, p. 26): "The physicians' place in industrial medicine . . . is auxiliary to the main purpose of the business: production and profit." This closeness of industrial medicine to the corporate class explains the sharing of views and beliefs among most industrial health professionals and that class. Both social groups believe that (a) most work-related accidents are caused by workers' carelessness, (b) there is a need for voluntary cooperation between management and labor and for voluntary enforcement of services and standards rather than compulsory government enforcement, (c) occupational health and safety professionals are scientists and therefore neutral, (d) most interventions need to be aimed at personal preventive devices and, (e) workers need to change their behavior and life styles.

These positions were and still are the dominant positions within industrial medicine and within the business establishment. However, this dominance was not, as Starr would have us believe, a result of the medical profession's persuasiveness. Rather, the rise of this position to dominance was based on a most brutal repression against alternate views of industrial medicine that saw most industrial accidents as caused by management's prioritization of productivity and profits over workers' lives, by faulty planning and equipment design, and by the use of toxic and hazardous materials that should either not be used or should be better controlled (8). This alternative view remained a repressed minority view because it conflicted with the interests of the employers who did not want to accept responsibility for the workplace damage, nor were they willing to change working conditions if this implied a reduction of their rights, privileges and benefits. The class of employers offered (a) rewards to those who favored the ideological position that reproduced their power, and (b) sanctions and repression against those who offered alternate explanations and solutions that challenged their power. The overwhelming influence of the class of employers in the funding of scientific endeavors, in the employment of occupational physicians, and on the agencies of the state explains why "the individual workers' responsibility" thesis became the dominant one in industrial medicine. The dominance of this position was based not on the power of persuasion of the industrial physicians but rather on the power of coercion and repression held by the dominant class whom those professionals served and whose ideology they accommodated to.

The rewarding of those medical positions that reproduced the dominant ideology and the repression and exclusion of those that conflicted with these positions *appeared in all areas of medicine*. In summary, dominant professional positions become dominant not because of the persuasiveness of their upholders but rather because of their articulation within the dominant/dominated power relations. Interpretations that conflict with the dominant relations are likely to be repressed while those that strengthen dominant explanations of reality are likely to be rewarded. Needless to say, and like the David-Goliath conflict, the dominated positions can occasionally win. Moreover, the dominant positions cannot just ignore the dominated ones. There is a continuous need to repress them and recycle those elements of the dominated positions that can be absorbed within the dominant ones. But here again, the point of the story is that most of the time, one position becomes dominant or not depending on how it articulates itself with the overall power relations in society.

I suspect that some would argue that occupational medicine is not representative of what happened with medicine in general; that most of the institutions of medicine did not have such a close relationship with the corporate class as the occupational medical institutions did. While it is true that the other branches of medicine did not have as close a relationship with the corporate class, the differences involve degree rather than substance. The reality is that, from its birth, the dominant medical ideology and position became hegemonic because it complemented and reproduced the dominant class ideology. For example, American medicine as we know it—Flexnerian medicine—was established in Germany in the 19th century with the active support of the German bourgeoisie whose dominant ideology was compatible and in accordance with what was later to be called scientific medicine. Positivism was the ideology of the nascent bourgeoisie, and positivism appeared in the interpretation of health and disease that became the dominant one within medicine (9). Consequently, disease came to be perceived as a biological phenomenon caused by one or several factors which were always associated and observed in the existence of that disease.

We have to realize, however, that side by side with this interpretation was an alternate one that saw disease as a result of the oppressive nature of the existent power relations of society at that time. The intervention was viewed as one modifying (Virchow) or smashing (Engels) those power relations. This version of medicine did not prevail. Rather, it was repressed by the dominant classes who, of course, felt threatened by those alternative explanations of disease and the operational proposals for its resolution. These classes preferred to support the biological and individual interpretation of disease which has since been reproduced in curative and preventive medicine. Thus, medical interventions were aimed at eliminating, eradicating and controlling the outside microagents—bacteria or viruses—that created the disease.

This interpretation of disease and of medicine was also the one that became dominant in the United States. And it became dominant for the same reasons. The established centers of power favored that interpretation of disease and medicine, repressing other interpretations that represented a potential threat to their power and privileges. Starr dismisses this explanation of the birth of American medicine. He actually belittles the explanation that the dominance of Flexnerian medicine also meant the repression of its alternative. He denies, for example, that capitalist ideology favored medicine over public health. He writes (1, p. 228), "It is difficult to see why capitalism as a system, would have benefited by favoring medical care over public health. . . . To be sure, many companies resisted public health measures that would have increased their production costs or limited their markets. On the other hand, for equally self-interested reasons, life insurance companies actively stimulated public health measures." By posing the question the way he does, however, he already provides the answers. The question that needs to be asked, however, is not so much why the capitalist class favored curative medicine over public health, but rather, why the dominant ideology of disease was the same in both (medicine and public health), i.e., the positivist biological one which led to medical and public health interventions focusing for the most part on individual interventions that minimized conflict with the power relations within and outside medicine. A clear example of this is the approach that both public health spokespersons and the life insurance industry took toward prevention. C. E. A. Winslow (one of the founders of what became the established public health position) included in his report prepared for the Metropolitan Life Insurance Company (10) the following analysis of what was wrong at the workplace and what should be done:

> *Do you know* that a great many men and women die every year on account of the conditions under which they work? *Do you know* that if a man goes into certain trades it means he will have five, ten or fifteen years less of life than if he earned his living in some other way?
>
> It is true. The death rate among cutlery grinders in Sheffield, England, for instance, is just about twice as high as it is for other men of the same age. Half the men who die in this trade die of *industrial disease* (chiefly tuberculosis), due, largely, to breathing in sharp particles of dust.
>
> Most industrial diseases are preventable. The bad conditions that exist in factories and other industrial establishments are due mainly to ignorance. They keep the worker uncomfortable, they hinder his work, and they make him an easy prey to sicknesses that come along. They are likewise harmful to the employer's interests, for he is a constant loser from poor and careless work, spoiled stock, absences and the breaking in of green hands. *Dangerous conditions continue to exist because neither employer nor employee knows what is going on.* They do not understand that dust and fumes, bad air, poor lighting and dirt make sick men and a poor product. This book is written to help its readers to think of these things; for conditions will be made better as soon as people begin to think about them. You cannot keep your shop healthful unless your employer does his part. Neither can he unless you do yours.

"Ignorance" was presented in that report as the primary source of the problem. Winslow's examination of the "dangerous trades," however, did not lead him to ask Metropolitan's subscribers to force their employers to clean up their factories. It is a rather hyperbolic statement to present, as Starr does, that call for information and health education as examples of "active" public health interventions. The reality is that the meaning of "active" is dramatically reduced within the parameters of nonconflictive solutions. A more updated version of this interpretation of public health is reflected in current Reagan health policies that focus on individual health education as the best measure of prevention, while weakening government regulations and other collective interventions.

It is important to understand that side by side with the dominant interpretation of public health focused on the individual, there has always been another interpretation which views public health as a set of interventions that frequently conflict with the dominant capitalist relations existent in the areas of work, consumption, environment, and residence. This latter interpretation has more often than not been repressed. The power of this alternative interpretation has primarily depended not on its power of persuasion but rather on its articulation with an alternate source of power, such as militant sectors of labor or other rebellious forces capable of facilitating its expression. Thus, the periods in which this alternate view has opened up new spaces have been those where militant sectors of the working class and related rebellious forces have been able to press for these types of interventions. As I will show later on, expansion of government public health interventions has occurred in periods when labor and allied rebellious forces have been in a relatively strong position.

AN ALTERNATIVE EXPLANATION: CLASS INTEREST AS THE DETERMINANT OF CHANGE

Another example of Starr's erroneous interpretation of history appears in his rather idyllic explanation of how workers' compensation laws were passed in the United States. Not uncharacteristically, Starr explains this event as a result of the powers of persuasion of the social reformers who were able to convince Americans of the merits of their specific legislation. Reality, however, was quite different. The passage of these laws had little to do with social reformers' persuasive powers, nor with the will or wants of Americans. These laws were passed because of the interests of American corporations. The latter had enormous power and influence over the legislatures of several states that passed workers' compensation laws after 1910. At that time, there was widespread worker unrest centered around poor working conditions and the large number of workers injured at the workplace. Consequently, large sections of labor were demanding an end to management prerogatives, including management's right to control the workplace. Moreover, many workers were suing management for damages, with the courts ordering settlements that proved to be quite costly for management. Because of these pressures, the voice of the major corporations, the National Civic Federation, actively supported workers' compensation legislation. Among other consequences, that law eliminated the workers' right to sue for damages (8). Today we are witnessing a similar type of response to the current individual workers' litigation against Johns-Manville and other asbestos producers. Johns-Manville, one of the most offensive corporations to the health of American workers, is in the forefront of the campaign for government compensation laws for asbestos workers which will shift the social costs of the corporations' criminal behavior to the government. It requires an overgenerous reading of corporate America, indeed, to define Johns-Manville or the earlier National Civil Corporation as "social reformers" and their political muscle and influence over the state legislatures as "persuasion." The implementation of those laws had little to do with "social reforms" or with persuasion. It had to do with the threat that workers' demands posed to American corporations and the enormous political muscle they have over the state legislatures. It is Starr's unawareness of these social and political conflicts that makes his explanations so erroneous.

Similarly, to see—as Starr does—the victory of the corporativist view within labor, which occurred after World War II, as representing labor's desire to change its image in order not to antagonize the middle classes is to ignore the enormous conflicts that took place in the 1940s and 50s, including a most brutal attack by the corporate class against the most militant section of the working class. McCarthyism represented brutal repression against any class threat to corporate class dominance. The Taft-Hartley Act, a result of that attack, was not a victory for labor, as Starr seems to believe, but rather a defeat. It forced labor to act as an interest group rather than as a class. Because of it, the United States is the only country in the Western developed world where labor cannot act as a class. For example, steel workers cannot strike in solidarity with a coal miners' strike. By law, each section of labor has to act as an interest group. Consequently, this piece of legislation weakened labor most dramatically; each fraction of labor has to act on its own (11, 12). Thus, some sectors of labor did achieve great advances through private collective agreements; however, for the working class as a whole, their level of benefits remained far more limited than that of their counterparts in Western Europe where the working class could still operate as a class. As a consequence, the United States has an underdeveloped welfare state. In terms of health benefits, the U.S. population has less coverage (in their private and public programs) than the majority of the populations in developed countries (13).

STARR'S INTERPRETATION OF RECENT EVENTS

The ideological and apologetic function of Starr's interpretation comes through most clearly in his interpretation of the current Reagan policies as the outcome of a popular mandate. He uncritically reproduces prevalent conventional wisdom that Americans' opinion follows a pendular swing, oscillating from pro- to anti-government. It speaks of the overwhelming influence that corporate America has on the means of information in the United States (including academia) that this interpretation is so widespread and reproduced in spite of overwhelming evidence to the contrary. Indeed, as I have shown elsewhere (14), popular opinion is not as volatile as it is assumed to be. For the years that I have analyzed popular opinion polls—1976-1983—the evidence is overwhelming: by large margins, the majority of Americans are in favor of increased rather than decreased health and social expenditures and strengthening rather than weakening government intervention to protect workers, consumers and the environment. Reagan's health policies do not follow a popular mandate.

Starr is also empirically wrong when he explains Reagan's 1980 electoral victory as the "outcome of the wishes of the majority of Americans and a general antipathy to government." The opinion polls for 1980 show a similar result as previous and subsequent polls: the majority of Americans were in favor of the same government programs that Reagan soon started cutting. Moreover, the majority of Americans did not vote or voted for candidates other than Reagan. Starr should get his facts straight and be less willing to join the chorus, following the establishment's tune. Moreover, even among the minority of the electorate who did vote for Reagan, many indicated that they had voted *against* Carter because of his perceived inability to reduce unemployment rather than *for* Reagan.

To believe that Carter was defeated in 1980 because he was too progressive is to uncritically reproduce what the establishment wants people to believe and to ignore all evidence to the contrary. Carter was elected in 1976 with a program that included an expansion of social consumption (including establishment of national health insurance) and a reduction of military expenditures—policies that he reversed in 1978, alienating large sectors of the population and, most importantly, large sectors of the grassroots element of the Democratic Party. This change of policies explains why his job rating in the opinion polls fell more precipitously from 1977 to mid-summer 1979 than had been the case for any other president since polling on the subject began in 1945 (15). In brief, there was not a popular mandate in 1980 for cutting social consumption and weakening government health regulations.

What we are witnessing in the 1980s is not the outcome of American wishes, if by Americans we mean the majority of Americans. What we are witnessing today is a most brutal class warfare, carried out by the most aggressive sector of corporate America against the advances that workers, women, blacks and other minorities, and environmentalists achieved in the 1960s and middle-1970s. Even Lane Kirkland, the head of the AFL-CIO and a person not known for radicalism, has expressed alarm that big business in this country is involved "in an unprecedented class warfare" (16).

Why this response? Because of labor shortages in the 1960s, we witnessed the strengthening of labor's power, responsible in large degree for the passage of social and health federal legislation. In addition, other rebellious movements, such as civil rights, black liberation, women's and ecological movements, pressed for government intervention. Contrary to conventional wisdom, the 1960s and 70s proved the effectiveness of government intervention in the social arena. By the second half of the 1970s, only 7–8 percent of the American public remained beneath the poverty level compared with about 18 percent in 1960. As Schwartz (17) has shown, this reduction of poverty was accomplished primarily through government transfer programs.

In the health care sector we witnessed a similar progress. In 1963, before the implementation of Medicare and Medicaid, fully one in five of those Americans living beneath the poverty level had never been examined by a physician. By 1970, the percentage of people living in poverty who had never been examined by a physician was reduced from its 1963 level of 19 percent to 8 percent. From 1965 to 1975, the overall infant mortality rate among the poor fell by 33 percent. Gains among blacks were particularly evident. Between 1950 and 1965, before the great expansion in federal medical and nutritional programs, the infant mortality rate among blacks barely fell, from 44.5 per 1000 births in 1950 to 40.3 in 1965. Following the expansion of the programs, the rate of black infant mortality declined quickly, from 40.3 in 1965 to 30.9 in 1970 and 24.2 in 1975. There thus occurred an approximately fivefold increase in the speed of decline in the black infant mortality rate after 1965.

Other social groups also improved their living conditions because of that growth of social consumption. In summary, the growth of social expenditures was an outcome of the relative strength of labor and other social movements. At the same time, that growth also strengthened the working class vis-à-vis the corporate class. Working families received collective and social wages that made them less vulnerable to the cyclical fluctuations of employment and thus less receptive to employers' pressures.

Government interventions took place not only by expanding expenditures but also by regulating the protection of workers, consumers, and of the environment. Regarding the environment, government interventions, in the Clean Air Act of 1970 and the Water Pollution Control Act in 1972, had a positive impact on improving water and air conditions in the United States. By 1979, the level of sulfur dioxide in the air had declined by about an additional 40 percent from its level in 1970, and concentrations of suspended particulate matter in the air in 1979 had declined by an additional 17 percent from their 1970 level. For carbon monoxide (from automobile exhaust), the decline was about 40 percent for the same period (17). Regarding water, the National Wildlife Federation indicates that fifty major bodies of water showed considerable improvement over the decade of the 70s (17).

Here again, the evidence is overwhelmingly clear that the growth of government health expenditures and of government regulations did improve the conditions of the majority of Americans and that the majority of Americans favor an expansion and strengthening of such interventions (14, 17). The fact that they were cut in 1978 and further cut in the 1980s was not because the majority of Americans changed their minds. The evidence is clear that they did not. The government social and health expenditure cuts and the weakening of government occupational and environmental regulations were an outcome of a most brutal repression from the most aggressive sectors of the U.S. capitalist class who saw those advances by the working population as threats to their privileges and interests (18).

To see those policies as aimed at "getting government off people's backs" is to indulge in the realm of apologetics, not rigorous analysis. The Reagan Administration is not anti-government. Actually, the percentage of public expenditures in the GNP has increased, not declined, under this administration. Primary characteristics of this administration have been (*a*) a dramatic transfer of federal funds from the social and health sectors to the military sectors, and (*b*) an enormous increase in the agencies of intervention and control, with a reduction of trade union, civil, women's, and ecological rights for the majority of the population. These interventions respond to a specific vision of the government role in today's United States, well defined by H. Salvatori (quoted in 19), a key member of the Reagan transitional team:

> In the history of man everyone has talked about expanding rights, having more and more freedom. But we have found that if you let people do what they want to do you have chaos . . . what we have to do is to restructure society. Frankly, we need a *more authoritarian state*. (emphasis added)

This is what we are witnessing today. In brief, the issue is not to be pro or anti-government. At issue, rather, is whose government and for what purpose. The overwhelming influence that those corporate class interests have over the media and political and academic institutions explains why a "new conventional wisdom" has been developed in which those government policies that are creating enormous pain and suffering are presented as responding to the wishes of the majority of Americans.

It is Starr's willingness to reproduce these ideological images that explains his popularity in the corridors of power. Here again, his "success" is not due to his persuasiveness but rather to his articulation with the dominant/dominated power relations in the United States. This fact also explains his repression of alternative antiestablishment views, represssion that appears in his book by stereotyping (to the point of ridiculing) or silencing all positions that clearly threaten the ideological reproduction of established class relations.

This deafening silence is not without costs, however. For example, in his chapter on the increased involvement of corporations in American medicine, Starr (1, p. 428) characterizes the creation of a medical-industrial complex as an "entirely unexpected" consequence of government interventions in the 60s. A better reading of U.S. realities would have led him to conclude that there was nothing "unexpected" in that development. Other authors (nowhere mentioned in this chapter) had predicted and explained this growth of corporate involvement in medicine. Actually, contrary to what Starr indicates, Arnold Relman, the editor of *The New England Journal of Medicine*, was not the first author to introduce the concept of the medical-industrial complex. Kelman (20), Salmon (21-23) and myself (6), among others, have explained how the rationale of the capitalist system and the enormous influence of corporate America in the organizations and agencies of the state determines that even when government, as a result of popular pressures, intervenes in the health and social spheres to improve the health and well-being of Americans, those interventions are limited and compromised by the need to respond to corporate interests as well, which in turn diminishes the initial intent of those interventions. All those authors predicted the establishment and enlargement of the medical-industrial complex (both in the financing and in the delivery of health services) before Relman and Starr.

The fact that Starr does not acknowledge or refer to these previous works is characteristic of the discrimination and repression against Marxist scholarship in the U.S. academia and media. By ignoring these previous works, however, he remains stuck in the same trenches with other "interest group" analysts. Indeed, this new version of the "corporatization of medicine," by ignoring the socio-economic-political context in which it takes place, and by seeing corporate America as one more interest group competing for government favors, is incapable of explaining why that corporatization is taking place now. It is not surprising that Starr finds that corporatization an unexpected event. That event, however, is expected and predictable. As those authors explained, this corporatization of medicine is the logical outcome of the dynamics of U.S. capitalism within a process of class struggle in which the dominant capitalist class continues to have an overwhelming influence over the organs of the state. This overwhelming dominance explains that even when government responds to popular demands from working America, that response takes place within the parameters and conditions defined by the hegemonic elements within that capitalist or corporate class. The very limited power of the working class in the United States (a situation unparalleled among developed capitalist societies) explains not only the underdevelopment of the U.S. welfare state but also the corporatization of its medicine.

In summary, government—as a branch of the state—is subjected to a matrix of influences, some of which are structurally more dominant than others. Dominant influences are not tantamount to absolute control. And the majority of Americans can have a voice after all. However, contrary to what Starr and the establishment would like us to believe, that voice is not the definitive one to explain our past, present or future. Other voices exist which limit, restrain and frequently even silence those majority voices. For example, the majority of Americans have desired for many years that the government assure that all persons in need of health care should receive it, or that whomever needs a job should have it (14, 25, 26). Neither popular wish has been fulfilled. The list of responsibilities that the majority of Americans feel their government should have and fails to take on is enormous. Whether government undertakes these responsibilities or not does not depend only or even primarily on what the majority of Americans feel or want. It depends on the sets of influences and dominances that shape government interventions, of which corporate America is a major one. And the majority of Americans know it. They believe, for example, that the major political parties are in favor of big business and that major American corporations tend to dominate and determine the behavior of our public officials in Washington (27, 28). It would be wrong to see corporate America as the only influence, with absolute control over government. But in a matrix of influences, theirs is a very powerful one indeed. And its power appears not only in political but also in civil, social and economic institutions. It is this overwhelming influence that compromises most significantly the meaning of democracy. Indeed, the public debate takes place within the parameters already defined by the dominant corporate class which influences, through its enormous varieties of communication agencies (academia, media, political institutions, etc.), the terms of the discourse and debate, through which that majority voice is supposed to appear. As an observer of the American scene has indicated (29), "The flaw in the pluralistic heaven is that the heavenly chorus sings with a very special accent. The system is askew, loaded, and unbalanced in favor of a fraction of a minority."

Thus, when government has to respond due to strong popular pressure (as in the 1960s and 70s), that response always takes place in a way that corporate class interests shape the nature of that response, continuing to be in a dominant position in those interventions. What alternatives are to be considered, and which ones are to be chosen depend not only on the majority of Americans but on many other forces as well, of which corporate class forces continue to be the dominant ones. Examples in the health sector are many. Witness the debate in the 1970s in the U.S. Congress about the type of national health insurance. The power of financial capital, the commercial insurance companies, forced a change in the Kennedy-Griffith proposal—the only proposal that excluded the insurance companies—and brought about the Kennedy-Mills proposal which accepted their role (6). As an editorial of the *New York Times* indicated (30):

> To retain the insurance companies' role was based on recognition of that industry's power to kill any legislation it considers unacceptable. The Bill's sponsors thus had to choose between appeasing the insurance industry and obtaining no national health insurance at all.

Even with these changes, the combined resistance of the dominant sectors of corporate America, side by side with the opposition of the major medical and hospital interest groups, defeated and silenced that alternative, in spite of the fact that the majority of Americans wanted then, and continue to want now, a tax-based program that could assure comprehensive and universal health coverage for the whole population.

Also, witness today's discussion of federal health policies. The discourse focuses on "consumer choice," "competitiveness," "rate of return" and the like, all heavily ideological terms that characterize the acceptable intellectual exchange. Anti-corporate positions are excluded by a most brutal force of repression from most of the communication agencies, including academia. Harvard University's Department of Sociology, incidentally the academic institution in which Paul Starr teaches, has not even one token tenured Marxist professor. Repression, not persuasion, explains this reality. The presentation of alternative explanations of reality and alternate socialist solutions to the population is dramatically reduced in the institutions of ideological reproduction—like the media and academia—by unhindered repression.

In brief, the element of "choice" that Starr assumes when he writes that the past, present, and future is what the majority of Americans have and will choose, assumes that there is no control of information, no limitation of the agenda for change, no predetermination of interest choices, and no limitation of instruments for change. The past and present of America deny these assumptions, however. Actually, what we are witnessing today is the increased alienation of people not from the values that (at least in theory) their government institutions should uphold (e.g., responding to the health needs of all people), but rather from the actual practice of those institutions that operate on their behalf.

The available evidence shows that the majority of Americans are dissatisfied with the major political, social and economic institutions of our country and the order of things that they sustain. They acquiesce to the existing order because they do not see the possibility of change, or do not see what alternatives exist or how the rules of the game can be changed. Indeed, the future of American medicine within the corporate order will not be the one that the majority of Americans would choose. Rather, it will be the outcome of enormous, heartbreaking struggle between the dominated and dominant classes, races, gender and other power categories, in which the corporate class will continue to have the major voice in defining the parameters, alternatives and discourses of that future. The future of the United States and its system of medicine will depend on the resolution of this struggle.

REFERENCES

1. Starr, P. *The Social Transformation of American Medicine.* Basic Books, New York, 1983.
2. Miliband, R. Marx and the state. In *The Socialist Register, 1965*, edited by R. Miliband and J. Saville. Merlin Press, London, 1966.

3. Navarro, V. Radicalism, Marxism, and medicine. *Int. J. Health Serv.* 13(2): 179–202, 1983.
4. Hunt, E. K. and Sherman, H. J. *Economics: An Introduction to Traditional and Radical Views.* Harper and Row, New York, 1972.
5. Ploss, J. A History of the Medical Care Program of the United Mine Workers of America's Welfare and Retirement Fund. Master's thesis, Johns Hopkins School of Hygiene and Public Health, 1980.
6. Navarro, V. *Medicine Under Capitalism.* Prodist, New York, 1977.
7. Berman, D. *Death on the Job.* Monthly Review Press, New York, 1979.
8. Navarro, V. The determinants of occupational health and safety policies in the United States (mimeograph).
9. Navarro, V. Work, ideology and science: The case of medicine. *Int. J. Health Serv.* 10(4): 523–550, 1980.
10. Winslow, C. E. A. The Health of the Worker: Dangers to Health in the Factory and Shop and How To Avoid Them. Metropolitan Life Insurance Company, New York, 1913.
11. Davis, M. Labour in American politics. *New Left Review* 123: 3–46, 1980.
12. Davis, M. The legacy of the CIO. *New Left Review* 124: 43–84, 1980.
13. Maxwell, R. *Health and Wealth: An International Study of Health Care Spending.* Lexington Books, Lexington, 1981.
14. Navarro, V. Where is the popular mandate? *N. Engl. J. Med.,* Dec. 9, 1982; *Int. J. Health Serv.* 13(1): 169–174, 1983.
15. Faux, J. Lessons for Democrats: Don't be conservative. *New York Times,* Jan. 6, 1984. p. A23; Countdown to Election: Presidential popularity. *National Journal* 11: 1729, 1979.
16. Raskin, A. H. Lane Kirkland: A new style for labor. *New York Times Magazine,* Oct. 28, 1979, p. 91.
17. Schwartz, J. E. *America's Hidden Success: A Reassessment of Twenty Years of Public Policy.* W. W. Norton, New York, 1983.
18. Navarro, V. The crisis of the international capitalist order and its implications for the welfare state. *Int. J. Health Serv.* 12(2): 169–190, 1982.
19. Reagan policy in crisis. *NACLA Report* 15(4): 10, 1981.
20. Kelman, S. Toward the political economy of medical care. *Inquiry* 8: 30–38, 1971.
21. Salmon, J. W. The health maintenance organizational strategy: A corporate takeover of health services delivery. *Int. J. Health Serv.* 5(4): 609–623, 1975.
22. Salmon, J. W. Monopoly capital and the reorganization of the health sector. *Review of Radical Political Economy* 9: 125–133, 1977.
23. Salmon, J. W. Corporate Attempts to Reorganize the American Health Care System. Doctoral dissertation, Cornell University, 1978.
24. Ollman, B. Academic freedom in America. *Monthly Review,* March 1984, p. 24.
25. Katznelson, I. and Kesselman, M. *The Politics of Power.* Harcourt, Brace, Jovanovich, New York, 1975.
26. Smith, K. M. and Spinard, W. The popular political mood. *Social Policy,* March–April 1981, p. 38.
27. Complete Hart Poll results. *Common Sense,* Sept. 1, 1975, pp. 16–17.
28. Bender, M. Will the bicentennial see the death of free enterprise? *New York Times,* Jan. 4, 1976, p. 27.
29. Schattschneider, E. E. *The Semi-sovereign People: A Realistic View of Democracy in America.* Holt, Rinehart and Winston, New York, 1960.
30. Health plan progress (editorial). *New York Times,* Apr. 7, 1974, p. E16.
31. Lipset, S. M. and Schneider, W. *The Confidence Gap: Business, Labor and Government in the Public Mind.* Free Press, New York, 1983.

CHAPTER 12

Physicians as Employees: Stanley Wohl's *The Medical Industrial Complex*

Joe Feinglass

Stanley Wohl, a California neurosurgeon, has written an eloquent indictment of bottom-line health care. Begun as a research project for a Wall Street brokerage firm, *The Medical Industrial Complex* (1) has loudened the populist alarm over "medical monopoly" first sounded in 1980 by Arnold Relman, editor of the *New England Journal of Medicine* (2). While describing the perverse incentives inherent in for-profit medicine, Wohl's physician-centered critique suffers from serious theoretical and empirical shortcomings which continue to plague the medical professions' reaction to the corporatization of medical care.

Wohl's critique is animated by the fear that a for-profit delivery system is undermining the professional autonomy and status of the medical profession. Wohl did not begrudge the corporate sector's role in supplying food, linens, diagnostic equipment, computers, health insurance, or pharmaceuticals so long as the supply firms stayed outside the "command structure" of health care. Ostensibly, the medical profession once stood as the ethical guardian of patient care, its professional authority serving as a safeguard against the regularized incidence of waste, fraud and abuse. With the rise of the "*new* medical industrial complex," however, Wohl believes that physicians have been "enticed" into "closing the circle" between an increasingly interlocked "corporate mosaic" of suppliers and providers. Wohl believes that the spread of mergers, acquisitions, interlocking directorates and common stock ownership has created a corporate "vested interest" in the "overutilization of all aspects of the health care system."

THE RISE OF BOTTOM LINE HEALTH CARE

Wohl's analysis of the rapid growth of for-profit hospital chains highlights many of the themes that are repeated in this book, *The Corporate Transformation of Health Care, Part I.* Access to venture capital through the sale of equity shares enabled listed corporations to absorb higher levels of debt financing and avoid complete dependency on high loan market interest rates. With large assets and earnings guaranteeing access to Wall Street, the earlier for-profit firms could raise the necessary capital to exploit the hospital industry's high-cash flow, low-inventory, and high-fixed, but declining variable cost function. A highly-capitalized, high-volume, cost-cutting, anti-union management style took advantage of the large resulting discrepancy between costs and revenue at the margin, especially when the hospital chains could benefit from the growing base of charge-paying patients in Sun-belt and suburban locations (3). The chains thus enjoyed great advantages in the virulent "non-price" competition of the 1970s, which sent hospital costs soaring as over-bedded hospitals scrambled to acquire the most extravagant equipment and amenities (4).

Wohl fails to address the complicity of the medical profession in laying the ideological foundations of for-profit medicine. Economist Uwe Rienhardt, in his debate with Arnold Relman, provides a rich description of the sym-biosis between organized medicine's "command structure" and the for-profit firms:

> We have here a profession that openly professes that its members are unlikely to do their best unless they are rewarded in cold cash for every little ministration rendered their patients. . . . Careful empirical research has estab-lished scientifically what was known to any cab driver all along: physicians, like everyone else, like to locate in pleasant areas where there is money to be had. Thus, our favorite areas have been said to be vastly overdoctored, while other areas, notably inner cities, have been sorely underserved. . . . But how does someone inputing a more lofty social role to physicians reconcile the physicians' locational choices with the lofty ideal? . . . Do you sincerely believe that our for-profit hospitals will leave in their wake as much neglect of uninsured, sick Americans as American physicians have, collectively, in the past and are likely to leave in the future? . . . Let us examine, then, what obligation for community service physicians believe they have shouldered in return for a largely tax-financed education. . . . They have refused to accept Medicaid patients because they considered the cash yield for treating such patients inadequate. They have "skimmed the cream," so to speak. . . . If it is all right for physicians to earn a handsome rate of return on their invest-ments, what is so evil about paying a handsome rate of return to the non-M.D.s who have let their savings be used for the brick and mortar of health care facilities against nothing more than the piece of hope-and-prayer lawyers refer to as a "common stock certificate?" . . . Suffice it to say that one would be hard put to distinguish organized American medicine from the trade asso-ciation of any other group of purveyors of goods and services (5, pp. 10–14).

Wohl's separating of the physician dominated not-for-profit system from the propriety chains leads him to ignore the all around corporatization of health care. The competitive struggle of recent years has forced "not-for-profit" hospitals into multi-institutional systems; their management style and preroga-tives appear to be evolving into essentially the same emphasis on the bottom line (3).

IS FOR PROFIT CARE MORE EFFICIENT?

Wohl rejects the view that vertical and horizontal integration of health care produces high volume economies of scale. He sees such claims as an ideological cover legitimating monopolistic pricing and provider-induced demand. In particular, he rejects the idea that the chaining of hospitals reduces cost:

> Americans have until now granted listed corporations license to own so many hospitals because they believed Madison Avenue glossies extolling the virtues of volume and efficiency as a potent cost-containment mechanism. . . . Therein lies the partial answer to how these companies have grown so rich so quickly while so many other hospitals were dying. . . . In medicine, unlike the clothing business, there really is not that much cost efficiency to be gained from high volume. I do not care how thin you slice it, the cost of running two hospitals is roughly double that of running one (1, pp. 90–91).

Wohl believes that the corporate hospital chains have only lowered their costs by skimping on quality:

> The typical NME hospital seems to me to have a Hilton exterior with a Motel Six interior. It looks like a hospital and has all the trappings, but where it really counts, there are deficiencies—fewer nurses per shift per ward, questionable quality of some hospital-based physicians, pathologists, and radiologists (1, p. 111).

Writing in late 1983, Wohl was forced to rely on anecdotal evidence to buttress his claims of corporate price gouging and overutilization. (He does cite the California study by Pattison and Katz which showed that proprietary chains charged 24 percent more than not-for-profit hospitals for the same services) (6). There is now little doubt that Wohl was correct despite his lack of extensive documentation. A review of 18 empirical studies and several hundred articles examining the impact of both for-profit and "not-for-profit" multihospital systems on the cost of hospital care, published in *Health Affairs*, found that business concentration has actually increased patient costs. Multihospital systems (which include over 1/3 of all U.S. community hospitals) have higher markup margins between costs and revenues for specific services; they provide more intensive and costly services per patient, and their facilities tend to be newer and have higher capital cost overhead expenses (7).

A major study comparing the two types of hospital systems in 1980 found that after adjusting for wage rates, case mix, location, third party payor mix, regulatory environment, and several other variables, investor-owned chains had 21 percent higher patient care revenues than "not-for-profit" chains. No significant differences were found in total costs for patient services; investor-owned chains had five times greater home office costs (8). Proprietary chains have often been defended for their relative tax burden, lack of philanthropic contributions, and restricted access to public funds as a justification for a high cost to charges ratio

(9). Yet higher for-profit patient care income was found to cover over twice the average tax and capital financing advantages of not-for-profit systems (7, 8). Forty-three percent of new hospital beds acquired by the six largest for-profit hospital chains were bought from other investor-owned hospitals; these purchases are symptomatic of high debt to equity ratios which drive up the for-profits' accounting and depreciation costs (10). When adjusted for geographic location, the for-profit hospitals were also found to be skimping on their relative share of uncompensated care (11).

THE CORRUPTION OF MEDICAL PRACTICE

The heart of *The Medical Industrial Complex* is the chapter, "Some of the Players," a colorful (but now a bit dated) introduction to key health industry firms. We learn that Jack Massey, co-founder of Hospital Corporation of America, was also one of the founders of Kentucky Fried Chicken, and how Humana failed to appoint even one of its 18,000 physicians to its quality control oversight committee until 1981. The company profiles illustrate Wohl's belief that an inferior quality of care and gross overutilization of services are inherent in medical care for profit. He is most outraged by the corporate corruption of medical practice:

> ARA believes that, "because the world will never outgrow its need for service," the company's fortunes are assured. The same company that pushes vending machines now pushes doctors. It is conceivable that one day it will develop a vending machine with a doctor inside to dispense hot or cold penicillin (1, pp. 103–104).

Wohl expresses disgust over the lavish corporate advertising effort, which he believes promotes superfluous products and procedures like vaginal sprays, tummy tucks, and face lifts. Humana comes in for especially harsh criticism for peddling "fast food," "drive through" medicine:

> No more going to the doctor's office; just about everyone in the country will line up at the drive-through window of a Humana Medfirst clinic. . . . Few self-respecting physicians—likewise few self-respecting chefs—will accept work at the drive-through window; so the Tuesday special at half price will probably feature somewhat less than a topnotch clinician (1, p. 114).

Even academic medical researchers, long subsidized by the National Institute of Health's supposedly altruistic basic science grants, have recently begun to be coopted by the medical industrial complex. Wohl singles out genetic scientists for special scorn:

> . . . yet another respected boundary of medicine as it has been traditionally practiced was now irrevocably breached. For many genetic scientists soon began reporting the results of their research first to the mass media and only

subsequently to the professional community. The *Wall Street Journal*, rather than the *New England Journal of Medicine*, became the forum of genetic research. . . . When a genetic scientist reports his or her results to the *Wall Street Journal*, the effect of the report is essentially to push the stock of the company involved up, regardless of the opinion of other scientists on the merits of the results. And when the scientists involved also owns a company that could financially benefit from certain research findings, it is truly amazing how frequently those breakthrough findings are made in the company laboratories. . . . While the shares of the jeans you were wearing went down, the shares of the gene splicers, who had no product to sell, were flying high (1, pp. 68–70).

Dr. Wohl shares the suspicions of other authors that the recent interest of for-profit chains in managing "flagship" academic medical centers has little to do with maintaining medical education, research and community service; rather, the chains would appear to be interested in the pursuit of profitable referral centers and a tertiary component to insurance marketing schemes (12). Wohl fears that integrated corporate provider-supply firms will soon exploit academic medical research contracts in order to patent profitable medical procedures. No doubt Wohl would also agree with the quoted observation of Dr. Quentin Young of the Health and Medicine Policy Research Group, that Humana's artificial heart program was undertaken as a "loss leader for the international marketing effort" (13).

FEE SPLITTING WRIT LARGE

While not explicitly stated in formal microeconomic terms, Wohl's opposition to the "Medical Moguls" is centered on the concept of "bounded rationality." This doctrine states that the market for medical care is unique insofar as the health care consumer lacks the expertise to correctly evaluate what is truly needed in times of sickness, or to judge the efficacy of the care actually received. The life-threatening aspects of serious illness preclude the repeated trials which underlie consumer "sovereignty" in normal goods and services markets. Wohl notes the difference between medical care and other commodities:

> . . . while executives of health corporations and commentators delight in referring to the chain hospitals as the McDonald's of health care, there is a crucial fact they are all forgetting. . . . If you don't like the fact that Pillsbury owns Burger King you can eat at your local greasy spoon. As a matter of fact you can go an entire lifetime without ever consuming a Wendy's hamburger but you have little chance of lasting through three score and ten without visiting a hospital (1, p. 98).

In order to protect the patients' interests in their "agency" relationship with physicians, the medical profession has traditionally been socialized to view their occupation as a "sacred trust, a science and art dedicated to the preservation of life." According to Wohl, physicians are awarded high social and economic status in order to resist the temptation to economically exploit their agency relationship with vulnerable patients; ethical concerns are better maintained when the incentives for their violation are reduced. Similarly, the hospital industry originally developed on the basis of a philanthropic, often religious, not-for-profit community service orientation. Unique health care "market imperfections" are further addressed by a host of government regulations and licensure laws, all supposedly designed to insulate the consumer from the naked greed of health care providers.

The *Medical Industrial Complex* bemoans the collapse of these traditional constraints in the wake of the "out of control" growth of corporate health care firms:

> For the medical profession this era may well be one of the most shameful and ethically questionable periods in its history. For all of us it is a really sad time, the passing of virtually a whole other way of life. The encounter between physician and patient used to involve a sacred trust. A physician was one of the few people one could confide in, sure he had nothing but one's best interests at heart. . . . Even legally a doctor-patient relationship has a special status. Now, what is the patient to think when his doctor's office is located within a hospital owned by a corporation listed on the New York Stock Exchange? . . . When strings of hospitals are owned by a corporation, by inference it is the corporation that is practicing medicine (1, pp. 95–97).

Wohl basically sees the for-profit "mediglomerates" as illegal fee-splitting operations:

> It does take the breath away—at least it takes away mine—to see clearly that, in the present state of affairs, the profits gained from the practice of medicine appear to show up in the pockets of stock market speculators—a particularly unpleasant instance, in my opinion, of illicit fee splitting. . . . What is legal in corporate law may be illegal or unethical in medicine. If a general practitioner examines you and then refers you to an orthopedist, it is illegal for that orthopedist to kick back a portion of his fee to the G.P. in consideration of the referral. Similarly a pharmacy cannot kick back a fee to a physician who writes a prescription that gets filled in the pharmacy. When an interconnected collection of corporate entities profits from acute care, chronic care, and pharmaceuticals, the lines of responsibility become rather blurred (1, pp. 87, 127).

THE CONQUEST OF THE MEDICAL PROFESSION

Wohl is horrified by what he terms "the conquest" (by "gentle persuasion") of the medical profession. He reserves his most bitter invective for corporations which have bought out medical partnerships (including an especially detailed indictment of hospital emergency room contracts with physician entrepreneurs). According to Wohl, physicians were rendered virtually powerless by a host of "adversary relationships" with government bureaucracies, hospital administrators, business purchasers and uppity consumers (particularly feminists). The confused and embattled medical profession went along quietly with the for-profit tide, greasing their own slide into proletarian status:

> In a few cases, as we have seen, doctors *are* the company, or they at least started the company. Whether they are employers or employees, however, corporate involvement results in a transformation of their methods and aims and ultimately the care they provide. Eventually, the alchemists who turn science into gold turn themselves into just another marketable product. . . . Physicians are looked upon as employees whose sole function is to fill the conglomerate's beds with "bodies" (1, p. 59).

Wohl's main explanation for the success of the corporate physician takeover is the so-called physician "glut." Medical school enrollments have doubled over the last decade, there has been a large influx of foreign medical graduates, and the ratio of active physicians per capita has been steadily growing (14). The resulting competitive pressure has reduced the opportunities for lucrative solo practices; few recent graduates can afford the climbing overhead cost (equipment, office space, malpractice insurance, etc.) of an individual practice, let alone pay off medical school debts. As the possibilities for lucrative self-employment vanish, physicians have succumbed to corporate advertising appeals:

> Most physicians still remember their medical school professors whose brilliant clinical acumen and impeccable ethics set the standard for the conduct of a medical practice. . . . But many physicians quickly sacrifice the ideal for the money. They opt for a nice office and buy a nice house in a nice suburb. They meet nice friends and join nice clubs. Instead of working at dark and drab inner-city hospitals, which they did as residents, they now work in sparkling new steel-and-glass Humana or NME facilities (1, pp. 180–181).

THE PHYSICIAN AS SCAPEGOAT

Throughout the *Medical Industrial Complex*, physicians are portrayed as innocent scapegoats in the public outcry over rising health care costs. Wohl minimizes the economic role of the medical profession by focusing exclusively on physician fees as a subcomponent of the 20 percent of health care spending which goes for "physician services." Nowhere does he acknowledge the fact that physician orders directly generate between 70 percent and 80 percent of all health care costs. Physicians have long been the "traffic cops" of the health care industry, directing the flow of money through their highly discretionary diagnostic and therapeutic decisions about hospitalization, surgery, drugs, laboratory tests, and the use of special care facilities. Numerous studies have repeatedly documented wide variations in physicians' care for patients with the same illnesses, and the exquisite sensitivity of physicians' medical practice habits to a variety of financial incentives (15).

Wohl frequently refers to physicians' historic role in limiting hospitals' ability to operate on purely profit-maximizing criteria. For instance, the "not-for-profit" hospital sector has traditionally avoided cost minimization for both labor and capital inputs, and investment has generally not been targeted towards the areas of highest profitability. Instead, output, pricing and investment decisions often reflected prestige, quality, and administrative "slack" considerations, which conflict with narrow institutional profitability. Wohl sees this type of market behavior as a response to medical staff concerns over providing high quality care (he does not acknowledge physicians' interests in hospital prestige, thick rugs, or administrative "slack"). He legitimately fears the results of recent price and product competition, given the corporate chains' reluctance to cross-subsidize unprofitable facilities or shift costs in order to care for less insured or medically indigent patients. What he misses, however, is the self-interested, profit-maximizing role of physicians in perpetuating the waste, mismanagement and inefficiency so evident in the industry's large-scale over-bedding, unnecessary duplication of facilities, and rapidly rising costs and charges.

In fact, most "not-for-profit" hospitals were run as a kind of physician co-operative, in which physicians used the hospital's non-profit status to benefit from public and philanthropic subsidies. By restricting the quantity and scope of outpatient physician services, the specialty saturated medical profession ensured that the increased demand for health services (whether falsely induced or in response to rising levels of income and insurance and the aging of the population) was primarily met by an increase in hospital capacity. This approach maximizes the productivity (and therefore the income or leisure) of staff physicians, while simultaneously reducing the productivity of hospital services. The hospital was organized to provide the maximum possible inputs to enhance physician input and economize the physicians' time; the notorious duplication of costly diagnostic, surgical, and intensive care facilities is a direct reflection of staff physicians' unwillingness to lose fees through referrals. Similarly, hospital medical staffs have favored cross-subsidizing hospital outpatient departments and emergency rooms which provide services for low-income patients. This relieves staff physicians to care for better insured patients in their offices or provide more remunerative acute-care inpatient services.

An especially contradictory aspect of medical staff influence over hospital management is the interest of staff physicians in increasing the number of medical residents. Residents provide services for which the teaching hospital physician is also reimbursed (often twice: once through patient fees and again through an academic staff salary). Ironically, the long-run increase in medical school enrollments and residencies is one of the prime factors currently undermining physicians' bargaining power, as the physician "glut" underlies a major rollback of the medical profession's dominance of the hospital industry.

THE POLITICAL AGENDA OF CORPORATIZATION

Physicians have continued their domination of the "not-for-profit" hospital sector on the basis of several conditions which are now changing. First, hospital market entry and price competition have been greatly restricted. In the past, this was often accomplished by large, established providers through adroit manipulation of Certificate of Need legislation or regulatory "capture" of regional Health System Agencies. Another necessary condition for physician dominance was the willingness of third party payors to maintain patients' elasticity of demand by passing through the cost of spiralling hospital bills.

The ability of providers to undercut patients' resistance to mounting hospital expenditures is usually explained in terms of legislative victories by "concentrated" special interest lobbyists from the American Medical Association or American Hospital Association over the "diffuse" interests of millions of health care consumers and premium payors. In reality, health policy has fluctuated around the relationship between the health care industry and the valuation of various types of medical care as human capital inputs by other economic sectors (and their affiliated foundations and subsidized policy planning agencies). Recent changes in the conditions for hospital market entry and the movement toward capitated and prospective payment systems have been attempts to limit overhead costs in a predominantly stagnant economy. Price competition is rapidly being injected into the hospital industry. Physicians are being pushed aside by profit-maximizing corporate managers and stockholders who will not tolerate the medical profession's material interest in "wasteful and inefficient," prestige-oriented investment policies.

Wohl indicates little awareness of the "pro-competition" coalition of corporate benefit officers (increasingly organized into regional Business Groups on Health), foundation, insurance company and media executives, and their academic and political operatives (16--18). He fails to see "the Fox's" hand in the recent restructuring of the organization and delivery of medical care, which he portrays as a spontaneous process:

> In truth, history shows that the corporations simply marched in because there was a profit to be made. Doctors, government, insurance companies, and so-called leaders in health care exerted about as much influence in the situation as a feather in the wind. All they could do was study the phenomenon after the fox had raided the chicken coop (1, p. 25).

Wohl's exclusive focus on the problem of overutilization blinds him to the *political* agenda of corporatization: reduction of what corporate and government leaders view as unacceptably high social capital outlays by rationing health expenditures on the basis of income. He does not explore the relationship between intensified corporate price and product competition and the proliferating variety of financial incentives (e.g., DRGs, for-profit HMOs, cost-sharing, etc.) for care avoidance, limitations on access for the poor, the elderly, the chronically sick and disabled, and restrictions on the quality and continuity of care for the majority of working Americans. These rationing incentives have already led to an epidemic of hospital patient dumping at the same time that budget cuts take their toll on the health of the poor families (19, 20).

Central to the corporatization of medical care is the attempt to improve medical productivity by asserting bureaucratic control over physician ordering decisions. To that end a new strata of health care managers is emerging. The new breed of health care MBAs, trained in marketing strategies of winning product lines, is rapidly gaining the expertise and cultural legitimacy to initiate surveillance of physician decision-making. Their success in gaining ideological hegemony (which will be crucial to directly disciplining physicians) is celebrated in trade journals like *Modern Healthcare*, but frequently lamented in medical journals like *The New England Journal of Medicine*, where one physician complains of the "New Language of Hospital Management:"

> The transformation of the hospital from a traditionally altruistic and humanistic institution into a series of profit centers has barely begun. . . . I have trouble understanding how Management can grow so rapidly in the face of a falling patient census. . . . Discussions of consumer demographics, target populations, product lines, and marketing compete with traditional concerns over service and the quality of care. Talented people from industry are being hired at high salaries in the hope of acquiring a magic money making touch. These newcomers speak of focus groups and pretesting and of advertising and image building. They tell of the way in which appliances are sold. Those who have a background in health care are intimidated. At meetings of their own, they are learning to parrot the jargon and fit in with that new thought process. Already accustomed to vague titles and sanitized job descriptions, they are perhaps less resistant to dubious new ideology and its human representatives (21, p. 1250).

Wohl's narrow view of bureaucratization focuses on the "interference" of medically uneducated managers in physicians' patient care decisions. He therefore misses the true proportions of what is in store for medical practice. As Derber has pointed out, physicians have long benefited by the division between "proprietary sponsors," who capitalize medical production, and "market sponsors," who provide capital to mediate and broker the sale of medical services:

> The traditional privileged and personal relation between physicians and patients created a critical market leverage for physicians that prevented either the private hospitals which capitalized them or the third parties which carried out other market-mediating functions for them from consolidating full control (22, p. 241).

Wohl is suspicious of what Derber calls the development of "unified" (corporate) sponsorship. Wohl expresses his views about sponsorship in terms of a traditional physician's irritation at the meddling of incompetent bureaucrats:

> The question that physicians are posing is whether one can entrust the changes that must come to the Blue Cross technocrats just because that company happens to insure so many Americans. Just like government, Blue Cross is notorious of working outside the usual medical channels. Rather than deal with medical staffs, it negotiates with hospital administrators. It avoids county, state, and national medical societies and chooses instead to bargain in the offices of government legislators and bureaucrats (1, p. 115).

Wohl particularly disdains hospital managers:

> Hospitals will bargain with physicians and nurses over the cost of a box of Band-Aids and then go out and buy a million-dollar machine nobody knows how to use. Before they learn what one machine can do they are already ordering the next model. Hospital administrators love to scurry about the hallways with computer printouts dangling from their pockets, as if to say, "Here I am, modern man completely in control." Never mind that the hospital is deep in debt and patients are still dying of cancer. The printout seems to function as a security blanket for those who don't understand it (1, p. 135).

Wohl has only a limited appreciation for the effects of unified sponsorship in an era of American economic stagnation, fiscal crisis, and declining competitiveness. He fails to fully grasp the implications of physicians' loss of control over the recruitment of patients as a new corporate style of practice is emerging, based on private sector negotiation of quality-cost tradeoffs for different patient populations.

PHYSICIAN PROLETARIANIZATION?

It is not surprising, given the book's populist analysis of "medical monopoly" and physician proletarianization, that Wohl has little to offer in his brief closing remarks on the future. Because he misrepresents previous relations of production within a period of relative economic expansion and prosperity, he never comes to grips with the political-economic logic of the current assault on physician autonomy. Instead, he relies on pleas for increased corporate "responsibility." (Wohl also briefly calls forth the panacea of preventive medicine, but does not address the costs of a real assault on the social origins of disease or the irrelevancy of prevention to the costs of a demand-inducing, for-profit medical care system) (23). Wohl seems to be saying that the real problem is what Moore has called the "infralinear obsession" of American business managers (24). Wohl argues that things might be O.K. if the businessmen relied more on physician input:

> Stating that widespread corporate involvement in health care is bad for us simply means that the wrong type of people are exerting a great measure of control over the nation's health. The laws and economics of corporate life mold the employee to behave in a manner that will advance his career and at

> the same time advance the common interests of his fellows. Corporate life is a team sport with decision by committee. Increasing corporate involvement in health care means, in human terms, that the gray flannel suit is replacing the white coat (1, p. 178).

If only all the medical industrial firms were like Baxter-Travenol, Wohl's idea of a socially-conscious firm (at least under its then current directors), then maybe they could be effectively regulated in the public interest. It is in these final chapters that *The Medical Industrial Complex* is revealed as the manifesto of an embattled professional-managerial class strata fighting for its privileged position by invoking progressive reforms (25).

HEARTS AND MINDS

In spite of recently advanced predictions of physician proletarianization and deteriorating hospital-physician relations (26–32), over the next decade physicians will likely retain considerable workplace autonomy and substantial authority within the relations of medical production (33). This will largely be a result of their virtually exclusive technical training and expertise, combined with the needs and expectations of patients for shared, face to face reassurance, trust and decision making. While the indispensability of physician specialists is being challenged and eroded by the substitution of cheaper labor from allied health professions, it will take a considerable period to translate the manpower requirements of the new era of "corporate medicine" into medical school and health professions education. To date, labor *saving*, equipment-embodied and coordinative technologies such as computerized artificial intelligence programs have had few applications in medicine; despite many attempts there has been little progress in modeling expert clinical decision-making, which does not follow narrowly probabilistic problem-solving techniques (34, 35).

What the future really holds will be in large part decided by whether physicians themselves defend access to medical care as an inviolable human right (36) or take their places in administering the new system (37, 38). The social prestige of the medical profession was once second only to that of the Supreme Court Justices. Television enshrined a benign, humanitarian image of the caring family doctor and the brilliant medical specialist. Today, the physician's standing is declining in the polls. While Americans continue to hold their own family doctors in high esteem, the medical profession as a whole is increasingly viewed with suspicion. The percentage of the population with "a great deal of confidence in medical leaders" has declined from 73 percent to 33 percent between 1966 and 1986 (39). More and more people are questioning mainstream medicine, and the role of financial incentives in shaping our system of medical care has never been clearer (40). Nevertheless, the economic and cultural power of physicians will be critical in the ongoing battle to determine whose interests are served in the "cost effectiveness" crusade. The younger generation of physicians, including increasing numbers of female and minority medical school graduates, is becoming more sensitive to issues of prevention, public health and environmental protection. As the economic and social position of the medical profession continues to deteriorate and physician labor is increasingly degraded, let us hope that many younger physicians will be looking beyond a self-interested critique of corporatization and will begin to question more basic premises of the corporate onslaught.

REFERENCES

1. Wohl, S. *The Medical Industrial Complex.* Harmony Books, New York, 1984.
2. Relman, A. S. The new medical-industrial complex. *New Engl J. Med.* 303(17): 963–970, October 23, 1980.
3. Ermann, D., and Gabel, J. Multihospital systems: issues and empirical findings. *Health Aff.* 3(1): 51–64, Spring 1984.
4. Robinson, J. C., and Luft, H. S. Competition and the Cost of Hospital Care, 1972 to 1982. *JAMA* 257: 3241–3245, 1987.
5. Relman, A. S., and Reinhardt, U. E. Debating for-profit health care and the ethics of physicians. *Health Aff.* , Summer 1986, pp. 5–31.
6. Pattison, R., and Katz, H. Investor-owned and not-for-profit hospitals: A comparison based on California data. *New Engl. J. Med.* 309(1983): 347–353, August 11, 1983.
7. Watt, J. E., et al. The comparative economic performance of investor-owned chain and not-for-profit hospitals. *New Engl. J. Med.* 314(2): 89–96, January 9, 1986.
8. Renn, S. C., et al. The effects of ownership and system affiliation on the economic performance of hospitals. *Inquiry* 22: 219–236, Fall 1985.
9. Herzlinger, R. E., and Krasker, W. S. Who profits from nonprofits? *Harv. Bus. Rev.,* January–February 1987, pp. 93–106.
10. Luft, H. S. For-profit hospitals: A cost problem or solution? *Bus. and Health,* January/February 1985, pp. 13–16.
11. Lewin, L. S., Eckels, T. J., and Miller, L. B. Setting the record straight: The provision of uncompensated care by not-for-profit hospitals. *New Engl. J. Med.* 318: 1212–1215, 1988.
12. Berliner, H. S., and Burlage, R. K. Proprietary hospital chains and academic medical centers. *Int. J. Health Serv.* 1986.
13. Kotulak, R. U.S. medicine going corporate. *Chicago Tribune,* December 2, 1984.
14. American Medical Association. Profile of medical practice. In *Trends in U.S. Health Care,* American Medical Association Center for Health Policy Research, 1987.
15. Wennberg, J. E. Dealing with medical practice variations: A proposal for action. *Health Aff.,* Summer 1984, pp. 6–32.
16. Meyerhoff, A. S., and Crozier, D. A. Health care coalitions: The evolution of a movement. *Health Aff.* 3(1): 120–127, Spring 1984.
17. Carter, M. F. Employers urged to overhaul benefits to promote use of alternate services. *Mod. Healthcare,* July 1984, pp. 58–62.
18. Feinglass, J. Future shuck: Experts on the new era in health care. *Health/PAC Bulletin* 15(6): 17–19, November/December 1984.
19. Schiff, R. L., et al. Transfers to a public hospital. *New Engl. J. Med.* 314(9): 552–557, February 27, 1986.
20. Mundinger, M. O. Health service funding cuts and the declining health of the poor. *New Engl. J. Med.* 513(1): 44–47, July 4, 1985.
21. Alper, P. R. The new language of hospital management. *New Engl. J. Med.* 311(19): 1249–1251, November 8, 1984.
22. Derber, C. Capitalism and the medical division of labor: The changing situation of physicians. In *Issues in the Political Economy of Health Care,* edited by John B. McKinlay. Methuen, New York, 1984.

23. McKinlay, J B., A case for refocussing upstream–the political economy of illness. *Behavioral Science Research Data Review*, American Heart Association Conference, Seattle Washington, June 17–19, 1974.
24. Moore, F. Who should profit from the care of your illness? *Harvard Magazine*, November–December 1985, pp. 45–54.
25. Ehrenreich, B., and Ehrenreich, J. The professional and managerial class. In *Between Labor and Capital*, edited by Pat Walker. South End Press, Boston, 1979.
26. McKinlay, J. B., and Arches, J. Towards the proletarianization of physicians. *Int. J. Health Serv.* 15(2), 1985.
27. McKinlay, J. B., and Stoeckle, J. D. Corporatization and the social transformation of doctoring. *Int. J. Health Serv.* 18(2): 191–205, 1988.
28. Shortell, S. M., Morrisey, M. A., and Conrad, D. A. Economic regulation and hospital behavior: The effects on medical staff organization and hospital-physician relationships. *Health Serv. Res.* 20(5): 597–628, December 1985.
29. Freedman, S. A. Megacorporate health care: Choice for the future. *New Engl. J. Med.* 312(9): 579–582, February 28, 1985.
30. Proprietary hospitals' boom: A boon for MDs–or a threat? *Med. World News,* January 18, 1982, pp. 26–29.
31. Levey, S., and Hesse, D. D. Bottom-line health care? *New Engl. J. Med.* 312(10): 644–646, March 7, 1985.
32. Hospital staffing structure on the way out as hospital-physician rivalry grows? *Med. World News*, September 10, 1984, pp. 18–19.
33. Young, D. W., and Saltman, R. B. *The Hospital Power Equilibrium: Physician Behavior and Cost Control.* The John Hopkins University Press, Baltimore and London, 1985.
34. McMullin, E. Diagnosis by computer. In *Logic of Discovery and Diagnosis in Medicine*, pp. 199–222. edited by Kenneth F. Schaffner.
35. McGuire, C. H. Medical problem-solving: A critique of the literature. *J. Med. Educ.* 60: 587–595, August 1985.
36. Nutter, D. O. Access to care and the evolution of corporate, for-profit medicine. *New Engl. J. Med.* 311(14): 917–919, October 4, 1984.
37. Hillman, A. L., Nash, D. B., Kissick, W. L., and Martin, S. P. Managing the medical-industrial complex. *New Engl. J. Med.* 315(8): 511–513, 1986.
38. Winkelwerder, W., and Ball, J. R. Transformation of American health care. *New Engl. J. Med.* 318: 317–319, 1988.
39. Blendon, R., and Altman, D. Public opinion and health care costs. In *Health Care and Its Costs: Can the U.S. Afford Adequate Health Care?*, edited by C. Schranm. W. W. Norton, New York, 1987.
40. *Alternative Medicines: Popular and Policy Perspectives*, edited by J. W. Salmon, Methuen, New York, 1984.

CHAPTER 13

Mystery as a Means of Raising Doubts about Health Care for Profit: Sara Paretsky's *Bitter Medicine*

Agatha M. Gallo

Recent writings in academic journals have begun to delineate issues and problems related to the corporatization of health care. These writings have examined the extent of for-profit ownership and management, the range of effects of the for-profit trend on access, cost and quality of care, and the effects of public policy on corporatization. However, not much has been published in the popular press to relay the breadth of these issues to the general public over the last two decades.

How do the concepts and criticisms addressed in academic writings make their way into the lay person's reality other than by personal experience, or through media such as television, newspapers and radio? One significant medium to pass important ideas to the general public and raise questions about issues such as health care is the novel. Sara Paretsky's mystery, *Bitter Medicine*, is a good example of contemporary fiction which explores potential perils of for-profit health care enterprises to patient care (1). This chapter analyzes how *Bitter Medicine* presents a plausible story to highlight concerns voiced by policy analysts who see the corporatization trend in health care as problematic. In addition, Paretsky's own attitudes and values about social injustices are examined within the context of her book.

THE STORY OF FOR-PROFIT HEALTH CARE

Bitter Medicine is the fourth in Sara Paretsky's V.I. Warshawski mystery series set in Chicago. V.I. (Vic to her friends) is a former public defender turned private investigator. In *Bitter Medicine*, Vic investigates the death of a friend's

16-year-old, diabetic daughter, Consuela Alvarado, who had become pregnant. Vic's involvement with Consuela begins with trying to help the baby's father, a street punk named Fabiano, get a job in the Chicago suburbs. Vic drives them to the job interview; while waiting for Fabiano, Consuela goes into premature labor. Vic takes Consuela to the nearest hospital, Friendship Five, which is located in an upscale suburb. This hospital is part of a nationwide corporate chain, its first Midwest venture after setting up 18 other hospitals in the Southeast Sunbelt.

Friendship Five advertises a full obstetrical service with a Level III perinatal center to care for premature babies and their pregnant mothers. Slick, four-color brochures with photographs proclaim, "Friendship Five: Your Full-Care Obstetrical Service." The copy reads, "Most women give birth without complications of any kind. But if you need extra help before or during birth, our perinatologist is on call twenty-four hours a day" (1, pp. 260–261). The young obstetrics head, Dr. Peter Burgoyne, describes for Vic the reasons why he chose to practice at Friendship Five after completing his obstetric residency, rather than accept a specialty residency position at a large Chicago hospital for perinatology training: "They offered me so much—not just money, but new facilities they were planning—I couldn't turn it down" (1, pp. 32–33).

Death, Dumping and Profit

That same night both Consuela and the baby die. Vic senses early on that something was not quite right. For example, Mrs. Kirkland, the admitting clerk exclaims her displeasure to Vic while she is filling out the admitting forms, "I learned she [Consuela] doesn't work for the plant. She's some Mexican girl who got sick on the premises. We do not run a charity ward here. We're going to have to move this girl to a public hospital" (1, p. 22). (This public hospital would most likely be Cook County Hospital in inner-city Chicago—an ambulance ride of at least 20 miles). Vic immediately questions if Consuela was being treated; as an attorney, Vic knew she could not be denied emergency treatment under Illinois public health law. The admitting clerk refers her to Alan Humphries, the Executive Director of Friendship Five. Humphries presents himself as a self-confident, smooth-talking administrator. He assures Vic that Dr. Burgoyne is doing what is necessary for Consuela and that she can speak with him when he is finished in the intensive care unit.

When Fabiano finally arrives at the hospital, obviously drunk and shouting obscenities, Humphries ushers him into his office offering Fabiano transportation home "after we're through talking." Vic was correct in thinking that Humphries was going to offer Fabiano money in exchange for signing a release on the death of the baby. Later, Fabiano, seen driving a late model luxury car, confesses to Vic reluctantly that Humphries gave him $5,000 to "say how sorry they were that the baby died and that she [Consuela] died, too" (1, p. 72).

More Death, and Deception

The next day Dr. Malcolm Tregiere, an associate of Dr. Lotty Herschel, Consuela's clinic physician, is brutally murdered in his apartment. Tregiere had been called to Friendship Five and arrived in the middle of Consuela's delivery, which he described to Vic when he was leaving the hospital that evening as "very chaotic up there—it's hard to come into the middle of a case and know for sure what the progress had been" (1, p. 28). The police concluded that his murder was done at random, being part of a crime wave by gang members in the Chicago Uptown area where Tregiere lived. At the request of her close friend, Dr. Herschel, Vic begins to investigate the circumstances surrounding the doctor's death.

Prompted by the police hunch that gang members may be involved, Vic contacts gang leader, Sergio, whom she once helped get his sentence reduced in her public defender days. He had become a "community leader," doing well for himself since his release from prison. She is able to meet with Sergio, but not without being roughed up and getting her face slashed in the process—obviously Sergio was not happy with the earlier court decision, and had continued his association with gang activities.

In the meantime, Burgoyne, the obstetrical head at Friendship Five and the physician who cared for Consuela, begins calling and courting Vic. He attends the Alvarado funeral with her, takes her to upbeat restaurants, and walks with her along Lake Michigan beaches. During their interludes, Burgoyne expresses concern about Consuela's death because she is the first obstetrical patient to die since he came to Friendship. He asks questions about the police process and Vic's progress in finding Malcolm's murderer.

The following day when Vic arrives at Dr. Herschel's store front clinic located in a low-income Hispanic area, she finds it beseiged by anti-abortionists led by Dieter Monkfish, the head of IckPiff (the Illinois Committee to Protect the Fetus). The aftermath of the confrontation left the clinic in disarray, with windows broken, furniture toppled, filing cabinets pulled down, and patient files dumped. Vic goes down to night court to intercede for her 70-year-old neighbor, Mr. Contreras, who came to the clinic earlier with wrench and bat in hand "to help the cause." There she sees her disagreeable ex-husband, Richard Yarborough, one of the city's top corporate lawyers, representing Dieter Monkfish, "a fanatic with a shoestring organization" as Vic describes him. Her curiosity is raised as Yarborough says it is none of her business how Monkfish can afford him, but "even fanatics have friends" (1, p. 151).

The Search for Answers

Vic then prepares to find out where Monkfish is getting the money to pay Yarborough's $200 per day legal fees. In her usual undercover style, Vic poses as an auditor for the State of Illinois who is checking lists of donors and non-profit organization's tax exempt status. After pressuring IckPiff's secretary, she obtains the badly kept ledgers and file cards with donors' names and addresses. She looks up Yarborough's name in the card file and finds a penciled note saying, "Bills to be mailed directly to donor." It is with this that Vic rushes off as Monkfish arrives on the scene. That night Vic returns to IckPiff. She leaves with the files intending to return them later, and covers up the theft by alerting a group of winos at the bottom of the stairs that they could find money in the opened office upstairs.

She arrives at her apartment to find Peter Burgoyne waiting for her. Burgoyne seems upset with her for "breaking and entering," but helps her carry the files upstairs to her apartment. While getting dinner that night, Burgoyne makes a phone call, and immediately asks Vic to accompany him on his 20 foot sailboat to spend a day on the waters of Lake Michigan; she accepts the offer.

Things begin to happen. Lotty realizes that all the Alvarado files from her storefront clinic are missing (including Consuela's) when she is sued for malpractice by Fabiano. It is assumed that one of the clinic vandals must have stolen them during the anti-abortion demonstration earlier. Vic then asks Burgoyne to get Friendship's file on Consuela for Lotty to review for the suit. He reluctantly agrees, but stalls until Friendship Five too is summoned in the law suit and Consuela's record is locked up at the hospital.

Meanwhile, Vic's apartment had been broken into while she was sailing with Burgoyne. The IckPiff files were the only items taken. Vic suspects that Burgoyne had something to do with this as he and Mr. Contreras were the only ones who knew she had them; she sets out to find out more. Posing as Yarborough's secretary, she calls Humphries' office to see if "the billing for Mr. Monkfish was to go onto the Friendship corporate account, or to be listed on a separate invoice and sent to Dr. Burgoyne directly" (1, pp. 204–205). As she suspected, Friendship Five is Yarborough's client and Humphries wanted Monkfish's bill to come directly to him at the hospital, but why?

As with most mysteries, the plot thickens. Vic decides to go to Friendship that night to search for Consuela's records. She easily enters the plush offices of Humphries and Burgoyne. She cannot help but think, "I was truly in the for-profit part of the hospital" (1, p. 244). Expensive wood parquet covered floors, Persian rugs, antique desks adorn the offices. Vic finds the files in Humphries office and also finds a handwritten note by Burgoyne indicating that the call to the perinatologist was delayed one hour after Consuela's arrival at the hospital and that the treatment started just prior to his arrival was inappropriate by today's medical standards. This caused Consuela to go into heart failure, loose the baby, and eventually die.

The files and reports that Vic takes from the offices tell an important story. She begins to piece the puzzle together. Both Humphries and Burgoyne receive hefty salaries, plus profit sharing from the operations of hospital and national franchise. After reading through the comprehensive corporate report, she finds a note from Humphries to one offender who went over the maximum reimbursement of Medicare, "Please remember we are a for-profit institution." Vic expresses her concern about Friendship Five, "They presented an approach to the practice of medicine I personally found unappetizing, since it seemed to place the health of patients secondary to that of the organization" (1, p. 257).

The Bottom Line

Lotty and her friend Max Loewenthal, executive director of a large Chicago hospital, explain to Vic about "bottom line" strategies in health care, which in this case contributed to Consuela and her baby's deaths. Although it seemed that Friendship has done nothing illegal based on documents that Vic found in Humphries' office, the hospital still attempts to present an image competitive with other hospital's obstetrical services. Thus, to advertise a full obstetrical service, including a perinatologist and a full complement of fetal monitors and a neonatal intensive-care unit, works to their marketing advantage. It helps them to sell their services to suburban, well-educated women who read about risks associated with childbirth.

However, a staff perinatologist on the premises can be quite an expensive ordeal when the women typically seen at Friendship are low-risk with few complications of pregnancy. To make a Level III, full-service obstetrics service pay, at least 2,500–3,000 infants need to be delivered a year, which is not the case at Friendship. Thus, to have a perinatologist on call twenty-four-hours a day for the occasional complication, rather than being paid as a full-time hospital staff member, cuts expenses at Friendship. As Max says, "You know, bottom line . . . can't offer unprofitable services" (1, p. 264).

Vic sums the situation all up, "So everything falls to the bottom line. Humphries and Peter are part owners of the hospital. It's important to them personally that every service make a profit. More important to Humphries, perhaps, since his potential take is bigger. So they advertise their full-care service. They get Abercrombie on a part-time basis and figure that's all they need because they're in a part of town where they won't need a lot of emergencies. . . . And then Consuela and I show up and put a spanner in the works. It wasn't exactly that they thought she was indigent that they didn't treat her. That might have been a part of it, but the other part was they were trying to locate the perinatologist, Keith Abercrombie" (1, p. 266–267).

As it turns out, the hospital executive Humphries' overwhelming and blinding personal greed is revealed as the main impetus associated with Malcolm, Consuela and eventually Fabiano's deaths. Humphries got Monkfish to organize the anti-abortion protest so that one of Sergio's gang members could steal Consuela's file hoping to find Malcolm's report of the birth and treatment at Friendship. When the report was not found in the file, he paid Sergio to break into Malcolm's apartment to find the dictating machine and tape; in the process

Malcolm was murdered. Malcolm's dictation, which he taped in his car while driving from Friendship, was eventually found at the Medical Transcription Room at the Chicago hospital where he worked. In the report, Malcolm specifies the failure to treat her for close to an hour and the incorrect medication used.

Vic now is more clear on why Burgoyne was so "obsessed" about Consuela's death; "Because he knew he'd let her die. . . . By agreeing to work in an environment where he was promising a service he couldn't deliver, he had created the situation that caused her death" (1, p. 282). In the end, the bereaved Burgoyne, "carrying the burden of death on his shoulders," and unable to forgive himself for not saving Consuela, confesses all and then takes his own life. The avarice of Humphries is stopped as he is arrested for the murders of Malcolm Tregiere and Fabiano, though the corporate structure which led the executive to such nefarious actions stays in place.

IS BITTER MEDICINE PLAUSIBLE?

The Paretsky novel, *Bitter Medicine*, weaves many true-to-life aspects into its story of profit and greed. When the author wrote this mystery in 1986–1987, profits had begun to plummet in the several large national hospital chains. Financial pressures mounted on individual hospital administrators to maintain profit margins amid declining admissions, tighter reimbursement, and growing competition with other neighboring hospitals (2). The behavior and reactions of Friendship's hospital administrator Humphries, including murder and coverup, while perhaps extreme, were motivated by an organizational structure similar to real proprietary institutions which reward managerial performance measured by the bottom-line. Humphries' own individual greed and personal monetary rewards are portrayed as total disregard for patient care at the expense of short-term profit maximization.

The setting of Chicagoland for a for-profit hospital chain to operate is quite appropriate. For-profit hospitals have sought out locations in well-to-do growing suburbs of large cities. For example, these chain-owned or managed hospitals increased in Illinois by 50% between 1981–1986; there has been a concomitant increase in beds (3). They had especially benefited across the 1970s from operations in the sunbelt states. This logistical placement of the hospital consciously presents spatial barriers for the poorer, uninsured patients (4, 5). Thus, the hospital chain is making a definite decision as to whom they are going to deliver health care.

Consuela's presentation at Friendship's Emergency Room is not a typical occurrence at most for-profit hospitals, and studies show that such patients are not admitted in the first place, being sent to public hospitals sometimes without being medically stabilized (6, 7). The hospital staff at Friendship *assumed* that

Consuela, being Hispanic and from the city, was a non-paying patient when they realized that she was not employed by the firm interviewing Fabiano, which had a preferred-provider arrangement for care of their employees. As Vic put it as she read over Consuela's admitting forms on her arrival to Friendship's Emergency Room, ". . . a source of payment, which a second guess had led them to list as "Indigent"–euphemism for the dirty four-letter word poor. Americans have never been very understanding of poverty, but since Reagan was elected it's become a crime almost as bad as child molesting" (1, p. 23). In fact, the staff's assumption was incorrect; Consuela had insurance coverage under her mother's group health insurance plan.

Friendship Five was advertised as a hospital providing Level III perinatal services. This was the reason Vic chose to take Consuela there on physician recommendation. Hospitals providing such services are co-directed by a full-time, board-certified obstetrician who has special training and certification in maternal-fetal medicine, and by a board certified pediatrician with sub-specialty certification in neonatal medicine. These physicians are responsible for coordination and evaluation of patient care services, research and teaching (8).

Clearly, Burgoyne was recruited to Friendship before he acquired the peri-natal specialty qualifications necessary for his appointment as obstetrical head of a designated Level III service. Like many medical school graduates with large debts, fearing that he would not be able to compete for advance residencies and fellowships, and lured by the "better life" of for-profit medicine, Burgoyne chose the well paying salaried position with extra amenities to offset these conditions (5, 9). This doctor's remorse over the association of Consuela's and the baby's death, along with his lack of training and the inappropriate treatment, ended in a sad, but uninstructive manner. As health care workers' concerns and similar remorse are engendered over serving corporate profit rather than patient needs, and as they are challenged by new management structures that inherently place them in ethical dilemmas, they will need to chose more useful actions and strategies to advocate for patient care rather than suicide, as Burgoyne did (10, 11).

The marketing practices at Friendship are questionable at best. In recent times, for-profit as well as "not-for-profit" hospitals have drawn criticism for their marketing practices—advertising services that they are unable to deliver or providing services of substandard quality. For example, to advertise Level III perinatal services, hospitals not only need to have the qualified personnel neces-sary to provide the care, but they also must be involved in the education of physicians and other health care practitioners; most for-profit hospitals, like Friendship Five, do not conduct teaching programs. However, there has been an attempt by for-profit chains to purchase teaching hospitals in order to increase prestige and provide a fuller compliment of medical care so to maximize short-term profits (12).

PARETSKY: ATTITUDES AND VALUES MADE EXPLICIT

While Paretsky does not see herself in her main character, Vic, they share their hometown of Chicago, and possess similar attitudes about social injustices, such as for-profit medicine, abortion restrictions and women's issues, and medical neglect of the poor.

For-Profit Medicine

Like Vic, Paretsky has a well-developed sense of suspicion toward the world of for-profit management (13). *Bitter Medicine*, she says, "was the first book in which I really make the decision to write about an issue I felt very strongly about." Her understanding of the corporate world stems from her ten years working for a large property casualty insurance company as a marketing manager. While there, she spent a few years in the professional liability division where she was exposed to cases of malpractice. Her interest in health care for profit was motivated by an article in the *Wall Street Journal* which talked about hospital chains buying up hospitals for the specific purpose of increasing their margins through high technology specialties. She continued to learn more by reading the continuing series of articles in *The New England Journal of Medicine* spurred on by its editor, Arnold Relman. Relman has admonished the medical profession to avoid conflict of interests over working in "new medical industrial complex" entities (14).

Abortion Issues

While *Bitter Medicine* is not about abortion per se, Paretsky's perspectives favoring prochoice and abortion rights more than subtly come through. They go back to her late 1960's memories of the doctors and other individuals concerned with legalizing abortion and associated with the Chicago abortion underground, Jane (13). She attempted to characterize Dr. Lotty Herschel particularly on the relationship "between the women and Jane and some of these doctors that I was thinking about." Paretsky continues to speak and write about these issues with the National Abortion Rights Action League. As she states, "I think reproductive freedom is the most fundamental freedom. There are other issues—jobs and housing and all these things that are just terribly critical—but I feel if abortion rights go away then the others are just not worth a whole lot" (15, p. 67). She backs up these convictions through support of Planned Parenthood of Chicago.

Women's Rights

Propelled by her feminist attitudes, Paretsky developed the character, Vic, as a strong, woman detective doing a job that has always been believed to be done by men from Sherlock Holmes to the television series of today. Vic is someone who is not just tough but also human. She makes mistakes and accepts responsibility for them. Mary Schmish in her article on Paretsky in the *Chicago Tribune* describes Vic in the following way, "She sips Scotch while lying in the bathtub of the North Halsted Street apartment. She sniffs her dirty running clothes before jogging her daily five miles around Belmont Harbor. She washes the dishes at most once a week and doesn't pay her bills until the third warning. She beds a man or two per book, but they usually want more commitment than she has to spare for men who aren't her equals, which the guys she meets never quite are" (16, p. 1).

Yet, while Paretsky spends a great deal of time telling her story through the eyes of this woman sensitive to all forms of social injustice, she misses an opportunity to make her minor women characters rise out from stereotypes embedded over the decades. For example, on three occasions in the reviewed book, she presents secretaries as easily coerced into relinquishing information to Vic either in person or on the telephone. The portrayal of the Emergency Room nurses at Friendship who are non-caring and detached may be more disturbing to health professionals. While conditions at Friendship under Humphries' leadership would not necessarily bring out the best in health workers, perpetrating the myth that nurses are gossips and more interested in their appearance or marriage prospects does nothing to promote a more positive image of the skilled, empathetic nurse who not only "superintends complex technologies," but "dispenses information and health education and strives for a holistic understanding of patients' needs" (17, p. 80). Buried in a few sentences at the conclusion of the book, Paretsky notes that the Emergency Room head nurse, who was worried about Consuela's condition, had provided Malcolm Tregiere with the information about what caused Consuela's cardiac arrest.

Medical Neglect for the Poor and Underinsured

The heroes of the book are individuals who, as *Medical Tribune* reviewer Nason so enthusiastically states, "share a continual struggle to salvage what's left of human integrity in a world that doesn't seem to give a damn about things like that" (18, p. 21). Over 37 million Americans are without health insurance and an additional 10–15 million are seriously underinsured (7, 19). These people are forced to fall back on the already overcrowded and poorly financed public hospitals and clinics for their health care, many of which are not easily accessible. Thus, "unsponsored patients" without insurance may delay seeking care until a more serious stage of illness develops.

In this day and age, people without adequate medical insurance coverage are not considered profitable and thus are not likely to get needed care (19). Because of their inability to pay, a growing number of the U.S. population is subject to transfers from private to publicly subsidized hospital emergency departments despite the enactment of the 1986 anti-dumping provisions. This phenomenon, as demonstrated in research conducted in Chicago, is part of a growing problem referred to as "patient dumping" (6, 7).

Paretsky, through her exposure to professional liability issues in her former employment, recognizes the travesty of poor patients being turned away from care in hospitals. These values come through in her characters of Vic, Malcolm and especially, Dr. Lotty Herschel. Lotty, who escaped the Nazi Holocaust as a child, is a competent obstetrician practicing in a large Chicago hospital, but also operates a low-income area clinic for women who do not have access to care elsewhere. The ideal within Lotty's commitment is made clear in *Bitter Medicine*.

PARETSKY: POLITICS THROUGH MYSTERY WRITING

Paretsky sees all writing as political. She feels that intentionally or not, authors write out of what they know, feel and care about (13). Thus, *Bitter Medicine* presents not only a fast-paced mystery with an exciting plot, but Paretsky's real-life attitudes and values weave together in a swirl of authentic Chicago. As she lays out her perspectives before us, the story reaches for more than just another entertaining read for pleasure. Thus, on one hand, *Bitter Medicine* entails purpose and vitality—a story consciously based on a decision to explore how profit maximization can affect health care and people's lives. In this way the novel introduces the public to this important trend in American health care. On the other hand, like most fiction, Paretsky personifies evil as a greedy and corrupt character, Humphries. Critiques of for-profit medicine call for a more direct analysis which implicates the structure and purpose of health care institutions rather than the individual person as villain (20, 21). Thus, we await fiction which appropriately incorporates such a broader perspective to help readers to fully comprehend dangers from for-profit medicine to real-life situations.

REFERENCES

1. Paretsky, S. *Bitter Medicine—A V.I. Warshawski Mystery*. William Morrow and Company, New York, 1987.
2. Salmon, J. W. Discussion of major findings from the symposium and public hearings on the corporatization of health care. In *Proceedings of "The Corporatization of Health Care: Two Day Symposium and Public Hearings,"* edited by J. W. Salmon and J. Todd. Illinois Public Health Association, Springfield, Ill., 1988.
3. Whiteis, D. G. Testimony. In *Proceedings of "The Corporatization of Health Care: Two Day Symposium and Public Hearings,"* edited by J. W. Salmon and J. Todd, pp. 160–176. Illinois Public Health Association, Springfield, Ill., 1988.
4. Whiteis, D. G., and Salmon, J. W. The proprietarization of health care and the under-development of the public sector. *Int. J. Health Serv.* 17(1): 47–64, 1987.
5. Feinglass, J. Physicians as employees: Stanley Wohl's medical industrial complex. In *The Transformation of Health Care*, edited by J. W. Salmon, Chapter 12. Baywood Publishing Company, Farmingdale, New York, 1989.

6. Schiff, R. C., Ansell, D. A., Schlosser, J. E., et al. Transfer to a public hospital: A prospective study of 467 patients. *New Engl. J. Med.* 314: 552–557, 1986.

7. Berliner, H. Patient dumping—No one wins and we all lose. *Am. J. Pub. Health* 78(10): 1279–1280, October 1988.

8. American Academy of Pediatrics, American College of Obstetrics and Gynecology. *Guidelines for Perinatal Care.* American Academy for Pediatrics, Evanston, Ill., 1983.

9. Feinglass, J. Living with bottom line health care. *Zeta Magazine* 1(10): 96–99, October 1988.

10. Relman, A. S. Salaried physicians and economic incentives. *New Engl. J. Med.* 319: 784, 1988.

11. Salmon, J. W. The medical profession and the corporatization of the health sector. *Theoretical Medicine* 8: 19–29, 1987.

12. Berliner, H. S., and Burlage, R. K. Proprietary hospital chains and academic medical centers. *Int. J. Health Serv.* 17(1): 27–45, 1987.

13. Personal interview with Sara Paretsky, April 14, 1988.

14. Relman, A. S. The new-medical industrial complex. *New Engl. J. Med.* 303(17): 963–970, 1980.

15. Shapiro, L. Sara Paretsky. *Ms.*, January, 1988, pp. 66–68.

16. Schmich, M. T. The case of the curious mystery writer. *Chicago Tribune*, July 16, 1988, Sec. 5, pp. 1, 5.

17. Wills, G. F. The dignity of nursing. *Newsweek*, May 23, 1988, p. 80.

18. Nason, R. A mystery that flaunts healthy prejudices. *Medical Tribune*, August 12, 1988, p. 21.

19. Salmon, J. W. The uninsured and the underinsured: What can we do? *The Internist* 29(4): 8–11, April 1988.

20. Navarro, V. *Medicine under Capitalism.* Prodist, New York, 1976.

21. Salmon, J. W. Profit and health care: Trends in corporatization and proprietarization. *Int. J. Health Serv.* 15(3): 395–418, 1985.

CHAPTER 14

Mindbend against a Corporate Intrusion into Health Care

Arthur R. Strobeck, Jr.

During recent years, an ever increasing proportion of health services delivery has come under the control and ownership of investor-owned enterprises. Wohl has observed that this development "signals the arrival in this country of health care as a corporate endeavor" (1, p. 1). These new business ventures—aside from companies that have traditionally manufactured and sold drugs, medical equipment, and supplies—are now the "new Medical Industrial Complex," including for-profit hospital systems; nursing homes; home care agencies; out-patient surgery; urgent care and hemodialysis centers; and a host of other corporate enterprises.

The rise of this addition to the Medical Industrial Complex has not gone unchallenged, and it has been criticized. Many question the ethics of treating medical care as an economic commodity subject to sale, purchase, or even speculation for private corporate gain. The academic critics represent a wide spectrum of social and political thought (1–16). Unfortunately, they are seldom read by the general public, their audience being largely composed of like-minded health professionals.

The general public shapes its opinions on health matters from both its own experiences with the health care system and the information it gleans from media sources of radio, television, newspapers, and periodicals. Public opinion is also influenced by popular culture found in tabloids and paperback books bought on newsstands or in supermarkets and discount pharmacies. Most ideas found at this level dealing with the Medical Industrial Complex normally appeal to the public's inherent populist distrust of large corporations. In fact, this type of anti-corporate opinion would probably argue to the worst aspects of an individual's personal experiences with the health care system (i.e., long waiting periods, discourteous treatment, high charges from overpaid physicians, expensive prescriptions, etc.) and be devoid of a type of analysis to aid in forming a more thorough opinion. It would almost certainly not be expected to link recent changes in healthcare with larger political economic forces shaping those changes.

In recent years, one writer in particular, Robin Cook, M.D., has authored several popular medical "thriller" novels that often made best-seller lists and sold millions of low-priced paperback editions: *Coma* (made into a moderately popular movie), *Brain, Fever, Godplayer, Mindbend,* and *Outbreak. Mindbend,* published in 1985, is especially significant because he appeals to his readers' anti-corporate sympathies by attacking the Medical Industrial Complex. This is possibly a first such anti-corporate health criticism in a mass market paperback edition. Even more to the point is Cook's frank admission that he has written the book as an anti-big business polemic.

At the end of the book, Cook enumerates several reasons for writing *Mindbend*. He is concerned about the "crisis in medicine" represented by corporate intrusion into the healthcare field (17, pp. 347–351). Cook describes the business mentality as being "diametrically opposed to the traditional aspects of altruism that have formed the foundation of the practice of medicine . . ." (17, p. 347). He also believes that corporations view ". . . the medical field as a high-cash-flow, high-profit, low-risk, and low capital investment industry that is now particularly ripe for takeover" (17, p. 348). Cook expresses disbelief over the small amount of criticism of this corporatization trend—the reason influencing him to write the book. He wants to focus greater public attention, believing that "by couching the problem in an emotional framework," it will bring the situation into a personal perspective and thus allow the reader to understand the implications through identification with the main character (17, p. 348).

Mindbend relates the story of Arolen Corporation, a large pharmaceutical enterprise, which through the use of violently coercive behavior modification techniques has recruited many renown physicians to do medical care and research work. The novel is set in locales which include: inner-city New York; a luxury Caribbean cruise; and Puerto Rico. Adam Schoenberg, the main character, is a third year medical student dropout who is seeking employment to support his pregnant wife, Jennifer. Adam is hired by Arolen, and while working there, he becomes aware of the company's illegal activities, especially its physician procurement methods. Adam seeks to expose the corporation, but he must also save Jennifer who has fallen under the Svengali-like influence of a corporate physician.

Obviously, the plot is at best an exaggeration and certainly at variance with the more subtle reality of everyday life. International pharmaceutical companies do not induce physicians to do their bidding by luring them on Caribbean cruises in which they are drugged and tortured with electrical shock treatment; in reality, physicians go freely in mind and finance. It is much easier for drug companies to use legal and more discrete methods, e.g., sufficient inducements such as an attractive payment and perquisites. However, the altrusitic physicians who inhabit Cook's *Mindbend* world seem to be beyond the influence of temptation offered by personal and financial gain.

Cook's doctors did not win any sympathy from book critics. In reviewing *Mindbend, New York Times* critic Dave Barry sided with the "giant evil corporation" because it victimized physicians not innocent civilians. Besides, he reasoned, the patients were treated well. The brainwashed Arolen doctors at least ". . . see their patients promptly and actually listen to them" (18).

If Cook were not trying to be serious, the book would be humorous. However, the author is attempting to send a message to his large readership, and his anti-corporate argument deserves more analysis within the context of recent developments. Likewise, his message needs to be compared and contrasted with realities of the Medical Industrial Complex, as well as with what others are saying about the corporatization of American healthcare.

Cook pursues three main arguments in his book: 1) he attacks the pharmaceutical industry; 2) he deifies the physicians and laments their "fall" from private practice into "salaried positions;" and 3) he uses his book as a vehicle to advance what appears to be an undeclared anti-abortion agenda.

Mindbend is primarily an attack on the pharmaceutical industry—one segment of the Medical Industrial Complex. Cook selects the drug industry ". . . not because it has been worse than any other group, but because it has been around longer than most businesses associated with medicine and it exerts a powerful and growing influence." It is an industry that does "not exist for the public weal," and its goal ". . . is to provide a return" on its investors' capital. Pharmaceutical firms promote their products through "an ungodly amount of money" which is mostly used to influence physicians who are "rather easy prey." Any contributions to society that have been made by the drug companies are "the by-product, not the goal" of the firms, and ". . . there have been cases in which the public good was ignored" (17, p. 349).

Cook especially criticizes the drug industry's sales promotion practices. The novel describes the work of Arolen Corporation's sales representatives. Adam Schoenberg, trained as one of these "detail men," witnesses how colleagues liberally distribute their free drug samples to physicians who are very eager to receive them. Cook barely conceals his contempt for this behavior in his fellow physicians. The Arolen representatives continually use narcissistic flattery on the gullible doctors who are portrayed as being somewhat ignorant of drug side-effects and contraindications. Schoenberg's mentor during his training period informs him that "They (the physicians) get their drug information, what little they get, from the likes of me, and I only tell them what I want to tell them" (17, p. 121). During a single day, Schoenberg and his companion distribute over five hundred free sample bottles of drugs to sixteen physician's offices.

Cook is emphatically critical of the pharmaceuticals' promotion of unsafe drugs. Arolen aggressively promotes the sale and use of pregdolen (a fictional creation of Cook), a drug for morning sickness, even though the medicine has toxic side effects and received negative reviews in medical journal articles. Pregdolen samples are freely given away to physicians so they will later prescribe them.

The author also exposes the dark side of Arolen's relationship with its Julian Clinic. The clinic is staffed by brainwashed physicians and allied health workers. The company uses the clinic to promote its products, and corporation doctors are seen shamelessly prescribing pregdolen during the course of their daily duties. Likewise, the health facility is a convenient place for obtaining fetuses that are necessary for Arolen's research. Most of these come from cases in which the doctor has lied to the patient by telling her that an abortion was medically necessary when it actually was not needed.

Since pharmaceuticals are also earning large amounts of money, Cook examines an opulent side of Arolen's wealth. The corporation's headquarters building with its huge bronze mirrored sides rises out of the New Jersey plains. Complete with a twentieth floor executive swimming pool, the corporate building complex provides an awesome sight to the visitor. Even the Julian clinic is not just another hospital building; it has fifteen stories of mirrored glass and the lobby of a "luxury hotel" (17, p. 83). And finally, Arolen's luxury cruise ship as well as its large and impressive research facility in Puerto Rico provide further evidence of the company's lucrative trade in pharmaceuticals.

Cook exhibits great confidence in the ability of government agencies to deal with abuses committed by the pharmaceutical industry. Adam Schoenberg's father, a physician, is a dedicated administrator of an important division within the Food and Drug Administration (FDA). Feeling a great degree of trust and confidence, the younger Schoenberg turns to the FDA for assistance after obtaining incontrovertible evidence of Arolen's illegal physician procurement program.

In contrast to Cook's seemingly blind faith in the FDA, others criticize that agency for its handling of matters pertaining to the drug industry. There have been charges of pharmaceutical influence in the FDA as well as complaints about its allegedly failing to do enough to regulate drug prices and unsafe drugs. Bodenheimer claims that large pharmaceutical companies have used their political campaign contributions to obtain favorable legislation and influence high appointments to positions within the FDA. In fact, Bodenheimer notes, "FDA officials have tended to go back and forth between the government and the drug industry itself" (19, p. 211). He cites persons who have alternately held government or FDA positions and jobs in the pharmaceutical industry including, for example, President George Bush, who at one time served as a director of Eli Lilly (19, p. 211).

Cook has chosen the pharmaceutical industry as an appropriate villain of the Medical Industrial Complex, but, nevertheless, he fails to demonstrate a working relationship between pharmaceuticals and the rest of the Complex. Furthermore, he does not mention the multinational aspects of Arolen Corporation despite the fact that the drug industry is now controlled by transnational interests, and there is also never any hint of an exploitative relationship between the corporation and Third World people even though Arolen's major research facility is located in the Third World.

In everyday reality, the pharmaceutical industry is connected with other health product companies through interlocking directorates. For example, the chief executive officer and chairman of the board of Hospital Corporation of America (HCA) is also a member of the board of directors of Johnson and Johnson; Gerald D. Laubach, a director of Connecticut General Insurance Company, is also the president of Pfizer, Inc., a large drug company (1, p. 27). Chase Manhattan, Citibank, and Morgan Guarantee Trust banks all have directors on the boards of pharmaceutical firms such as American Home Products, Bristol Myers, Eli Lilly, Merck, SmithKline, Beckman, Abbott, and Searle (19). In fact, Strelnick observes that J. P. Morgan and Company is among the top ten shareholders in 26 major medical supply and pharmaceutical concerns (20, p. 10), and Bodenheimer adds that the average large pharmaceutical company had 13 interlocks with financial institutions in 1976 (19, p. 194).

Through mergers, acquisitions, and diversification, the pharmaceutical industry is undergoing a development similar to other multinational corporations. Two significant mergers that have happened during recent years are SmithKline, a drug company, merging with Beckman, a manufacturer of scientific instruments. In 1985, Baxter Travenol, a drug concern, merged with the American Hospital Supply Corporation, the largest manufacturer and supplier of medical and hospital equipment in the United States. The latter followed an aborted attempt by Hospital Corporation of America, the largest corporate hospital chain, to merge with the hospital supply company. In both mergers above, the firms gained a foothold in each other's fields including sales forces, markets, and mechanisms for obtaining FDA approval of products.

Many drug corporations are also diversifying. A drug company such as Warner-Lambert manufactures Bromo-Seltzer, chewing gum, sunglasses, razors, and a fiber optic enclososcope by American Optical, and Eli Lilly and Upjohn have approximately 30 percent of their sales in nonpharmaceutical items (19, p. 195). Even nonpharmaceutical corporations such as Standard Oil, Coca Cola, Ligget and Myers, and the United Fruit Company have acquired pharmaceutical firms.

On an international level, the global drug industry is controlled by a relatively small number of firms based in the United States, Western Europe, and Japan. These companies plan their sales and production on a worldwide scale and organize them to achieve a maximum profit which includes pricing products at artificially high prices in Third World countries. Bodenheimer describes their organization scheme as follows: ". . . a pharmaceutical company might have its corporate headquarters in the United States, produce its drugs in Ireland, assemble its capsules in Brazil, and sell the product in Bolivia. The details depend on where raw materials are obtainable most cheaply, where labor costs are lowest, where taxes most easily can be evaded and where marketing regulations are least strict" (19, pp. 188-189).

Perhaps the most serious abuse committed by the pharmaceutical companies has been the sale, and in some cases, the promotion of unsafe drugs in Third World countries. Since prescriptions are not often required for drug purchases, the situation has become quite aggravated. Some drugs such as Chloroaphenicol, widely banned for most uses in the United States, until recently was widely available over the counter in most of Latin America. Everyone is now familiar with infant formulas, such as Nestle's, which were heavily marketed in the Third World, even after their withdrawal from the U.S. market. The misuse of such products is said to have been a contributing factor in the deaths of one million infants each year (22).

Multinational pharmaceuticals have resisted disseminating sufficient information concerning toxicity of their drugs being sold in Latin America. In a study of various drugs being marketed by multinational firms in Latin America, Silverman found that the listings of the drugs' hazards in reference books ". . . are curtailed, glossed over, or totally omitted. In some cases, only trivial side effects are described, while serious or possibly fatal reactions are not mentioned" (23, p. 106). Contrariwise, he found the reverse situation existing in the United States where the laws concerning a drug's side effects are seriously enforced (23, p. 106).

Pharmaceuticals' ownership and monopolization of patent rights for seventeen years on each invention has enabled them to keep their prices high and receive a return on the costs of research and development of a product. While the patent is in effect, a company can act as the sole producer of a product. Even after a drug patent expires, a firm can still earn money since it has the advantage of having previously marketed the product, and it still has the rights to the brand name. In an attempt to maintain sales of their brand name drugs, the pharmaceuticals have historically supported legislation that would prohibit the substitution of a more often lower-priced generic equivalent for a brand name (24, pp. 138-170).

The industry's methods of drug sales promotion have been seriously questioned. Pharmaceuticals routinely attempt to influence physicians by giving away free drug samples from company detail men. The influence usually begins in medical schools where the students receive free gifts such as stethoscopes and black bags. Pressure on Third World physicians is reported to be far greater. Bodenheimer cites the experience of a Brazilian physician who was visited by 69 detail men in a three week period. The doctor received 452 free drug samples and twenty-five other gifts (19, p. 203).

Drug companies also sponsor large amounts of advertising in medical journals. Critics charge that this commercialism may affect the editorial content of the publications by both silencing critics of the pharmaceutical firms and winning over medical associations as lobbies for the drug industry (24, pp. 67–75). Furthermore, the almost universally used *Physicians Desk Reference* (PDR) is nothing more than "a compilation of *paid advertising purchased by the major brand-name companies*" and without reference to generic names for drugs (24, pp. 75–76, italics are Silverman's).

By his choice of the pharmaceuticals, Cook set up a villain that could be easily struck down. So easily, in fact, that his fictional exaggerations seem entirely unnecessary. He could build his case against the drug industry with the available wealth of factually supported evidence. Likewise, he could easily demonstrate how patients rather than doctors have been the real victims in the real world of the drug industry.

In his second main argument, Cook deifies the physician. None of the doctors are villains who willingly cooperate with Arolen Corporation. They are innocent victims; all are forced through violent physical and mental coercion to serve the company. The physicians are inherently good and the corporation is inherently evil. For example, a supporting character, Dr. Vandermer, initially refuses to prescribe pregdolen for his patients because "It's not safe" (17, p. 141). Unfortunately, the good doctor is invited on a "mindbending" Arolen Caribbean cruise and changes his mind about pregdolen. He now prescribes the drug while denying he ever criticized it as unsafe. Dr. Vandermer—like other physicians in *Mindbend*—is corrupted by the corporation. One cannot imagine Cook writing a scenario in which physicians would ever think of placing their own economic interests first. Such would not conform to Cook's idyllic view of doctors.

Cook laments the ongoing changes in the physicians' status. He decries the loss of doctors' personal practices, and their subsequent acceptance of a salaried position with Arolen Corporation. Dr. Vandermer, formerly quite satisfied in a private practice, accepts a position with Arolen and confides to Adam Schoenberg that "fee-for-service medicine is a thing of the past" (17, p. 174).

In *Mindbend*, the intentional machinations of Arolen Corporation cause physicians to leave their comfortable practices to work for the company. In real life, the reasons are quite different. Physicians are adjusting to rapid changes in health care, many of which are a result of the expansion of the Medical Industrial Complex. Some of the growing change in physician status is often referred to as the proletarianization of physicians—a gradual process by which a growing number of doctors are losing many of their prerogatives.

McKinlay and Arches note that the prerogatives lost through proletarianization are associated with the power of an occupation and have to do with loss of control over (*a*) criteria for entrance; (*b*) content of training; (*c*) autonomy regarding terms and control of work; (*d*) objects of labor; (*e*) tools of labor; (*f*) the means of labor; and (*g*) amount and remuneration for labor (25, pp. 161–162). According to them, "the net effect of proletarianization then is the eventual reduction of all workers in a particular occupation to some common level in the service of the broader interests of capital accumulation" (25, p. 162).

Such change is not demonstrating itself equally or in a similar manner among all physicians. With some types of physician activity, the change is rapid and visible. In other activities (i.e., a large bureaucracy), the rate of change is slow and imperceptible. The change is often occurring at such a slow rate that it is historically comparable to the gradual change in twentieth century American agriculture—a situation in which ". . . the encroachment of capitalist prerogatives slowly shunted aside small scale production" (25, p. 162).

The high degree of bureaucratization of medical care today has also influenced the trend toward proletarianization. Bureaucracy has increasingly encroached on physicians who are being forced to give up control over the disposition of their labor power. As a consequence, their labor is now assuming more of the features of a market commodity, and it is "increasingly sold in exchange for wages and salaries and is involved in the creation of surplus value for some other party at an increasing rate of exploitation" (25, p. 171). Derber predicts that physicians will come under even more control in the future because both profit and nonprofit organizations will have greater economic incentives to exercise such control. At that point, the physician will be in a further weakened position because of his dwindling role as a market sponsor in a hospital (i.e., more patients will come to him via HMOs and other provider institutions rather than from individual physicians). Likewise, the dramatic increase in the number of physicians points to an oversupply of doctors thus giving employers more leverage for extracting concessions (26, p. 249).

Other general developments have affected the physician privileges including the deskilling of doctors caused by their narrowing specializations which in turn leads to a loss of many general applications of skills. McKinlay and Arches suggest that the growth of segmentalization in medicine (i.e., reducing medical care to more manageable components that can be performed by lesser skilled health workers) could eventually lead to the replacement of the physician. Braverman observed and described a comparable process of deskilling and replacement among office workers (27).

The physician is affected by changes in the organization of medical practice. Prepaid insurance coverage for ambulatory care has often led to the "demanding patient" who insists on service based on contractual rights. Observers such as Mechanic have also seen the role of the physician under capitation systems being transformed from a patients' advocate to an allocator of health care resources—the physician becomes the gatekeeper to forms of more specialized treatment (28). The physician's position in his immediate job setting may also change when working more as a team member with allied health workers in a bureaucratic setting. Eventually, suggests Gerber, physicians may even have to deal with corporate moves into private practice (29). Certainly, real changes already occurring with physicians suggest far more sophisticated causes than the violent corporate coercion depicted by Dr. Cook.

Cook's third main argument seems to be part of an undeclared agenda, and it is a point which he pursues with almost greater vigor than his critique of the Medical Industrial Complex. The argument consists of the anti-abortion tone and bias which is found throughout the novel. There are remarks, innuendos, and opinions of an anti-abortion nature. Adam Schoenberg even speaks out against abortion, and the condition of his wife merely reinforces Schoenberg's anti-abortion beliefs. At the very outset, Cook uses a fictional newspaper account to demonstrate Arolen Corporation's alliance with opponents of the anti-abortion movement. The book also describes a link between the corporation's obtaining fetuses; the Arolen-owned Julian clinic; and a fetal research program. The entire novel apparently serves as a vehicle for Cook's undeclared offensive against abortion.

Finally, there are two significant weaknesses in Cook's overall attempt to critique the Medical Industrial Complex. By emphasizing the pharmaceutical industry in his narrative, he ignores the expansion of the investor-owned hospital chains and the horizontal and vertical integration of providers and suppliers in the for-profit sector (i.e., Cook does not hint at the enormous power and influence arising as a result of concentration of ownership among fewer economic interests).

Cook also fails to mention the increased lack of access to care for many poor and uninsured persons and the marketing practices by which investor-owned firms locate facilities in areas having large numbers of privately insured patients. Omission of this social issue together with Cook's exaggerated concern for the declining status of physicians reveal a seeming disregard for the plight of poor and uninsured patients.

Cook obviously does not understand the true implications of a situation in which private profit dictates the distribution of a social good, such as medical care. Nor does he see the relationship of corporatized health care to a larger society in which profit also reigns over the production and distribution of most socially needed goods and services. Instead, the reader is given an anti-corporate argument to appeal to an emotional, and not political instinct. As such, it may result in minimal provocation of thought.

On a different level of criticism, liberal observers of the Medical Industrial Complex such as Relman, Wohl, and Starr have remarked beyond Cook's simple appeal and depicted an awareness of the possible consequences of corporatized health care. While they appear to display a greater understanding of economic processes involved, there is still not much questioning of the consequences of private profit determining the distribution of a public good such as health care.

Relman, a major spokesperson for the medical profession against the new Medical Industrial Complex, (2) fears growth in its power and influence. He charges that investor-owned hospitals already treat less than their fair share of the indigent. Relman observes that "the continued expansion of the investor-owned hospital companies is likely to increase the unfairness in the U.S. health care system and make it less responsive to community needs" (3, p. 60).

Relman further believes that health care ". . . is a public rather than a private good . . ." (2, p. 966). In fact, if Americans really believed that health care were a private business, ". . . American society would not have subsidized medical education research and development so heavily" (4, p. 32). He makes a clear distinction between the surplus (profit) of the investor-owned and "not-for-profit" sectors. Surplus in the latter sector guarantees an institution's survival, while surplus in the investor-owned sector is returned as earnings to private investors who can decide the distribution of health services. Unfortunately, rather than taking a broader approach to the problem, Relman is more concerned with simply disassociating physicians from the commercial exploitation of health care.

Wohl, another physician observer, examined organizations active in the corporatization trend in his *The Medical Industrial Complex* (1). Wohl claims to be an ideological neutral explaining that "While I strongly criticize some of the activities of big business, I also clearly recognize their positive contribution and the fact that they must be included in any scheme for reforming the system" (1, p. 2). There is no hint that he understands the reasons for widespread concern over private profits influencing the fulfillment or nonfulfillment of health needs.

Starr's *The Social Transformation of American Medicine* won a Pulitzer Prize in 1984 and has received more attention and a wider readership than most non-fiction health books. Like Relman and Wohl, Starr misunderstands the class forces propelling the expansion of for-profit health care, though he does comprehend some of the social consequences. Unfortunately, Starr centers his analysis of the Medical Industrial Complex around investor-owned hospital chains. He is concerned about "not-for-profit" institutions being forced into for-profit ventures (5). Starr simply ignores or barely mentions related health services, pharmaceuticals, nursing homes, etc. He also analyzes this situation from the physician's perspective and, as a result, fails to examine many of the implications for patients or the public. Starr does not lament the proletarianization of physicians because he believes that they may only lose some autonomy and income, but the corporations will still need their active cooperation (5, pp. 444–449).

Cook, Relman, and Starr have all failed to understand the nature and consequences of large-scale corporate involvement in American health care. Brown has noted the "The crisis in today's health care system is deeply rooted in the interwoven history of modern medicine and capitalism" (7, p. 1). Kelman has further observed that ". . . developments in the medical care system are but reflections of developments in the larger society" (30, p. 30). Corporate class influence is felt at all levels of society and increasingly in the health care field as evidenced by the concern expressed by the writers reviewed in this chapter.

Robin Cook's *Mindbend*, while a serious attempt to focus public attention on these current trends, is still a narrow appeal to the populist anti-corporate attitude. It briefly affects emotions but leaves the reader without a fuller understanding of the nature of the corporatization of health care or what to do about it.

Despite its lack of a more meaningful analysis, *Mindbend* does represent deep-seated concern for health care as a public good in the United States, and to its credit, it realizes that such a goal cannot be easily accomplished, if at all, in a system in which so many decisions affecting our health are based upon the power and influence of private corporations. And certainly, despite its weaknesses, Robin Cook's *Mindbend* contributes by focusing public attention on the Medical Industrial Complex. Hopefully, those who understand the class nature of corporatization and proprietarization in health care will provide a lens to fine focus most of that attention.

REFERENCES

1. Wohl, S. *The Medical Industrial Complex*. Harmony Books, New York, 1984.
2. Relman, A. S. The new medical industrial complex. *New Engl. J. Med.* 303(17): 963–970, October 23, 1980.
3. Relman, A. S. Meeting community needs is a major concern raised by for-profit health care. *Bus. and Health*, January/February, 1985, p. 60.
4. The medical industrial complex. (Debate between A. S. Relman and J. Bedrosian.) *Urban Health* 13(6): 30–51, July, 1984.
5. Starr, P. *The Social Transformation of American Medicine*. Basic Books, New York, 1982.
6. Brown, E. R. He who pays the piper: Foundations, the medical profession and medical education reform. *Int. J. Health Serv.* 10(1): 71–88, 1980.
7. Brown, E. R. *Rockefeller Medicine Men: Medicine and Capitalism in America*. University of California Press, Berkeley, 1979.
8. Navarro, V. Medical history as justification rather than explanation. *Int. J. Health Serv.* 14(4): 512–528, 1984.
9. Salmon, J. W. Profit and health care: Trends in corporatization and proprietarization. *Int. J. Health Serv.* 15(3): 395–418, 1985.
10. Berliner, H. S. Starr Wars. *Int. J. Health Serv.* 13(4): 671–675, 1983.
11. Berliner, H. S., and Burlage, R. Proprietary hospital chains and academic medical centers. *Int. J. Health Serv.* 17(1), 1987.
12. Kennedy, L. Hospitals in chains: The transformation of American health institutions. *Health PAC Bulletin* 12(7): 9–14+, September/October, 1981.
13. Kennedy, L. The proprietarization of voluntary hospitals. *Bull. N.Y. Acad. Med.* 61(1): 81–89, January–February, 1985.
14. Kennedy, L. Voluntary compulsion: The transformation of American health institutions, Part II. *Health PAC Bulletin* 12(8): 11–18, November/December, 1981.
15. Young, Q. D. The danger of making serious problems worse. *Bus. and Health* 2(3): 32–33, January/February, 1985.
16. Young, Q. D. Impact of for-profit enterprise on health care. *J. Publ. Health Policy* 5(4): 449–452, December, 1984.
17. Cook, R. *Mindbend*. New American Library, New York, 1986.
18. Barry, D. Mindbend. *New York Times*, March 3, 1985.
19. Bodenheimer, T. S. The transnational pharmaceutical industry and the health of the world's people. In *Issues in the Political Economy of Health Care*, edited by J. B. McKinlay, pp. 187–216. Tavistock Publications, London, 1984.

20. Strelnick, H. Billions from Bandaids. *Health PAC Bulletin* 13(3): 7–10+, May/June, 1982.
21. Strelnick, H. Profits without honor. *Health PAC Bulletin* 13(5): 7–8, September/October, 1982.
22. The breast vs. the bottle. *Newsweek*, June 1, 1981, pp. 54–55.
23. Silverman, M. *The Drugging of the Americas*. University of California Press, Berkeley, 1976.
24. Silverman, M., and Lee, P. R. *Pills, Profits, and Politics*. University of California Press, Berkeley, 1974.
25. McKinlay, J. B., and Arches, J. Towards the proletarianization of physicians. *Int. J. Health Serv.* 15(2): 161–195, 1985.
26. Derber, C. Physicians and their sponsors: The new medical relations of production. In *Issues in the Political Economy of Health Care*, edited by J. B. McKinlay, pp. 217–254. Tavistock Publications, London, 1984.
27. Braverman, H. *Labor and Monopoly Capital: The Degradation of Work in the Twentieth Century*. Monthly Review Press, New York, 1974.
28. Mechanic, D. The transformation of health providers. *Health Aff.* 3(1): 65–72, Spring, 1985.
29. Gerber, P. C. Will hospital corporations move into private practice. *Physician's Management* 24(9): 202+, September, 1984.
30. Kelman, S. Toward the political economy of health care. *Inquiry* 8(3): 30–38, September, 1971.

Contributors

LINDA BERGTHOLD is currently a health care consultant with National Medical Audit, a division of Mercer Meidinger Hansen, Inc. She is directing the long-term care and aging consulting activities for the western region. She was formerly Assistant Professor in the Department of Social and Behavioral Sciences at the University of California, San Francisco and the Project Director at the Institute for Health and Aging of a national study on post-hospital care for the elderly. She holds a Ph.D. in political sociology from the University of California, Santa Cruz, and was a Pew Health Policy Doctoral Fellow at the University of California, San Francisco.

HOWARD S. BERLINER is Associate Professor and Chair of the Health Services Administration Program at the New School for Social Research. Previously he was Assistant Commissioner for Research, Policy, and Planning, State of New Jersey Department of Health and Associate Research Scientist at Conservation of Human Resources, Columbia University. He has held several other academic appointments. He received his M.P.S. from Cornell University and Sc.D. from Johns Hopkins University School of Public Health. He authored *A System of Scientific Medicine: Philanthropic Foundations in the Flexner Era* (Tavistock, 1985); *Strategic Factors in U.S. Health Care* (Westview, 1987); and with Eli Ginzberg and Miriam Ostow, *Young People at Risk: Is Prevention Possible?* (Westview, 1988).

ROBB K. BURLAGE is Associate Professor and Director of the Division of Urban Planning in the Graduate School of Architecture and Planning at Columbia University. His current research interests include the proprietarization of U.S. health care and the regionalization of community health care services. He is author of *New York City's Municipal Hospitals* (Institute for Policy Studies, 1967).

RAISA B. DEBER is Assistant Professor in the Department of Health Administration at the University of Toronto. She received her Ph.D. in political science from the Massachusetts Institute of Technology. Her current research interests include Canadian health policy, medical decision-making, and technology assessment. She has served on the editorial boards of *Dimensions in Health Service* and *Medical Decision Making*. Professor Deber is currently compiling a book of case studies in Canadian health policy; writing (with Steven Heiber) a book on the development and implementation of the Canada Health Act; and (with Peggy Leatt) investigating the process by which Ontario hospitals acquire and use new technologies.

271

JOE FEINGLASS is Research Assistant Professor of Medicine, Section of Internal Medicine, Northwestern University Medical School, Chicago, Illinois; and Research Associate at the Northwestern University Center for Health Services Research and Policy, Evanston, Illinois. He received his Ph.D. in Public Policy Analysis from the Health Policy and Planning Specialization in School of Urban Planning and Policy at the University of Illinois at Chicago. He is also the Project Director of the Housestaff Cost Awareness Project at Northwestern Memorial Hospital. His dissertation, "A Severity-Adjusted Statistical Model of Physicians' Impact on Hospital Resource Use: Identifying Cost-Effective Patterns of Inpatient Medical Care," examines medical practice variations in a teaching hospital.

BRUCE FRIED is Assistant Professor in the Department of Health Administration at the University of Toronto. He received his doctorate in health policy and administration from the University of North Carolina at Chapel Hill and holds a master's degree in social service administration from the University of Chicago. Professor Fried is on the editorial board of *Healthcare Management Forum* and *Dimensions in Health Service*, and is a contributing editor of *Canadian Health Care Management*. He recently co-authored *Multi-Institutional Arrangements and the Canadian Health System* and is currently conducting research on general hospital psychiatry units, multi-institutional arrangements, and decentralized hospital management structures.

AGATHA M. GALLO has extensive clinical background as a pediatric nurse practitioner, staff nurse in a variety of settings, and nurse educator. Within these positions her emphasis has been on family-oriented care. Her recent research has focused on a grounded theory approach to how families define and manage a child's chronic illness. Dr. Gallo received her Ph.D. in Health Professions Education and her Master of Science in Nursing from the University of Pennsylvania. She is Assistant Professor in the Department of Maternal Child Nursing at the University of Illinois at Chicago.

PEGGY LEATT is Professor and Chair of the Department of Health Administration at the University of Toronto. She received her Ph.D. in sociology from the University of Alberta, and holds degrees in health administration and nursing. Professor Leatt has published extensively in the area of organizational theory and design, and is past board chairperson of the Association of University Programs in Health Administration. Her current research interests include medical staff organization, decentralized hospital management structures, multi-institutional arrangements, technology acquisition in hospitals, and hospital foundations.

JOHN B. McKINLAY is Vice President and Director of the New England Research Institute and Professor of Sociology and Research Professor of Medicine, Boston University. He is presently engaged in several large scale epidemiologic studies of hormone profiles in aging men, menopause in women, black help-seeking behavior and several studies of older populations. He recently received a National Institutes of Health MERIT award which "provides long-term stable support to investigators whose research competence and productivity are distinctly superior and who are likely to continue to perform in an outstanding manner."

VICENTE NAVARRO is Professor of Health Policy at Johns Hopkins University; founder and editor-in-chief of the *International Journal of Health Services*; and series editor for this Policy, Politics, Health and Medicine Series for Baywood Publishing Company, Inc. An advisor to several governments and international agencies as well as labor organizations, he has written extensively on the sociology, political sociology, and the political economy of medical and social services. Dr. Navarro is the author of *Medicine Under Capitalism; Social Security and Medicine in the U.S.S.R.: A Marxist Critique*; and *Class Struggle, the State and Medicine: An Historical and Contemporary Analysis of the Medical Sector in Great Britain*. He is the editor of the collections: *Health and Medical Care in the U.S.: A Critical Analysis; Imperialism, Health and Medicine*; and (with D. Berman) *Health and Work Under Capitalism: An International Perspective*, all previous volumes in this Baywood Policy, Politics, Health and Medicine Series.

GEOFFREY RAYNER is a Health Liaison Officer, London Borough of Lambeth, devising policy strategies on Health Service and public policy issues. He is also a consultant to the World Health Organization, an advisor to the Association of London Authorities, and formerly a consultant to the Greater London Council. He writes regularly on health policy, and taught at South Bank Polytechnic, University of London, and Brooklyn College, City University of New York. He is a joint author of *Banking on Sickness: Commercial Medicine in Britain and the U.S.A.* (Lawrence and Wishart, 1987).

CAROL REGAN is a Health Policy Specialist for the American Federation of State, County and Municipal Employees in Washington, D.C. Previously she was with the Service Employees International Union's national office. Her M.P.H. is from the University of Michigan School of Public Health. For the past several years she has been involved in health advocacy with a variety of community groups and labor organizations.

J. WARREN SALMON is Professor and Coordinator of the Health Policy and Planning Specialization in School of Urban Planning and Policy; and Professor of Health Resources Management in the School of Public Health at the University of Illinois at Chicago. Previously he was Associate Professor of Community Medicine and Environmental Health at Hahnemann University in Philadelphia and has held several other administrative, planning and consulting positions in the health care field. He is the editor of the "Special Section on the Corporatization of Medicine" for the *International Journal of Health Services*. His research interests have also focused on public sector health care delivery, comparative health care systems, altnative and complimentary medicines, and selected health policy issues. He edited *Alternative Medicines: Popular and Policy Perspectives* (Tavistock/Methuen, 1984); (with Jeffrey W. Todd) *The Corporatization of Health Care: A Two Day Symposium and Public Hearing* (Illinois Public Health Association, 1988); and *The Corporate Transformation of Health Care, Part II: Perspectives and Implications* (Baywood Publishing Co., forthcoming).

ARTHUR R. STROBECK, JR. is a Research Associate at the American College of Healthcare Executives in Chicago where he has worked since 1984. He received his Masters degree in Urban Policy and Planning in the Health Policy and Planning Specialization at the University of Illinois at Chicago in 1987 and his Masters of Arts degree in Latin American history from Northern Illinois University in 1969. He has previously worked in community organizing and adult education in Chicago. He has also been employed as a project editor for GED books in social sciences and reading skills.

JOHN D. STOECKLE is Professor of Medicine at Harvard Medical School and Chief of Medical Clinics at the Massachusetts General Hospital in Boston. He is internationally respected for his teaching and research in the area of primary health care and for studies of the doctor-patient relationship. He edited *Encounters Between Patients and Doctors* (MIT Press, 1987).

LOUIS TANNEN currently makes a career of designing and conducting worker training programs mandated by federal and state "right-to-know" laws, combined with a carpentry and cabinet-making business. He was previously an Instructor in the Department of Community Medicine and Environmental Health at the Hahnemann University in Philadelphia. His Masters in City Planning degree specializing in health planning is from the University of Pennsylvania.

DAVID WHITEIS is Research Associate in the Center for Health Services Research in the School of Public Health at the University of Illinois at Chicago. Now completing his Ph.D. in Public Policy Analysis from the Health Policy and Planning Specialization in School of Urban Planning and Policy at the University of Illinois at Chicago, his thesis is entitled "U.S. Urban Hospital Closure, 1980–87: Internal Hospital Characteristics and Community Socio-economic Characteristics Correlated with Risk of Closure." He received his M.P.H. degree in community health sciences from the University's School of Public Health in 1984. He has worked as consultant and health planner for several public agencies and in community organizing. He is also a free-lance writer for local Chicago newspapers.

Index